The Role of Artificial Intelligence in Cybersecurity

Darcel Tolliver

ISBN:

Dedication

To those who believe that knowledge is a responsibility and innovation is a calling. May this work serve as a light in an increasingly complex digital world.

Acknowledgment

I extend special recognition to the Raptors Cyber Team, whose untiring time, discipline, and commitment to excellence continue to inspire this work. Your countless hours spent training, analyzing threats, competing, and pushing beyond limits embody the very intersection of artificial intelligence and cybersecurity defense discussed in these pages.

Your resilience, teamwork, and relentless pursuit of knowledge demonstrate that the future of cybersecurity is not only intelligent but determined. It is an honor to mentor and learn alongside you.

Contents

About the Author

Dr. Darcel Tolliver has over 20 years of experience working with technology, cybersecurity, and teaching at colleges and universities. She has led technology projects, helped design secure computer networks, and created hands-on cybersecurity training used in defense and business settings. She is well known for guiding and mentoring students as they learn how to solve real cyber problems and prepare for cybersecurity careers.

Dr. Tolliver loves teaching, learning, and sharing cybersecurity knowledge. She is especially interested in how artificial intelligence (AI) can help protect computers and networks. She is the author of The Role of Artificial Intelligence in Cybersecurity, a book that explains how AI is changing the way cyber threats are found and stopped. As a professor, she teaches cybersecurity, computer systems, and network design using hands-on learning and real-world examples.

Dr. Tolliver is strongly committed to helping students succeed. She supports students through coaching, mentoring, and research projects. She works hard to create a welcoming learning environment where students feel supported and encouraged to grow.

Dr. Tolliver holds a bachelor's degree in Mathematics, two master's degrees in Information Systems and Cybersecurity, and a Ph.D. She also holds professional cybersecurity certifications, including CEH, CHFI, and CompTIA Security+, showing her strong knowledge and skills in cybersecurity.

Page Blank Intentionally

Chapter 1: The New Battlefield: Cybersecurity in the Age of AI

A Digital Deception That Shook the World

On what appeared to be an ordinary Tuesday morning, a finance employee at Arup, one of the world's most prestigious engineering consultancies responsible for designing iconic structures like the Sydney Opera House and Beijing National Stadium, joined what seemed to be a routine video conference call. The meeting invitation had come from the company's UK-based Chief Financial Officer, urgently requesting a discussion about a time-sensitive acquisition opportunity that required immediate attention and discretion.

The employee, experienced in handling complex international financial transactions, entered the video call without suspicion. The CFO's familiar face appeared clearly on screen, his voice carrying the distinctive British accent that the employee had heard countless times in previous meetings. His mannerisms and speaking patterns matched perfectly with past interactions. Several other senior colleagues joined the discussion throughout the call, each appearing exactly as they did during regular virtual meetings same backgrounds, same lighting, same professional demeanor that had become routine in the post-pandemic era of remote work.

The conversation progressed naturally over the course of nearly an hour. They discussed the strategic importance of acquiring a smaller engineering firm, reviewed projected financial benefits, examined potential regulatory challenges, and addressed competitive threats from rival companies also interested in the target. The CFO emphasized the critical nature of timing, explaining that their primary competitor had already submitted a preliminary offer and that quick action was essential to secure the opportunity. The documentation appeared legitimate, the business rationale was sound, and the familiar faces of trusted colleagues provided the reassurance needed for such a significant financial decision.

Following established internal protocols for high-value international transactions, the employee carefully processed the requested transfers. Over the course of the discussion, fifteen separate wire transfers were authorized, each ranging from several hundred thousand to several million dollars, totaling HK$200 million approximately US$25.6 million. Each transaction was methodically executed according to the company's refined procedures, with appropriate documentation and verification steps that had been developed and tested over years of handling similar complex deals (World Economic Forum, 2025).

It was only weeks later, when the supposed acquisition failed to materialize and routine quarterly financial audits began raising questions about the unusual series of transfers, that the devastating truth emerged. A comprehensive internal investigation, supported by external cybersecurity experts and law enforcement agencies, revealed the shocking reality: every single person on that video conference call, except for the employee who authorized the transfers, had been an artificial intelligence-generated deepfake.

The sophisticated criminal organization behind this attack had invested considerable time and resources in reconnaissance and preparation. They had systematically studied Arup's organizational structure through publicly available information, analyzed hours of footage from corporate conferences and interviews where executives had spoken, and collected voice samples from earnings calls, promotional videos, and other public appearances.

Using advanced artificial intelligence technology that has become increasingly accessible and sophisticated, they created convincing digital doubles capable of real-time interaction, natural conversation, and believable responses to unexpected questions during the video conference.

This attack represented something fundamentally different from traditional cybercrime. There was no malware to detect, no suspicious email attachments to flag, no unusual network traffic to monitor, and no technical vulnerabilities to exploit. The criminals never attempted to penetrate Arup's computer systems, bypass their firewalls, or compromise their security infrastructure. Instead, they weaponized artificial intelligence to target something far more fundamental and difficult to protect: human trust and the psychological mechanisms we rely upon to verify identity and authenticity in digital communications.

The Arup incident stands as a watershed moment in cybersecurity history, marking the emergence of a new category of threats that operate at the intersection of advanced technology and human psychology. It demonstrated how artificial intelligence has fundamentally transformed the digital battlefield, creating attack vectors that even the most security-conscious organizations with robust technical defenses struggle to anticipate and prevent.

The Staggering Reality of AI-Enabled Cybercrime

The Arup case, while shocking in its sophistication and financial impact, represents just one example of a rapidly expanding global phenomenon that is reshaping the entire cybersecurity landscape. According to comprehensive research conducted by leading cybersecurity organizations, the statistics reveal the staggering scale and explosive growth of AI-enabled cybercrime that has emerged in recent years.

Data from multiple authoritative sources paints a troubling picture of this new threat landscape. Deepfake fraud cases have surged by an astronomical 1,740% in North America between 2022 and 2023, with financial losses exceeding $200 million in the first quarter of 2025 alone (Cobalt, 2025). These numbers represent not just statistical abstractions, but real organizations, employees, and individuals whose trust has been systematically exploited and whose financial security has been permanently compromised.

A comprehensive survey conducted by Deloitte revealed that 25.9% of executives reported their organizations had experienced one or more deepfake incidents specifically targeting financial and accounting data in the twelve months prior to the study.

Even more concerning for future threat assessments, 50% of all surveyed executives indicated they expected a significant increase in such attacks over the following year, suggesting that the Arup incident may represent just the beginning of a new wave of AI-powered financial crime (Incode, 2025).

The democratization of artificial intelligence tools has fundamentally altered the economics and accessibility of sophisticated cybercrime. Where traditional fraud schemes once required extensive technical expertise, access to expensive tools, substantial financial resources, and often direct insider knowledge of target organizations, today's AI-powered attacks can be orchestrated by individuals with relatively modest technical skills and limited budgets.

According to current research, voice cloning technology now requires just 20 to 30 seconds of target audio to create convincing vocal replicas, while persuasive video deepfakes can be produced in as little as 45 minutes using freely available software applications (World Economic Forum, 2025).

The global AI voice cloning market, which serves as a key enabler for many of these attacks, was valued at $2.1 billion in 2023 and is projected to reach $25.6 billion by 2033, representing a compound annual growth rate that reflects both legitimate applications and malicious exploitation of the technology (Tech Advisors, 2025).

This explosive growth in the availability and sophistication of AI tools has created what cybersecurity experts describe as a "force multiplier effect" for criminal organizations.

Recent research by IBM and the Ponemon Institute provides additional context for understanding the broader impact of AI on cybersecurity.

Their 2025 Cost of a Data Breach Report, based on analysis of 600 organizations globally, found that 97% of breached organizations that experienced an AI-related security incident lacked proper AI access controls. Even more concerning, 63% of organizations surveyed revealed they had no AI governance policies in place to manage AI systems or prevent employees from using unauthorized "shadow AI" applications (IBM, 2025).

The financial implications of this governance gap are substantial. Organizations with high levels of shadow AI usage, where employees download or use unapproved internet-based AI tools, experienced an additional $670,000 in average breach costs compared to organizations with proper AI governance frameworks.

This represents a significant premium that organizations pay for failing to properly manage their AI adoption and security practices.

The Dual Nature of Artificial Intelligence in Cybersecurity

The story of artificial intelligence in cybersecurity represents one of the most fascinating and complex paradoxes in modern technology. The same technological capabilities that provide cybersecurity professionals with unprecedented abilities to detect, analyze, and respond to threats also empower malicious actors with sophisticated new methods of attack. This duality is not merely theoretical it plays out daily in corporate networks, government systems, and critical infrastructure worldwide, shaping every strategic decision made in the realm of digital security.

Understanding this paradox requires examining both sides of the AI equation with equal rigor and respect for their capabilities. The technologies that strengthen our digital defenses and the identical technologies that create new vulnerabilities often emerge from the same research laboratories, use the same algorithms, and rely on the same computational principles. This creates a unique situation where defenders and attackers often have access to similar tools, making the difference between successful defense and successful attack dependent on factors such as implementation strategy, resource allocation, organizational commitment, and human expertise.

The Defensive Revolution: AI as a Cybersecurity Game-Changer

On the defensive side of cybersecurity, artificial intelligence has revolutionized virtually every aspect of threat detection, analysis, and response. The transformation has been so significant that many security professionals describe it as the difference between fighting with conventional weapons and deploying advanced military technology. Modern AI-powered security systems can process and analyze vast amounts of data in real-time, identifying patterns, anomalies, and threat indicators that would take human analysts weeks or months to discover, if they could identify them at all.

According to the 2025 State of AI in Cybersecurity Report conducted by the Ponemon Institute, organizations have dramatically improved their security postures through AI adoption. Seventy percent of survey respondents reported that AI increases the productivity of IT security personnel, representing an increase from 66%. More specifically, 51% of respondents indicated that AI improves the efficiency of junior analysts, enabling senior analysts to focus on critical threats and strategic projects rather than routine monitoring and initial threat assessment tasks (Ponemon Institute, 2025).

The IBM Cost of a Data Breach Report 2025 provides compelling quantitative evidence for the defensive value of AI in cybersecurity operations. Organizations that made extensive use of AI and automation in their security operations experienced average breach costs of $3.84 million, compared to $5.72 million for organizations that did not use these technologies, a savings of $1.88 million per incident. Even more significantly, AI-powered security systems enabled organizations to identify and contain breaches within a mean time of 241 days, the lowest detection and containment period recorded in nine years of research (IBM, 2025).

Google's Project Zero, working in collaboration with DeepMind, has developed groundbreaking AI systems that represent a paradigm shift in proactive vulnerability research. Their "Big Sleep" AI agent autonomously searches for and discovers previously unknown security vulnerabilities in software systems, effectively transforming cybersecurity from a reactive discipline to a proactive one. Big Sleep had successfully identified its first real-world security vulnerability, and by 2025, the system had discovered multiple critical vulnerabilities, including CVE-2025-6965 in SQLite, a database system used by millions of applications worldwide (Google, 2025).

The significance of these achievements cannot be overstated in the context of traditional cybersecurity practices. Conventional vulnerability research has long been a manual, labor-intensive process that relies heavily on human expertise to analyze source code, identify potential weaknesses, develop proof-of-concept exploits, and coordinate responsible disclosure with software vendors. This approach, while effective when properly resourced, is inherently limited by human cognitive capacity, time constraints, and the exponential growth in software complexity across modern digital systems.

Leading cybersecurity companies have also demonstrated the practical benefits of AI implementation in real-world security operations. Darktrace has deployed sophisticated AI systems such as FACADE (Fast and Accurate Contextual Anomaly Detection), which has been performing insider threat detection since 2018, processing billions of daily security events across enterprise infrastructures to identify internal threats and anomalous behavior patterns. What makes FACADE particularly innovative is its unique contrastive learning approach, which doesn't require historical attack data to function effectively. Instead, the system learns what constitutes normal behavior within each specific organizational context and flags deviations that might indicate malicious activity (Google, 2025).

The maturity of AI adoption in cybersecurity has increased significantly over the past year. According to Ponemon Institute research, 53% of organizations have achieved either the full adoption stage (31% of respondents) or the mature stage (22% of respondents) in their AI security implementations. This represents a substantial increase, when only 47% of respondents had reached similar levels of AI maturity in their security operations (Ponemon Institute, 2025).

The Offensive Threat: AI as a Weapon Against Security

However, the same technological capabilities that strengthen cybersecurity defenses are equally available to malicious actors, creating a continuous arms race where the sophistication of attacks evolves in lockstep with defensive capabilities. The offensive applications of AI in cybersecurity represent some of the most concerning developments in the modern threat landscape, precisely because they leverage the same advanced technologies that defenders rely upon, often with fewer ethical, legal, or operational constraints.

Cybercriminals and nation-state actors have quickly recognized and exploited the offensive potential of AI technologies. The same machine learning algorithms that enable security systems to identify threats can be repurposed to create more sophisticated attack vectors that adapt in real-time to defensive countermeasures, automatically modify their behavior to avoid detection systems, and scale to levels that would be impossible with traditional manual approaches.

The statistics surrounding AI-enabled attacks are particularly alarming. According to comprehensive industry research, AI now generates 40% of phishing emails targeting businesses, representing a dramatic shift from traditional manually-crafted social engineering approaches (Cobalt, 2025). These AI-generated phishing campaigns achieve significantly higher success rates, with 78% of people opening AI-generated phishing emails and 21% clicking on malicious content contained within them. Generative AI tools and automation help attackers compose phishing emails up to 40% faster than traditional methods, while also enabling mass personalization and localization that makes detection more difficult (Tech Advisors, 2025).

The emergence of deepfake technology as an attack vector represents one of the most significant developments in AI-enabled cybercrime. Industry projections suggest that deepfake attacks will increase by 50% to 60%, with an estimated 140,000 to 150,000 global incidents. Particularly concerning is the fact that 75% of identified deepfakes impersonated a CEO or other C-suite executive, directly targeting the highest levels of organizational decision-making authority (Cobalt, 2025).

North Korean Advanced Persistent Threat (APT) groups have demonstrated sophisticated applications of AI in state-sponsored cyber operations. In July 2025, cybersecurity researchers documented a spear-phishing attack where the Kimsuky group used ChatGPT and other generative AI tools to create convincing fake military identification cards as part of a campaign targeting South Korean defense-related institutions. The attackers crafted AI-generated ID cards that were sufficiently realistic to serve as credible social engineering tools in highly sensitive government and military contexts (Genians Security Center,

2025).

These attacks represent a significant evolution in the sophistication and accessibility of nation-state cyber operations. Previously, creating convincing fake documents required specialized skills in graphic design, detailed knowledge of authentic document formats and security features, access to high-quality printing equipment, and often insider information about target organizations. AI tools have eliminated many of these traditional barriers, enabling threat actors to generate convincing fake credentials, documents, and communications with minimal technical expertise, financial resources, or operational infrastructure.

The scaling effect of AI in offensive operations is perhaps even more concerning than its increased sophistication. Traditional cyberattacks, even those conducted by well-resourced criminal organizations or nation-states, were inherently limited by human capacity constraints. Each target required individual attention, customized research and approach development, and manual execution of complex attack sequences. AI removes these bottlenecks, enabling attackers to simultaneously target hundreds or thousands of potential victims with personalized, sophisticated attack campaigns that adapt dynamically to individual target characteristics and defensive responses.

The Arms Race Dynamic and Escalating Complexity

The dual nature of AI in cybersecurity has created what researchers describe as a continuous "arms race dynamic" between attackers and defenders. As defensive AI systems become more sophisticated at detecting traditional attack patterns and behavioral anomalies, attackers develop AI-powered methods specifically designed to evade these detection mechanisms. When defenders implement new AI-based authentication systems, attackers respond with deepfake technologies capable of bypassing biometric security measures. When organizations deploy AI-powered network monitoring systems, attackers develop AI techniques for mimicking legitimate traffic patterns and user behaviors.

This dynamic creates a continuous cycle of technological escalation where both sides must constantly innovate, adapt, and invest in new capabilities to maintain their effectiveness. Unlike traditional cybersecurity arms races that evolved over months or years, AI-enabled competition operates at machine speed, with new attack and defense techniques emerging, being tested, and being countered within days or weeks rather than traditional development cycles.

The complexity of this arms race is further compounded by the fact that many of the most advanced AI technologies are developed and published by academic and commercial research organizations with legitimate, beneficial purposes. The same research that enables breakthrough medical diagnoses, enhances educational applications, advances scientific discoveries, and improves quality of life also provides the foundational knowledge and tools that can be repurposed for more sophisticated cyberattacks. This dual-use nature of AI technology creates complex ethical, policy, and governance challenges that traditional cybersecurity frameworks struggle to address effectively.

The Evolution and Transformation of Cyber Threats in the AI Era

The integration of artificial intelligence into cybersecurity represents far more than incremental technological advancement or the simple automation of existing processes. It signifies a fundamental evolution in the very nature of cyber threats, their development methodologies, execution techniques, and potential impact on organizations and society. To understand the magnitude of this transformation, it is essential to examine how traditional cyber threats have evolved and what entirely new categories of threats have emerged, specifically in the AI era.

From Human-Mediated to Machine-Mediated Cyber Operations

Traditional cyberattacks, while often sophisticated and frequently successful, typically followed predictable patterns that security professionals could anticipate, prepare for, and defend against using established methodologies and proven techniques. These attacks relied primarily on exploiting known vulnerabilities in software systems, deploying social engineering techniques that required significant human interaction and psychological manipulation, or distributing malware that followed recognizable behavioral patterns and left detectable forensic evidence.

While these traditional attacks could be highly sophisticated and often achieved their objectives, they were inherently constrained by human limitations in terms of scale, speed, adaptability, and operational complexity. Attackers needed to manually research targets, craft individualized approaches, make real-time decisions during attack execution, and adapt to unexpected defensive responses using human judgment and experience.

The integration of AI into cyber operations has fundamentally altered these traditional constraints and limitations. Between 2020 and 2025, the threat landscape experienced what researchers describe as a "volatility explosion," characterized by the emergence of zero-click exploits, advanced supply chain attacks, AI-assisted infiltration techniques, and automated attack systems that operate at machine speed and scale while requiring minimal human oversight.

Modern AI-powered attacks like EchoLeak, which emerged in 2025, exemplify this fundamental evolution. EchoLeak demonstrated how cybercriminals could exploit Microsoft Copilot's natural language interface to extract sensitive data from organizational systems without requiring any user interaction, suspicious downloads, or traditional indicators of compromise. Unlike traditional attacks that depend on users clicking malicious links, opening infected attachments, or interacting with suspicious content, EchoLeak operates entirely through AI-to-AI communication channels, representing a new category of threats that bypass human-centric security measures entirely (Sangfor, 2025).

This evolution represents a critical shift from what cybersecurity professionals classify as "human-mediated" cyberattacks to "machine-mediated" cyber operations. Where traditional attacks required human decision-making, adaptation, and manual execution at each step of the attack lifecycle, AI-enhanced attacks can operate autonomously, adapting to defensive countermeasures in real-time, simultaneously scaling across thousands of targets, and executing complex multi-stage campaigns without continuous human oversight.

The Acceleration of Attack Timelines and Response Requirements

Perhaps the most significant impact of AI on cybersecurity has been the dramatic transformation of both attack and defense timelines. Traditional cybersecurity operations functioned on human timescales, where threats were identified, analyzed, and responded to over periods of hours, days, weeks, or in some cases, months. This relatively slow pace allowed security teams time for investigation, consultation, planning, and coordinated response efforts.

AI has compressed these traditional timelines to seconds, minutes, or at most hours, creating an operational environment where the speed of detection, analysis, and response often determines the difference between successful defense and catastrophic compromise. According to IBM's latest research, organizations equipped with extensive AI-powered security systems were able to identify and contain breaches within an average of 241 days the fastest containment time recorded in nine years of data collection. In contrast, organizations without AI assistance required significantly longer periods for detection and containment (IBM, 2025).

However, this acceleration effect applies equally to both defensive and offensive operations. AI-powered attacks can now progress from initial reconnaissance through data exfiltration or system compromise within hours or even minutes, compared to traditional attacks that might require weeks or months to achieve similar objectives. This compression of attack timelines places unprecedented pressure on defensive systems and security teams to operate at machine speed and scale.

The Expansion of Attack Surfaces and Vulnerability Categories

AI has not only accelerated existing threats but has also created entirely new categories of vulnerabilities and attack surfaces that did not exist in traditional cybersecurity frameworks. The proliferation of AI systems, machine learning models, and automated decision-making systems has introduced novel vulnerability classes that require specialized knowledge, tools, and defensive strategies.

According to comprehensive industry research, the four most common types of cyberattacks specifically targeting AI systems are poisoning attacks (which corrupt training data to manipulate model behavior), inference attacks (which extract information about training data or model architecture), extraction attacks (which steal model parameters or intellectual property), and evasion attacks (which fool AI systems into making incorrect decisions) (Tech Advisors, 2025).

These AI-specific attack vectors represent a fundamental expansion of the traditional cybersecurity threat landscape. Organizations must now defend not only against conventional threats targeting their traditional IT infrastructure but also against specialized attacks targeting their AI systems, machine learning models, and automated business processes. This dual responsibility significantly increases the complexity and cost of maintaining effective cybersecurity postures.

The rise of "shadow AI" usage within organizations has created additional attack surfaces that are particularly difficult to monitor and secure. IBM's research found that 63% of organizations lack AI governance policies to manage AI systems or prevent the proliferation of unauthorized AI tools, while organizations with high levels of shadow AI usage experienced an average of $670,000 in additional breach costs (IBM, 2025). This represents a new category of insider threat where well-intentioned employees inadvertently create security vulnerabilities by using unmanaged AI applications for legitimate business purposes.

Nation-State Actors and the Industrialization of AI-Powered Cyber Operations

The adoption of AI by nation-state actors represents one of the most concerning developments in the evolution of cyber threats. Unlike traditional cybercriminal organizations that are primarily motivated by financial gain, nation-state actors possess significant resources, long-term strategic objectives, and fewer operational constraints, enabling them to develop and deploy AI-powered cyber capabilities at unprecedented scale and sophistication.

Recent intelligence assessments indicate that major nation-state actors have established dedicated AI research and development programs specifically focused on cyber operations. These programs combine cutting-edge AI research with traditional intelligence tradecraft, creating hybrid capabilities that merge technological sophistication with a deep understanding of geopolitical objectives and target vulnerabilities.

The Kimsuky group's use of AI-generated fake military identification cards represents just one example of how nation-state actors are integrating AI into traditional intelligence and cyber espionage operations. This approach allows them to scale their operations while maintaining operational security and plausible deniability that would be difficult to achieve with traditional human-intensive approaches (Genians Security Center, 2025).

Intelligence agencies and cybersecurity researchers are particularly concerned about the potential for AI to enable "influence operations" that go beyond traditional information warfare. AI-powered systems can generate convincing disinformation content, create fake social media personas, manipulate online discussions, and even generate synthetic media designed to influence public opinion, political processes, and economic decisions in target countries.

The Economic and Business Impact of AI-Enabled Cybersecurity Threats

The financial implications of AI-enabled cybersecurity threats extend far beyond the immediate costs of individual cyber incidents. They represent a fundamental shift in the economic landscape of cybersecurity risk, business continuity planning, and organizational strategic decision-making. Understanding these economic impacts is crucial for business leaders, policymakers, and cybersecurity professionals working to develop effective risk management strategies in the AI era.

The Rising Costs of Cybersecurity Incidents and Breach Response

IBM's comprehensive Cost of a Data Breach Report provides authoritative quantitative data on the financial impact of cybersecurity incidents in the AI era. The global average cost of a data breach reached $4.88 million, representing a 10% increase from the previous year and the largest annual increase since the pandemic era. However, these headline figures only tell part of the story about the true economic impact of modern cybersecurity threats (IBM).

The breakdown of these costs reveals how AI-enabled attacks create particularly expensive incident response requirements. Of the total average breach cost, $2.8 million came specifically from lost business due to operational downtime and customer churn, combined with post-breach activities such as increased customer support staffing, regulatory fines, legal fees, and reputation management efforts. This component represents the highest cost category for business disruption and recovery activities recorded over the past six years (Barracuda Networks).

Industry-specific analysis reveals even more concerning trends. The healthcare sector, which has been consistently targeted by cybercriminals due to the high value of medical data and the critical nature of healthcare operations, experienced average breach costs of $9.77 million. The financial services industry faced average costs of $6.08 million per incident, which is 22% higher than the global average and reflects the sophisticated nature of attacks targeting financial institutions (IBM).

For organizations dealing with "mega breaches" involving one to ten million compromised records, the financial impact becomes exponentially more severe. These incidents, while representing only a small fraction of total cybersecurity incidents, cost an average of $42 million per breach nearly nine times more expensive than the global average. When breaches involve 50 million or more records, average costs reach $375 million, representing existential threats to all but the largest organizations (Zscaler, 2025).

The Hidden Costs of AI Governance Failures and Shadow AI

Beyond the direct costs of cybersecurity incidents, organizations face significant hidden costs related to AI governance failures and unmanaged AI adoption. IBM's 2025 research revealed that organizations with high levels of shadow AI usage, where employees download or use unapproved internet-based AI tools, experienced an additional $670,000 in average breach costs compared to organizations with proper AI governance frameworks in place (IBM, 2025).

These shadow AI costs reflect a broader pattern of "security debt" that organizations accumulate when they adopt AI technologies without implementing appropriate security controls, governance frameworks, and risk management processes. This security debt manifests in several ways: increased vulnerability to AI-specific attacks, higher breach costs when incidents occur, extended recovery times due to complex AI system dependencies, and regulatory compliance failures in industries with strict data protection requirements.

The Ponemon Institute's research on insider risks provides additional context for understanding these hidden costs. Their 2025 Cost of Insider Risks Global Report found that the average cost of insider incidents has reached $17.4 million, with organizations now dedicating 16.5% of their annual IT security budget to insider risk management more than double the 8.2% allocated in 2023 (DTEX Systems, 2025). A significant portion of these insider risks is now attributed to employees' unmanaged use of AI tools and systems.

The Economic Benefits of AI-Powered Security Investments

While AI-enabled threats create new costs and risks, organizations that invest strategically in AI-powered security technologies achieve substantial economic benefits that often justify the required investments. IBM's research demonstrates that organizations making extensive use of AI and automation in their security operations experienced average breach costs of $3.84 million, compared to $5.72 million for organizations that did not deploy these technologies a net savings of $1.88 million per incident (IBM, 2025).

These cost savings result from several factors enabled by AI-powered security systems. Organizations with AI-enhanced security capabilities detect breaches faster, contain incidents more quickly, reduce the scope of data compromise, minimize business disruption, and require fewer human resources for routine security monitoring and incident response activities.

The productivity gains alone are substantial: 70% of survey respondents in Ponemon Institute research reported that AI increases the productivity of IT security personnel, while 69% indicated that AI adoption improved job satisfaction by eliminating tedious manual tasks (Ponemon Institute, 2025).

The return on investment for AI security technologies extends beyond immediate cost savings to include strategic business benefits that are difficult to quantify but critically important for long-term organizational success. These benefits include enhanced customer trust and confidence, improved regulatory compliance capabilities, reduced cyber insurance premiums, faster time-to-market for digital products and services, and increased competitive advantage through superior security postures.

Market Growth and Investment Trends in AI Cybersecurity

The economic significance of AI in cybersecurity is reflected in the explosive growth of market investment and commercial activity in this sector. The global artificial intelligence cybersecurity market was valued at $22.4 billion in 2023 and is projected to grow at a compound annual growth rate of 21.9%, reaching $60.6 billion by 2028 (Markets and Markets, 2023). This growth rate significantly exceeds most other technology sectors and reflects both the urgent need for AI-powered security solutions and the substantial economic opportunity they represent.

Investment patterns within this market reveal interesting trends about organizational priorities and risk management strategies. According to industry research, 82% of IT decision-makers planned to invest in AI-driven cybersecurity solutions within two years, with 48% planning to make these investments before the end of 2023 (Lakera, 2025). These investment commitments represent a fundamental shift in how organizations allocate cybersecurity resources and approach risk management in the AI era.

The cybersecurity workforce market also reflects the economic impact of AI adoption. The global cybersecurity workforce grew by 12.6% in 2023, but demand continues to significantly outstrip supply, with an estimated shortage of four million cybersecurity professionals. This skills gap could reach 85 million professionals by 2030 if not addressed through technological solutions, training programs, and innovative recruitment strategies (SentinelOne, 2025).

Organizations that successfully implement AI-powered security solutions can partially address this workforce shortage while reducing their dependence on scarce human cybersecurity expertise. This creates a competitive advantage for early AI adopters and puts additional pressure on organizations that delay their AI security investments.

The Trust Infrastructure Under Siege: Psychological and Social Implications

The emergence of AI-powered cybersecurity threats represents more than a technological challenge it constitutes a fundamental assault on the trust infrastructure that underlies all digital communications, business transactions, and social interactions in our interconnected world. The Arup incident and similar deepfake attacks illuminate critical vulnerabilities that extend far beyond technical systems to encompass the social and psychological foundations upon which digital society is built.

The Erosion of Digital Trust and Authentication Assumptions

For decades, cybersecurity frameworks have been built upon certain foundational assumptions about digital trust and human authentication capabilities. These assumptions include the reliability of familiar voices and faces as identity verification mechanisms, the authenticity of communications from known contacts using established channels, the trustworthiness of video and audio evidence for decision-making purposes, and the ability of trained professionals to distinguish between genuine and fraudulent communications based on contextual clues and behavioral patterns.

AI-powered attacks systematically undermine each of these foundational assumptions. When video calls, audio messages, written communications, and even behavioral patterns can be convincingly generated by artificial intelligence systems, the traditional methods of establishing trust and verifying identity become fundamentally unreliable. This creates what security researchers describe as an "authenticity crisis" in digital communications that challenges the basic premises upon which business, government, and social interactions are conducted.

The psychological impact of this authenticity crisis extends beyond immediate security concerns to affect human behavior, decision-making processes, and social relationships. As Rob Greig, Arup's Chief Information Officer, reflected on their incident: "Like many other businesses around the globe, our operations are subject to regular attacks, including invoice fraud, phishing scams, WhatsApp voice spoofing, and deepfakes. What we have seen is that the number and sophistication of these attacks have been rising sharply in recent months" (World Economic Forum, 2025).

This statement captures a critical reality facing modern organizations: traditional security awareness training becomes less effective when the fundamental assumptions about digital communication authenticity can no longer be trusted. Employees who have been trained to be suspicious of unexpected emails, to verify unusual requests through alternative communication channels, and to question anything that seems suspicious now face situations where routine business meetings conducted through established, trusted channels with familiar colleagues can be entirely fabricated.

The Weaponization of Human Psychology and Evolutionary Biology

AI-powered attacks like the Arup incident succeed precisely because they exploit millions of years of human evolutionary psychology using technology that has existed for less than a decade. Human beings have evolved sophisticated mechanisms for recognizing faces, voices, and behavioral patterns as a survival mechanism, enabling us to distinguish between friends and threats, establish social hierarchies, and maintain group cohesion. These recognition systems operate largely at a subconscious level and are extremely difficult to override through conscious effort or training.

The criminals behind the Arup attack understood this psychological vulnerability and designed their approach to exploit it systematically. They created convincing visual and auditory representations of trusted individuals, maintained consistent behavioral patterns throughout the interaction, provided plausible explanations for the unusual request, and structured the conversation to feel natural and unremarkable. The attack succeeded not despite the employee's training and experience, but precisely because it was designed to bypass the conscious security awareness mechanisms that might have flagged a more traditional phishing or social engineering attempt.

This represents a fundamental shift in the nature of social engineering attacks. Traditional social engineering relied on psychological manipulation, pressure tactics, creating false urgency, or exploiting human emotions like fear, greed, or desire to be helpful. These approaches often triggered conscious warning signs that well-trained individuals could recognize and resist. AI-powered social engineering, by contrast, operates by creating experiences that feel completely normal and authentic, bypassing conscious security awareness entirely.

Organizational and Societal Implications of Trust Erosion

The broader implications of AI-enabled trust erosion extend far beyond individual organizations to affect entire industries, economic systems, and social structures. The European Union's AI Act, which entered force, represents an early attempt to address these challenges through regulatory frameworks that mandate transparency obligations and technical marking for AI-generated content. However, the global nature of AI development and deployment makes comprehensive regulatory solutions extremely challenging to implement and enforce (World Economic Forum, 2025).

With industry projections suggesting that AI-enabled fraud could reach

$40 billion annually by 2027, the stakes extend far beyond financial losses to encompass the basic assumptions that enable digital commerce, remote work, international business relationships, and global communication networks (World Economic Forum, 2025). If individuals and organizations cannot trust the authenticity of digital communications, the efficiency gains and cost reductions that have driven digital transformation over the past decades could be severely compromised.

The psychological impact of this trust erosion is already becoming visible in organizational behavior and decision-making processes. Security professionals report increasing levels of paranoia and suspicion in workplace communications, with employees becoming reluctant to trust video calls, audio messages, or even written communications from colleagues they haven't physically seen recently. This "trust recession" creates operational inefficiencies, slows decision-making processes, and can undermine the collaborative relationships that modern organizations depend upon.

The Cultural and Generational Divide in AI Threat Perception

Research reveals significant generational and cultural differences in how individuals perceive and respond to AI-enabled threats. According to comprehensive survey data, 71% of people worldwide don't know what deepfakes are, while 25% of individuals have difficulty distinguishing deepfake audio from authentic recordings (Keepnet Labs, 2025). These knowledge gaps create uneven vulnerability patterns across different demographic groups and organizational levels.

Younger employees, who have grown up with digital technology and social media, often demonstrate greater skepticism about online content but may lack the business experience to recognize sophisticated financial fraud schemes. Older executives, who possess extensive business judgment and decision-making authority, may be less familiar with AI capabilities and more vulnerable to technologically sophisticated attacks that mimic traditional business communications.

This generational divide creates particular challenges for organizational security training and awareness programs. Traditional cybersecurity education approaches that focus on technical indicators or behavioral red flags may be ineffective against AI-powered attacks that are specifically designed to appear normal and authentic. Organizations must develop new training methodologies that address the psychological and perceptual aspects of AI-enabled threats while remaining practical and actionable for employees across different age groups and technical sophistication levels.

The New Defensive Paradigm: Adapting Security Frameworks for the AI Era

The emergence of AI as both weapon and shield has necessitated a fundamental rethinking of cybersecurity strategies, frameworks, and operational approaches. Traditional cybersecurity methodologies, which were developed for defending against human-operated attacks with predictable patterns and timelines, are insufficient for addressing AI-enabled threats that operate at machine speed and scale while continuously adapting to defensive countermeasures.

Zero Trust Architecture and the "Never Trust, Always Verify" Model

The proliferation of AI-powered attacks has accelerated organizational adoption of Zero Trust security architectures, which operate on the principle that no user, device, or communication should be trusted by default, regardless of their location within or outside the organizational network perimeter. This approach represents a fundamental shift from traditional "trust but verify" models that assumed some level of inherent trustworthiness in communications and systems based on source credentials, network location, or previous authentication events.

Zero Trust frameworks are particularly well-suited for defending against AI-enabled attacks because they require continuous verification of identity, device integrity, and behavioral patterns for every access request or communication. Rather than relying on initial authentication events that could be compromised through deepfake or social engineering attacks, Zero Trust systems continuously monitor and verify user behavior, device health, network traffic patterns, and data access patterns to detect anomalies that might indicate compromise.

Implementation of Zero Trust architectures requires significant technological and organizational changes. According to industry research, organizations that have successfully deployed comprehensive Zero Trust frameworks report substantial improvements in their ability to detect and respond to sophisticated attacks, including AI-enabled threats. However, the complexity of implementing Zero Trust across legacy systems, diverse technology environments, and global organizational structures presents significant challenges that many organizations struggle to address effectively.

AI-Powered Defense Systems and Autonomous Security Operations

The same AI technologies that enable sophisticated attacks also provide defenders with unprecedented capabilities for threat detection, analysis, and response. Modern AI-powered security systems can process and analyze vast amounts of network traffic, user behavior data, and threat intelligence in real-time, identifying patterns and anomalies that would be impossible for human analysts to detect manually.

According to Ponemon Institute research, the maturity and effectiveness of AI-powered defense systems have improved dramatically over the past year. In 2025, 53% of organizations achieved either the full adoption stage (31%) or mature stage (22%) in their AI security implementations, compared to 47%. These organizations report significant improvements in their security postures, including enhanced threat prioritization capabilities (56% of respondents), increased SOC team efficiency (51%), and faster threat analysis capabilities (43%) (Ponemon Institute, 2025).

The development of autonomous security operations represents one of the most significant advances in defensive cybersecurity capabilities. These systems can automatically detect, analyze, and respond to threats without human intervention, operating at machine speed to counter AI-powered attacks. Google's FACADE system, which processes billions of daily security events to identify insider threats, exemplifies this approach by using contrastive learning techniques that don't require historical attack data to function effectively.

However, the deployment of autonomous security systems also creates new challenges and risks. Organizations must carefully balance the benefits of machine-speed response capabilities with the need for human oversight, accountability, and strategic decision-making. Poorly configured autonomous systems can create false positive alerts, interfere with legitimate business operations, or even be manipulated by sophisticated attackers who understand their operational parameters.

Collaborative Threat Intelligence and Information Sharing

The global nature of AI-enabled threats requires unprecedented levels of collaboration and information sharing between organizations, industries, and government agencies. Traditional approaches to cybersecurity, which often emphasized secrecy and competitive advantage through superior security capabilities, are insufficient for addressing threats that can rapidly adapt and scale across multiple targets simultaneously.

Industry initiatives for collaborative threat intelligence sharing have expanded significantly in response to AI-enabled threats. These programs enable organizations to share anonymized threat data, attack indicators, and defensive techniques while maintaining competitive confidentiality about their specific security implementations and vulnerabilities. The effectiveness of these collaborative approaches is demonstrated by faster threat detection times, improved attack attribution capabilities, and more effective countermeasures against sophisticated threat actors.

Government agencies and regulatory bodies are also playing increasingly important roles in coordinating defensive responses to AI-enabled threats. The European Union's AI Act, various national cybersecurity strategies, and international cooperation frameworks provide policy foundations for addressing AI-related security challenges. However, the rapid pace of AI development and deployment often outpaces regulatory processes, creating gaps between emerging threats and available policy responses.

Privacy-Preserving AI and Federated Learning Approaches

One of the significant challenges in deploying AI for cybersecurity purposes is the need to analyze sensitive data while maintaining privacy and regulatory compliance requirements. Traditional AI systems often require access to large datasets that may contain personally identifiable information, proprietary business data, or other sensitive information that organizations are reluctant or legally prohibited from sharing.

Federated learning approaches address this challenge by enabling AI systems to learn from distributed datasets without requiring centralized access to the underlying data. This technique allows organizations to benefit from AI capabilities while maintaining control over their sensitive information and complying with data protection regulations such as GDPR, CCPA, and industry-specific requirements.

The adoption of privacy-preserving AI techniques is particularly important for industries such as healthcare, financial services, and government agencies that handle highly sensitive information but also face sophisticated AI-enabled threats. These organizations require AI-powered security capabilities but cannot compromise their data protection obligations or regulatory compliance requirements to achieve them.

Future Implications: Strategic Recommendations The Quantum Computing Threat Horizon

As AI continues to evolve and mature, cybersecurity professionals must also prepare for the next generation of technological disruptions that could fundamentally alter the threat landscape. Quantum computing represents one of the most significant potential disruptions to current cybersecurity frameworks, with the potential to render many current encryption and security protocols obsolete.

While practical quantum computers capable of breaking current encryption standards remain several years away, the timeline for their development is uncertain, and the potential impact would be catastrophic for organizations that are unprepared. AI-powered quantum computing systems could potentially break RSA encryption, compromise PKI infrastructures, and undermine the cryptographic foundations that secure modern digital communications and transactions.

Organizations must begin preparing for the quantum threat by implementing quantum-resistant encryption algorithms, developing quantum-safe communication protocols, and ensuring that their AI-powered security systems can be updated to address quantum-enabled attacks when they emerge. This preparation requires significant technical expertise, strategic planning, and financial investment that many organizations are not yet prepared to undertake.

Regulatory and Policy Evolution

The regulatory landscape surrounding AI and cybersecurity continues to evolve rapidly as policymakers struggle to keep pace with technological developments and emerging threats. Current regulatory frameworks such as the EU AI Act, various national cybersecurity strategies, and industry-specific requirements provide important foundations for addressing AI-related security challenges, but significant gaps remain.

Future regulatory developments are likely to focus on mandatory AI governance requirements, liability frameworks for AI-related security incidents, international cooperation mechanisms for addressing cross-border AI threats, and technical standards for AI system security and transparency. Organizations must monitor these regulatory developments closely and ensure that their AI adoption strategies are compatible with emerging compliance requirements.

The challenge for policymakers is to create regulatory frameworks that provide meaningful protection against AI-enabled threats without stifling innovation or creating excessive compliance burdens that disadvantage legitimate organizations compared to malicious actors who operate outside regulatory constraints.

Workforce Development and Skills Evolution

The AI transformation of cybersecurity is creating significant changes in workforce requirements, skill development needs, and career progression paths for cybersecurity professionals. Traditional cybersecurity roles that focused primarily on network monitoring, incident response, and vulnerability management are evolving to require an understanding of AI systems, machine learning algorithms, and automated security operations.

According to industry projections, the cybersecurity skills shortage could reach 85 million professionals by 2030 if not addressed through technological solutions and innovative training programs (SentinelOne, 2025). AI-powered security systems can help address this shortage by automating routine tasks and enabling junior analysts to focus on more strategic and complex security challenges.

However, the integration of AI into cybersecurity operations also creates new skill requirements for security professionals. They must understand how AI systems work, how they can be attacked, how to configure and maintain AI-powered security tools, and how to interpret and act upon AI-generated threat intelligence and recommendations.

Educational institutions, professional certification programs, and corporate training initiatives must adapt their curricula to address these evolving skill requirements. This includes developing new courses in AI security, machine learning for cybersecurity applications, AI governance and risk management, and human-AI collaboration in security operations.

Conclusion: Navigating the AI Cybersecurity Paradox

The Arup incident serves as both a warning and a catalyst for transformation in how we understand, approach, and implement cybersecurity in the age of artificial intelligence. It demonstrates that traditional boundaries between technical and social engineering attacks have dissolved, requiring new frameworks for understanding, detecting, and responding to threats that operate at the intersection of advanced technology and human psychology.

The statistics and research presented in this chapter reveal the magnitude of the challenge facing organizations worldwide. With deepfake fraud increasing by 1,740% in recent years, AI generating 40% of phishing emails, and organizations facing average breach costs of nearly $5 million, the stakes have never been higher. Yet the same research also demonstrates that organizations making strategic investments in AI-powered security capabilities achieve substantial benefits, including cost savings of nearly $2 million per incident and significantly faster threat detection and response capabilities.

The path forward requires organizations to embrace a fundamentally different approach to cybersecurity one that acknowledges both the tremendous potential and the significant risks of AI technology. This approach must combine technical solutions such as Zero Trust architectures and AI-powered defense systems with human-centric strategies that address the psychological and social dimensions of AI-enabled threats.

Success in this new environment will require unprecedented levels of collaboration between organizations, industries, and government agencies, along with substantial investments in new technologies, workforce development, and organizational transformation. The organizations that successfully navigate this transition will gain competitive advantages through superior security postures, enhanced operational efficiency, and greater resilience against evolving threats.

The battle for digital security in the age of AI is not merely a technological contest it is a struggle for the preservation of trust, authenticity, and human agency in an increasingly automated world. Understanding this struggle and developing effective responses to it will determine whether artificial intelligence becomes humanity's greatest tool for digital security or its most formidable threat.

As we stand at this critical juncture in cybersecurity history, the choices made by business leaders, policymakers, technology developers, and security professionals over the next few years will shape the digital security landscape for decades to come. The Arup incident reminds us that the future of cybersecurity is not a distant possibility it is here now, requiring immediate attention, strategic investment, and coordinated action to protect the digital foundations upon which modern society depends.

References

Barracuda Networks. (2024, August 20). *2024 IBM Breach Report: More breaches, higher costs.* Retrieved from https://blog.barracuda.com/2024/08/20/2024-IBM-breach-report-more-breaches-higher-costs

Cobalt. (2025, June 24). *Top 40 AI cybersecurity statistics.* Retrieved from https://www.cobalt.io/blog/top-40-ai-cybersecurity-statistics

DTEX Systems. (2025, February 25). *2025 Cost of Insider Risks Global Report.* Retrieved from https://www.dtexsystems.com/newsroom/press-releases/2025-ponemon-insider-threat-report-release/

Genians Security Center. (2025, September). *AI-driven deepfake military ID fraud campaign by Kimsuky APT.* Retrieved from https://www.genians.co.kr/en/blog/threat_intelligence/deepfake

Google. (2025, July 15). *A summer of security: Empowering cyber defenders with AI.* Google AI Blog. Retrieved from https://blog.google/technology/safety-security/cybersecurity-updates-summer-2025/

IBM. (2024, July 30). *IBM Report: Escalating data breach disruption pushes costs to new highs.* Retrieved from https://newsroom.ibm.com/2024-07-30-ibm-report-escalating-data-breach-disruption-pushes-costs-to-new-highs

IBM. (2025, August 7). *2025 Cost of a Data Breach Report: Navigating the AI rush without sidelining security*. Retrieved from https://www.ibm.com/think/x-force/2025-cost-of-a-data-breach-navigating-ai

IBM. (2025). *Cost of a data breach 2025.* Retrieved from https://www.ibm.com/reports/data-breach

Incode. (2025, July 14). *Top 5 cases of AI deepfake fraud from 2024 exposed.* Retrieved from https://incode.com/blog/top-5-cases-of-ai-deepfake-fraud-from-2024-exposed/

Keepnet Labs. (2025, April 18). *Deepfake statistics about cyber threats and trends 2025.* Retrieved from https://keepnetlabs.com/blog/deepfake-statistics-and-trends-about-cyber-threats-2024

Lakera. (2025). *AI Security Trends 2025: Market overview & statistics.* Retrieved from https://www.lakera.ai/blog/ai-security-trends

Markets and Markets. (2023, December 19). *Artificial Intelligence in Cybersecurity Market Share, Forecast.* Retrieved from https://www.marketsandmarkets.com/Market-Reports/artificial-intelligence-ai-cyber-security-market-220634996.html

Ponemon Institute. (2025, June). *The 2025 study on the state of AI in cybersecurity.* Retrieved from https://ponemonsullivanreport.com/2025/06/the-2025-study-on-the-state-of-ai-in-cybersecurity/

Sangfor. (2025, July 3). *AI-powered cyber threats: From zero-day exploits to deepfakes.* Retrieved from https://www.sangfor.com/blog/cybersecurity/ai-powered-cyber-threats-zero-day-deepfakes

SentinelOne. (2025, July 30). *Key cyber security statistics for 2025.* Retrieved from https://www.sentinelone.com/cybersecurity-101/cybersecurity/cyber-security-statistics/

Tech Advisors. (2025). *AI cyber attack statistics 2025.* Retrieved from https://tech-adv.com/blog/ai-cyber-attack-statistics/

World Economic Forum. (2025, February 4). *Cybercrime: Lessons learned from a $25m deepfake attack.* Retrieved from https://www.weforum.org/stories/2025/02/deepfake-ai-cybercrime-arup/

World Economic Forum. (2025, July). *Detecting dangerous AI is essential in the deepfake era.* Retrieved from https://www.weforum.org/stories/2025/07/why-detecting-dangerous-ai-is-key-to-keeping-trust-alive/

Zscaler. (2025, April 2). *7 key takeaways from IBM's Cost of a Data Breach Report 2024.* Retrieved from https://www.zscaler.com/blogs/product-insights/7-key-takeaways-ibm-s-cost-data-breach-report-2024

Chapter 2: Cybersecurity Basics: Understanding the Digital Threat Landscape

Introduction: The Foundation of Digital Defense

In an interconnected world where virtually every aspect of modern life, from banking and healthcare to education and entertainment, relies on digital systems, understanding the fundamentals of cybersecurity has become not merely advisable but essential. The rapid digital transformation accelerated by global events such as the COVID-19 pandemic has exponentially increased both our dependence on technology and our vulnerability to cyber threats. According to the International Monetary Fund, the frequency of cyberattacks has doubled since the pandemic, creating an environment where organizations and individuals face constant bombardment from increasingly sophisticated threat actors (SentinelOne, 2025).

The economic impact of these threats is staggering and continues to escalate. Cybersecurity Ventures estimates that global cybercrime costs will reach $10.5 trillion by 2025, with some forecasts suggesting this figure could soar to $23 trillion by 2027 (Viking Cloud, 2025). These astronomical figures represent not just direct financial losses but also the broader economic impact of business disruption, reputational damage, regulatory penalties, and the massive investments required to defend against evolving threats.

To effectively navigate this challenging landscape, it is crucial to first understand the foundational concepts that underpin cybersecurity as a discipline. This chapter provides a comprehensive exploration of cybersecurity basics, examining the fundamental principles that guide security practices, the common types of threats and attacks that organizations face, the essential defensive strategies employed to protect digital assets, and the critical importance of data protection in maintaining organizational resilience and trust.

Understanding these fundamentals is not merely an academic exercise; it represents the first critical step in developing effective security postures, implementing appropriate defensive measures, and fostering the security awareness necessary to protect against the sophisticated threats that characterize the modern digital threat landscape. As we will see throughout this chapter, the principles established decades ago continue to guide contemporary security practices, even as the specific threats and technologies continue to evolve at unprecedented rates.

The CIA Triad: Foundational Principles of Information Security

At the heart of cybersecurity lies a deceptively simple yet profoundly important conceptual framework known as the CIA triad. This model, which has guided information security practices for decades, comprises three fundamental principles: Confidentiality, Integrity, and Availability. Despite the coincidental acronym, this CIA has nothing to do with the intelligence agency; instead, it represents the three pillars upon which virtually all effective security strategies are built (Fortinet, 2025).

The CIA triad emerged organically over time through the evolution of early computing and information security research. While no single individual is credited with creating this model, its conceptual foundations can be traced to several influential documents from the 1970s and 1980s. A 1976 paper written for the U.S. Air Force explored early concepts related to information confidentiality, while David Clark and David Wilson's 1987 paper titled "A Comparison of Commercial and Military Computer Security Policies" examined integrity requirements in commercial computing environments. The concept of availability became more widely incorporated during the late 1980s, and by 1998, security professionals were commonly referencing these three principles together as the CIA triad (SecurityScorecard, 2025).

The enduring relevance of the CIA triad in 2025 speaks to the fundamental nature of the challenges it addresses. It remains embedded in virtually every modern security framework, from ISO 27001 to the General Data Protection Regulation (GDPR). Article 32 of the GDPR explicitly references these principles when defining the necessary security measures for protecting personal data, demonstrating how regulatory frameworks continue to rely on these foundational concepts (IT Governance, 2025).

Confidentiality: Protecting Information from Unauthorized Access

Confidentiality represents the first pillar of the CIA triad and focuses on ensuring that sensitive information remains accessible only to authorized individuals or systems. In essence, confidentiality is about maintaining secrecy and privacy, keeping private data private, and ensuring that unauthorized entities cannot view, access, or misuse information to which they have no legitimate claim (Norton, 2023).

The principle of confidentiality addresses several critical aspects of information security. At its most fundamental level, confidentiality protects against unauthorized disclosure of information, whether that disclosure occurs through deliberate theft, accidental exposure, or technical vulnerabilities. This protection extends to all forms of sensitive data, including but not limited to personal identifying information, financial records, medical data, intellectual property, trade secrets, and confidential business communications.

Common threats to confidentiality include sophisticated cyberattacks such as man-in-the-middle (MITM) attacks, where adversaries intercept communications between two parties to steal sensitive information, and phishing schemes designed to trick individuals into voluntarily surrendering their credentials or confidential data. However, confidentiality breaches are not solely the result of malicious activity; human error and insufficient security protocols frequently play significant roles in unauthorized information disclosure (Norton, 2023).

Organizations employ multiple technical and administrative controls to maintain confidentiality. Encryption stands as one of the most powerful tools for protecting confidentiality, transforming readable plaintext into unreadable ciphertext that can only be decrypted by parties possessing the appropriate cryptographic keys. Access control mechanisms, including both physical restrictions on who can enter secure areas and logical controls determining who can access specific digital resources, form another critical line of defense. Multi-factor authentication (MFA), which requires users to provide multiple forms of verification before gaining access to systems, significantly strengthens confidentiality protections by making it much more difficult for unauthorized individuals to masquerade as legitimate users (American Public University).

Data classification systems also play crucial roles in maintaining confidentiality by clearly identifying which information requires protection and at what level. By categorizing data according to sensitivity, for example, distinguishing between public, internal, confidential, and highly confidential information, organizations can apply appropriate protective measures proportional to the risks associated with unauthorized disclosure.

The importance of confidentiality extends beyond mere regulatory compliance or risk mitigation. In many industries, maintaining confidentiality is fundamental to organizational survival and competitive advantage. Healthcare organizations must protect patient privacy as mandated by regulations such as the Health Insurance Portability and Accountability Act (HIPAA). Financial institutions are required to safeguard customer financial information under numerous regulations, including the Payment Card Industry Data Security Standard (PCI DSS). Technology companies must protect proprietary intellectual property and trade secrets that represent the foundation of their competitive positioning.

Integrity: Ensuring Accuracy, Trustworthiness of Data

The second pillar of the CIA triad, integrity, focuses on maintaining the accuracy, consistency, and trustworthiness of data throughout its lifecycle. Integrity ensures that information remains genuine, unaltered, and true to its original state, free from unauthorized or undetected modification, corruption, or manipulation (University of Tulsa).

While confidentiality addresses who can view information, integrity addresses whether that information can be trusted. In the context of cybersecurity, integrity provides assurance that data has not been tampered with by unauthorized entities and that any authorized modifications are properly documented and traceable. This concept extends beyond simple data accuracy to encompass authentication (verifying the source of information), non-repudiation (ensuring that actions cannot be denied by those who performed them), and data lifecycle management.

Integrity violations can occur through multiple vectors and motivations. Malicious actors may deliberately alter, corrupt, or destroy data to manipulate information for personal gain, competitive advantage, or ideological purposes. Data tampering attacks targeting corporate information such as emails, employee records, financial data, and customer information can have devastating consequences for business operations, regulatory compliance, and organizational reputation (NIST, 2020).

Malware and ransomware represent particularly insidious threats to data integrity. While ransomware is often discussed primarily in terms of availability (since encrypted data becomes inaccessible), it also fundamentally compromises integrity by altering data into an unusable encrypted state. Other forms of malicious software can modify data subtly and persistently, making detection difficult and potentially allowing attackers to manipulate systems over extended periods.

Organizations employ various technical mechanisms to detect and prevent integrity violations. Hash functions play a central role in verifying data integrity by creating unique digital fingerprints of information. These cryptographic algorithms, including MD5, SHA-1, and more secure modern variants like SHA-256 and SHA-3, take input data of any size and produce fixed-length hash values. The deterministic nature of hash functions, always producing the same output for the same input, makes them ideal for integrity verification (GeeksforGeeks, 2025).

The process of integrity verification through hashing follows a straightforward but effective pattern. When data is transmitted or stored, a hash value is calculated and associated with that data. Later, when the data is retrieved or received, a new hash value is calculated and compared with the original. If the hash values match, integrity is confirmed the data has not been altered. Even minor modifications, such as changing a single character, produce completely different hash values, making unauthorized alterations immediately detectable.

Digital signatures represent another powerful tool for maintaining integrity, particularly in scenarios requiring both integrity verification and authentication. By combining cryptographic hashing with public key encryption, digital signatures provide mathematical proof that data originated from a specific source and has not been modified since signing. This technology underpins numerous critical applications, from secure email communications to software distribution and blockchain transactions.

Version control systems, change management processes, and comprehensive audit trails provide additional layers of integrity protection. These mechanisms create detailed records of who accessed data, when modifications occurred, and what specific changes were made. This audit capability not only deters unauthorized modifications but also enables organizations to detect integrity violations and, when necessary, roll back to known-good states.

The principle of integrity is explicitly referenced in one of the eight Data Protection Principles that form the foundation of the UK Data Protection Act 2018, which mandates that data must be "kept accurate and up to date." Organizations have legal obligations to implement appropriate measures, ensuring data accuracy, and preventing unauthorized modifications (VinciWorks, 2022).

Availability: Ensuring Timely and Reliable Access to Information

The third pillar of the CIA triad, availability, ensures that information and systems remain accessible and functional for authorized users whenever they are legitimately needed. While confidentiality and integrity focus on protecting data from unauthorized access and modification, availability addresses the fundamental requirement that legitimate users must be able to access and use information and systems without undue delay or disruption (Washington University, n.d.).

Availability encompasses multiple dimensions of system accessibility and reliability. At the most basic level, it requires that networks, servers, applications, and data repositories function properly and respond to legitimate requests in acceptable timeframes. However, availability extends beyond simple uptime to include concepts such as system performance, scalability, disaster recovery capabilities, and resilience against various forms of disruption.

Threats to availability come in many forms. Distributed Denial of Service (DDoS) attacks represent one of the most prominent and damaging availability threats. In these attacks, adversaries overwhelm target systems with massive volumes of traffic from numerous sources, consuming bandwidth, exhausting system resources, and rendering services unavailable to legitimate users. DDoS attacks increased by 31% in 2023, with cybercriminals launching an average of 44,000 attacks daily. The first half saw a 25% rise in multi-vector attacks, where attackers employ multiple simultaneous attack techniques to maximize impact and complicate defensive responses (University of San Diego, 2025).

Ransomware attacks represent another critical threat to availability. By encrypting organizational data and systems, ransomware renders information and services inaccessible until victims pay ransom demands (if then) or restore from backups. The devastating impact of ransomware on availability was illustrated in numerous high-profile incidents throughout, with attacks demonstrating an alarming 81% year-over-year increase (University of San Diego, 2025).

Natural disasters, equipment failures, power outages, and human errors also threaten availability, often with less malicious intent but equally serious consequences. The CrowdStrike incident, where a faulty software update affected 8.5 million Microsoft Windows devices globally, demonstrated how even well-intentioned security measures can catastrophically compromise availability when implemented without adequate testing and safeguards (Secureframe, 2025).

Organizations employ numerous strategies and technologies to maintain availability. Redundancy represents a fundamental principle, involving the duplication of critical systems, data, and infrastructure components so that backup resources can immediately assume operations if primary systems fail. This concept manifests in various forms, from redundant network connections and power supplies to geographically distributed data centers that can maintain operations even if entire facilities become unavailable.

High availability architectures incorporate automated failover mechanisms that detect system failures and automatically redirect operations to backup resources without requiring manual intervention. Load balancing technologies distribute traffic and processing across multiple systems, preventing any single component from becoming overwhelmed and ensuring that capacity scales to meet demand.

Regular backups constitute another essential element of availability strategies. By maintaining current copies of critical data and system configurations, organizations can recover from failures, attacks, or disasters by restoring to known-good states. Modern backup strategies often employ multiple approaches, including local backups for rapid recovery, off-site backups for disaster recovery, and cloud-based backups for geographic redundancy and accessibility.

Business continuity planning and disaster recovery protocols provide organizational frameworks for maintaining availability during adverse events. These comprehensive plans document procedures for responding to various disruption scenarios, identify critical systems and processes that must be prioritized for recovery, and establish recovery time objectives (RTOs) and recovery point objectives (RPOs) that define acceptable levels of downtime and data loss.

Continuous monitoring and proactive maintenance help prevent availability issues before they occur. Performance monitoring tools track system health, resource utilization, and potential bottlenecks, enabling IT teams to address emerging problems before they result in service disruptions. Regular patch management, hardware refreshes, and capacity planning ensure that systems remain capable of meeting operational demands.

Balancing the CIA Triad: Trade-Offs and Practical Considerations

While the CIA triad provides a clear framework for thinking about information security, implementing these principles in real-world environments often involves navigating complex trade-offs and balancing competing priorities. Security controls that strengthen one principle may inadvertently weaken another, creating situations where organizations must carefully consider their specific requirements, risk tolerance, and operational constraints (SailPoint, n.d.).

Consider the relationship between confidentiality and availability. Implementing strong confidentiality controls, such as multi-factor authentication, significantly reduces the risk of unauthorized access, but it can also hinder availability if users lose access to their authentication methods or find the authentication process cumbersome enough to impede productivity. Similarly, encrypting data protects both confidentiality and, to some extent, integrity, but if encryption keys are lost, corrupted, or inadequately managed, that same encryption can completely destroy the availability of the protected data.

Integrity controls, such as strict change management processes and multiple approval requirements for system modifications, enhance data trustworthiness but can slow operational agility and responsiveness. Organizations operating in fast-paced competitive environments may find that overly restrictive integrity controls impede their ability to rapidly deploy updates, respond to market changes, or capitalize on emerging opportunities.

The balance between security and usability represents a persistent challenge in CIA triad implementation. More robust security measures, such as complex password requirements, frequent re-authentication, and restrictive access policies, make systems more secure but can also reduce usability, increase user frustration, and even motivate attempts to bypass security protocols through unsanctioned workarounds. Conversely, prioritizing user convenience by reducing security layers can weaken defenses and leave systems vulnerable to attacks (SailPoint, n.d.).

Effective CIA triad implementation requires risk-based thinking and contextual decision-making. Organizations must conduct thorough risk assessments that identify threats to confidentiality, integrity, and availability; evaluate the potential impact of security failures in each area; and determine appropriate security controls based on the specific sensitivity of data, criticality of systems, regulatory requirements, and business needs. Frameworks such as ISO 27001 and the GDPR explicitly mandate this risk-based approach, requiring organizations to implement "a level of security appropriate to the risk" (IT Governance, 2025).

Different types of data and systems may warrant different balances among CIA triad principles. Public-facing websites may prioritize availability over confidentiality, as their purpose is broad accessibility. Financial transaction systems require extremely high integrity to prevent fraud and maintain trust, even if this means accepting slower processing times or more complex user authentication. Healthcare systems must balance stringent confidentiality requirements mandated by privacy regulations with the critical need for availability during medical emergencies when delays in accessing patient information could have life-threatening consequences.

Understanding Common Cybersecurity Threats and Attack Vectors

Having established the foundational principles that guide cybersecurity practice, we now turn to examining the specific threats and attack vectors that these principles are designed to address. The threat landscape has evolved dramatically over the past decade, with attackers developing increasingly sophisticated techniques, motivations ranging from financial gain to geopolitical objectives, and targets spanning individual users, private enterprises, critical infrastructure, and government agencies (CrowdStrike, 2025).

Understanding common attack types, their mechanisms, and their potential impacts enables organizations to implement appropriate defensive measures, develop effective security policies, and foster the security awareness necessary to detect and respond to threats before they result in successful compromises. This section explores the major categories of cyber threats that organizations face in 2025, providing detailed examinations of attack methodologies, real-world examples, and defensive strategies.

Malware: Malicious Software in Its Many Forms

Malware, a portmanteau of "malicious software," represents one of the most pervasive and diverse categories of cybersecurity threats. This broad classification encompasses any software specifically designed to damage, disrupt, or gain unauthorized access to computer systems. Malware can take numerous forms, each with distinct characteristics, behaviors, and objectives (CrowdStrike, 2025).

Traditional malware types include viruses, which attach themselves to legitimate programs and replicate when those programs execute; worms, which self-replicate and spread across networks without requiring host programs; and Trojans, which masquerade as legitimate software while secretly performing malicious activities. These classic malware categories continue to evolve, incorporating new evasion techniques and distribution methods that make them increasingly difficult to detect and remediate.

Ransomware has emerged as one of the most economically damaging and operationally disruptive forms of malware. This category of malicious software encrypts victims' files or entire systems, rendering data inaccessible until victims pay ransom demands, typically in cryptocurrency, to maintain attacker anonymity. The median ransomware variant can encrypt nearly 100,000 files totaling 53.93 gigabytes in just 42 minutes and 52 seconds, leaving organizations with minimal time to detect and respond before critical data becomes inaccessible (Splunk, n.d.).

The ransomware threat landscape has evolved from opportunistic attacks against individual users to sophisticated campaigns targeting large organizations, critical infrastructure, and even entire supply chains. Ransomware-as-a-Service (RaaS) business models have democratized these attacks, enabling technically unsophisticated criminals to launch devastating ransomware campaigns using tools and infrastructure provided by specialized cybercrime groups. The emergence of groups like FunkSec, which plans to offer ransomware subscriptions and training courses for novice hackers, demonstrates how the ransomware ecosystem continues to mature and expand (PT Security, 2025).

The financial impact of ransomware extends far beyond ransom payments themselves. IBM's Cost of a Data Breach Report found that the average ransomware attack costs organizations $4,450,000 when accounting for business disruption, recovery efforts, legal fees, regulatory penalties, and reputational damage (Cobalt, 2025). Organizations that involve law enforcement in ransomware incidents save an average of nearly $1 million in breach costs compared to those that don't, and 63% of victims who engaged law enforcement were able to avoid paying ransoms entirely (IBM).

Spyware represents another significant malware category, designed to covertly gather information about users, organizations, or systems without their knowledge or consent. This category includes keyloggers that record keyboard inputs to steal passwords and sensitive data, screen capture tools that periodically photograph user activity, and sophisticated espionage tools deployed by nation-state actors for intelligence gathering. The Hot Topic retail breach, which affected at least 54 million customers, was traced to an infostealer infection on a company computer that provided attackers with credentials for accessing corporate cloud infrastructure (PT Security, 2025).

Cryptojacking, while less immediately visible than other malware types, poses significant risks by hijacking computer resources to mine cryptocurrency without authorization. Unlike ransomware or data theft, cryptojacking focuses on generating revenue through unauthorized resource utilization rather than directly stealing data or demanding payment. However, the degraded system performance, increased electricity costs, and potential hardware damage resulting from sustained unauthorized cryptocurrency mining can significantly impact organizational operations (University of San Diego, 2025).

Fileless malware represents one of the most concerning recent developments in malware evolution. Rather than writing malicious code to disk, where traditional antivirus software can detect it, fileless malware leverages scripts or loads modules directly into system memory (RAM). This approach makes detection significantly more difficult, as the malware leaves minimal forensic evidence and often exploits legitimate system administration tools like PowerShell, WMI, or built-in scripting engines (University of San Diego, 2025).

Phishing and Social Engineering: Exploiting Human Psychology

While malware attacks target technical vulnerabilities in systems and software, phishing and social engineering attacks exploit vulnerabilities in human psychology and behavior. These attacks manipulate people into voluntarily performing actions or divulging information that compromises security, often by creating artificial urgency, exploiting trust relationships, or leveraging authority (ConnectWise, 2025).

Phishing remains one of the most effective tools available to cybercriminals due to its ability to bypass technical security controls by targeting human decision-making. According to Verizon's Data Breach Investigations Report, social engineering represents the most prevalent form of cyberattack, reported by 56% of organizations. Phishing, web-based attacks, and credential theft represent the most prevalent attack trends across industries (Ponemon Institute, referenced in Cobalt, 2025).

The success rates of phishing attacks are alarming. Human error represents the common root cause of 68% of data breaches, with phishing playing a central role in many of these incidents (SentinelOne, 2025). Traditional phishing emails required significant effort to craft convincing messages, often containing obvious grammatical errors, suspicious sender addresses, or implausible scenarios that alert recipients to raised defenses. However, the integration of artificial intelligence into phishing operations has dramatically increased both the sophistication and effectiveness of these attacks.

AI now generates 40% of phishing emails targeting businesses, and these AI-crafted messages achieve significantly higher success rates than traditional manually-crafted attempts. Research indicates that 78% of people open AI-generated phishing emails, and 21% click on malicious content contained within them. Generative AI tools enable attackers to compose phishing emails up to 40% faster than traditional methods while simultaneously enabling mass personalization and localization that makes detection more difficult (Tech Advisors, 2025).

Spear phishing represents a more targeted and sophisticated variant of standard phishing attacks. Rather than broadcasting generic messages to thousands of potential victims, hoping a small percentage will respond, spear phishing campaigns carefully research specific individuals or organizations and craft highly personalized messages designed to exploit particular relationships, roles, or circumstances. These targeted attacks achieve much higher success rates but require more effort and reconnaissance.

There was a surge in phishing attacks exploiting legitimate file-hosting services such as SharePoint, OneDrive, and Dropbox for identity theft. By hosting malicious content on trusted platforms, attackers leverage the inherent trust users place in these services while also potentially bypassing security filters configured to allow content from these legitimate domains (ConnectWise, 2025).

Vishing (voice phishing) and smishing (SMS phishing) extend social engineering attacks beyond email into voice communications and text messaging. According to CrowdStrike's 2025 Global Threat Report, voice phishing attacks increased by 442% between the first and second halves, driven by AI-generated phishing and impersonation tactics (Hacker News, 2025). These attacks often impersonate IT support staff, financial institutions, or government agencies to trick victims into revealing sensitive information or performing unauthorized actions.

The psychological principles underlying successful social engineering are well-documented and consistently exploited by attackers. These include:

- **Authority:** People tend to comply with requests from perceived authority figures. Attackers impersonate executives, IT administrators, or government officials to leverage this tendency.

- **Urgency:** Creating artificial time pressure reduces careful deliberation. Phishing messages often claim accounts will be suspended, legal action is imminent, or opportunities will be lost unless immediate action is taken.
- **Trust:** Exploiting existing relationships or impersonating trusted entities reduces skepticism. Attackers research organizational structures and communication patterns to craft convincing impersonations.
- **Fear:** Threatening negative consequences motivate rushed decisions. Messages claiming security breaches, legal violations, or financial problems trigger emotional responses that override rational analysis.
- **Greed:** Offering rewards, bonuses, or unexpected windfalls exploits the desire for gain. "Too good to be true" offers continue to successfully compromise victims despite widespread awareness of these tactics.

The "Contagious interview" campaign that targeted developers demonstrates how attackers combine multiple social engineering principles. By inviting targets to fake job interviews, leveraging both professional ambition and the trust placed in recruitment processes, attackers successfully tricked numerous victims into downloading malicious code disguised as technical assessments or company information (PT Security, 2025).

Advanced Persistent Threats (APTs): Sophisticated Long-Term Intrusions

Advanced Persistent Threats represent some of the most sophisticated and dangerous category of cyberattacks, typically conducted by well-resourced nation-state actors or sophisticated criminal organizations pursuing long-term strategic objectives rather than immediate financial gain. The term "persistent" reflects these attackers' determination to maintain access to compromised systems over extended periods, often months or years, while conducting espionage, stealing intellectual property, or positioning themselves for future disruptive actions (University of San Diego, 2025).

APT campaigns distinguish themselves through several characteristics: extensive reconnaissance and target research before initial compromise; use of custom malware and zero-day exploits not available to typical attackers; sophisticated techniques for maintaining persistent access while evading detection; lateral movement through networks to identify and compromise high-value targets; and patient, methodical data exfiltration designed to avoid triggering security alerts.

The geopolitical dimension of APT activities has become increasingly visible. Chinese cyber espionage operations surged by 150% overall, with attacks against financial, media, manufacturing, and industrial sectors rising up to 300% according to recent intelligence assessments. These campaigns targeted government agencies, manufacturing operations, telecommunications providers, and media organizations across Southeast Asia, Hong Kong, and Taiwan (CSIS, 2025).

The Salt Typhoon campaign, attributed to Chinese state-sponsored actors, demonstrated the scope and ambition of modern APT operations. This campaign successfully breached at least eight major U.S. telecommunications companies, potentially compromising communications infrastructure and accessing sensitive customer data across millions of users. The strategic value of such access extends far beyond immediate intelligence collection to include potential capabilities for future disruption or influence operations (CSIS, 2025).

Russian cyberattacks on Ukraine surged by nearly 70%, with 4,315 reported incidents targeting critical infrastructure, including government services, energy sector operations, and defense-related entities. These attacks employed tactics ranging from malware distribution and phishing to account compromises, demonstrating how APT groups integrate multiple attack vectors into comprehensive campaigns (CSIS, 2025).

North Korean APT groups have demonstrated particular innovation in blending cyber operations with other forms of illicit activity. Beyond traditional espionage and disruptive attacks, North Korean actors have conducted numerous cryptocurrency thefts, with one operation stealing $1.5 billion in Ethereum from the Dubai-based exchange ByBit. These financially motivated attacks appear designed to generate revenue for the regime while simultaneously developing offensive cyber capabilities (CSIS, 2025).

The challenge of defending against APTs stems from their sophisticated tradecraft and patient operational security. Unlike opportunistic attacks that seek quick wins and move on after initial compromise or detection, APT actors invest significant time and resources in maintaining access, conducting reconnaissance, and achieving their strategic objectives. Detection often occurs only when attackers make operational errors, when defenders implement new detection capabilities that reveal previously invisible activity, or when intelligence sharing among government agencies and private sector partners identifies indicators of compromise associated with known APT groups.

Denial of Service Attacks: Disrupting Availability at Scale

Denial of Service (DoS) and Distributed Denial of Service (DDoS) attacks specifically target the availability component of the CIA triad, seeking to render systems, networks, or services unavailable to legitimate users. These attacks overwhelm targets with excessive traffic or resource requests, consuming bandwidth, exhausting processing capacity, or exploiting application vulnerabilities to cause crashes or performance degradation (Norton, 2023).

DDoS attacks amplify the basic DoS concept by coordinating attacks from numerous sources simultaneously, making them significantly more difficult to defend against through simple traffic filtering or IP address blocking. Attackers build botnets, networks of compromised devices under their control, that can generate massive volumes of attack traffic on command. The proliferation of insecurely configured Internet of

Things (IoT) devices has dramatically expanded the pool of potential botnet participants, with billions of connected cameras, routers, smart home devices, and other embedded systems vulnerable to compromise and co-option for DDoS attacks.

The scale and sophistication of DDoS attacks have increased dramatically. DDoS attacks increased by 31% in 2023, with cybercriminals launching an average of 44,000 attacks daily. The first half saw a 25% rise in multi-vector attacks, where attackers employ multiple simultaneous techniques such as volumetric floods, protocol exploits, and application-layer attacks to maximize impact and complicate defensive responses (SentinelOne, 2025; University of San Diego, 2025).

Amplification attacks represent a particularly efficient form of DDoS that leverages publicly accessible services to multiply attack traffic. Attackers send small requests to vulnerable DNS, NTP, or SNMP servers using spoofed source addresses that appear to originate from the intended victim. These servers respond with much larger replies directed to the victim, amplifying the attacker's bandwidth by factors of 50 or more. This technique allows relatively modest botnet resources to generate devastating attack volumes (University of San Diego, 2025).

The motivations behind DDoS attacks vary widely. Some attacks aim for direct extortion, with attackers launching or threatening attacks unless victims pay protection money. Others seek competitive advantage, taking down rival organizations' services during critical business periods. Ideologically motivated "hacktivists" use DDoS attacks to disrupt organizations whose policies or practices they oppose. Nation-state actors employ DDoS as components of broader campaigns to destabilize adversaries or create diversions for more targeted intrusion operations.

The business impact of successful DDoS attacks extends beyond the immediate unavailability of services. Organizations suffer financial losses from lost sales, degraded customer experiences, damage to brand reputation, and the costs of implementing defensive measures and recovering from attacks. For organizations providing critical services, healthcare providers, financial institutions, and emergency services, DDoS attacks can have consequences extending far beyond financial impacts to affect public safety and welfare.

Insider Threats: When Trust Becomes Vulnerability

Not all cybersecurity threats originate from external adversaries seeking unauthorized access to organizational resources. Insider threats, risks posed by individuals who have legitimate access to systems and data but abuse that access for malicious purposes or through negligence, represent a uniquely challenging category of security concern (ConnectWise, 2025).

According to Cybersecurity Insiders' Insider Threat Report, 83% of organizations reported at least one insider attack in the past year, with approximately 51% experiencing six or more attacks. The average cost of remediating insider incidents exceeded $1 million for 29% of respondents. These statistics underscore both the prevalence and financial impact of insider threats across industries (ConnectWise, 2025).

The Ponemon Institute's 2025 Cost of Insider Risks Global Report provides even more sobering data, finding that the average cost of insider incidents has reached $17.4 million. Organizations now dedicate 16.5% of their annual IT security budgets to insider risk management, more than double the 8.2% allocated in 2023. Notably, 65% of organizations with insider risk management programs reported that these programs were the only security strategy that enabled them to preempt data breaches by detecting insider risks early (DTEX Systems, 2025).

Insider threats manifest in three primary categories: malicious insiders who deliberately abuse their access for personal gain, revenge, or ideological motivations; negligent insiders who inadvertently compromise security through careless behavior, poor security hygiene, or failure to follow established procedures; and compromised insiders whose credentials have been stolen by external attackers who then operate under the guise of legitimate users.

The challenge of addressing insider threats stems from several factors. Insiders possess legitimate access credentials, making their activities more difficult to distinguish from normal behavior. They understand organizational systems, security controls, and valuable data locations, enabling more targeted and effective attacks. Traditional perimeter security measures designed to keep external attackers out provide no defense against insiders who already have access. Detection often requires sophisticated behavioral analytics capable of identifying subtle deviations from normal patterns.

The top three drivers behind the surge in insider attacks identified in recent research are complex IT environments (39%), adoption of new technologies including AI tools (37%), and inadequate security measures (33%) (ConnectWise, 2025). The proliferation of shadow AI and employees using unauthorized AI tools and services has created new insider threat vectors as sensitive data is shared with external AI systems that may lack appropriate security controls or may be operated by vendors with inadequate data protection practices.

A notable incident at security training company KnowBe4 demonstrated the evolving sophistication of insider threats. A North Korean fake IT worker successfully infiltrated the company's recruitment process using AI-generated credentials and synthetic identities. While detected before causing significant damage, this incident illustrates how nation-state actors are adapting traditional insider threat tactics with modern AI capabilities to position operatives within target organizations (ConnectWise, 2025).

Supply Chain Attacks: Exploiting Trust Relationships

Supply chain attacks represent an increasingly prevalent and dangerous category of threats where adversaries compromise trusted third-party vendors, service providers, or software suppliers to gain access to ultimate targets. Rather than directly attacking well-defended primary targets, attackers penetrate less secure supply chain partners who have trusted relationships and access to target environments (ConnectWise, 2025).

The SolarWinds attack discussed in Chapter 1 stands as perhaps the most significant and well-documented supply chain attack in recent history, but it is far from an isolated incident. The MOVEit mass data breach in 2023 demonstrated how a vulnerability in widely used file transfer software could cascade across hundreds of organizations that relied on this third-party solution. The Kaseya ransomware attack in 2021 showed how compromising managed service provider software could enable simultaneous attacks against hundreds of that provider's customers.

In November 2024, supply chain software provider Blue Yonder disclosed a ransomware attack that caused widespread disruptions across its managed services-hosted environment. Blue Yonder provides critical supply chain optimization services for major organizations, including Starbucks, Morrisons, and Sainsbury's. The attack temporarily incapacitated payroll and scheduling systems at Starbucks while UK retailers faced disruptions in inventory management and product availability, demonstrating how single points of failure in supply chains can have cascading effects across multiple industries (ConnectWise, 2025).

Cybersecurity experts believe that supply chain attacks are increasing due to several factors: increased reliance on open-source platforms, third-party vendors, and application programming interfaces (APIs); poor security practices among supply chain partners who may lack the resources or expertise to implement robust security measures; the efficiency of compromising one supplier to reach many targets simultaneously; and the difficulty of detecting attacks that leverage trusted relationships and legitimate access channels.

The challenge of defending against supply chain attacks extends beyond technical security measures to encompass vendor risk management, contractual security requirements, continuous monitoring of supplier security postures, and incident response coordination across organizational boundaries. Many organizations lack visibility into the security practices of their supply chain partners or the ability to enforce security standards on vendors upon whom they depend but over whom they have limited control.

Essential Defensive Strategies and Security Controls

Understanding the threat landscape provides necessary context for developing effective defensive strategies, but knowledge of threats alone is insufficient. Organizations must implement comprehensive security controls, adopt proven defensive frameworks, and foster security-aware cultures to effectively protect against the diverse and evolving threats described in the previous section.

Defense in Depth: Layered Security Approach

Modern cybersecurity best practices embrace a concept known as "defense in depth" implementing multiple layers of security controls so that if one layer fails, additional layers provide backup protection. This approach recognizes that no single security measure is foolproof and that determined attackers will eventually find ways to bypass individual controls. By implementing diverse, overlapping security measures at multiple levels, organizations significantly increase the difficulty and cost of successful attacks while improving their chances of detecting intrusions before attackers achieve their objectives (CrowdStrike, 2025).

Defense in depth typically encompasses security controls at several levels:

Physical Security: Physical access controls prevent unauthorized individuals from accessing facilities, server rooms, network infrastructure, and endpoint devices. While often overlooked in discussions focused on cyber threats, physical security remains foundational; attackers with physical access to systems can bypass many digital security controls.

Network Security: Firewalls, intrusion detection systems (IDS), intrusion prevention systems (IPS), network segmentation, and virtual private networks (VPNs) provide security at the network layer. Next-generation firewalls combine traditional packet filtering with application-layer inspection, threat intelligence integration, and advanced features that provide more granular control and visibility.

Endpoint Security: Antivirus software, endpoint detection and response (EDR) solutions, host-based firewalls, and application whitelisting protect individual devices. Modern endpoint security has evolved beyond signature-based malware detection to incorporate behavioral analysis, machine learning, and integration with broader security ecosystems.

Application Security: Secure coding practices, regular security testing, input validation, and authentication mechanisms protect applications from exploitation. DevSecOps approaches integrate security into software development lifecycles rather than treating it as an afterthought.

Data Security: Encryption, data loss prevention (DLP) systems, rights management, and access controls protect data regardless of where it resides or how it moves through the environment. These controls ensure that even if attackers breach perimeter defenses, they cannot access or exfiltrate valuable information in usable forms.

Identity and Access Management: Strong authentication mechanisms, least privilege principles, role-based access control, and privileged access management ensure that users have appropriate access to resources they need while preventing unauthorized access to sensitive systems and data.

The effectiveness of defense in depth depends on careful planning and implementation. Controls at different layers must complement rather than conflict with each other, and security teams must have visibility across all layers to detect and respond to attacks that may bypass individual controls.

Identity and Access Management: Controlling the Keys to the Kingdom

Identity and Access Management (IAM) represents one of the most critical elements of modern cybersecurity strategies. With credential theft continuing to be problematic, experiencing a 71% year-over-year increase in attacks using compromised credentials, IAM has evolved from a convenience feature to a fundamental security necessity (IBM, 2025).

According to IBM's research, stolen or compromised credentials represented the most common initial attack vector at 16% of all breaches studied. Breaches initiated through compromised credentials also took the longest to identify and contain, averaging nearly 10 months (292 days) and resulting in some of the highest breach costs (IBM).

Multi-Factor Authentication (MFA) stands as a cornerstone of modern IAM strategies. MFA requires users to provide multiple forms of verification before gaining access to systems, typically combining something they know (password), something they have (security token or mobile device), and/or something they are (biometric identifier). The security value of MFA is substantial; even simple implementations dramatically reduce the success rate of credential-based attacks by ensuring that stolen passwords alone are insufficient for unauthorized access.

However, the evolution of attack techniques has demonstrated that traditional MFA implementations are not impervious. Attackers have developed techniques for MFA bypass, including phishing for MFA tokens, exploiting authentication protocol vulnerabilities, and social engineering attacks targeting users to approve fraudulent authentication requests. This has driven the adoption of more sophisticated authentication methods, such as FIDO2/WebAuthn standards that provide phishing-resistant authentication through cryptographic protocols rather than shareable secrets (American Public University).

Identity Fabric architectures have emerged as a comprehensive approach to managing identity across complex, multi-cloud, hybrid IT environments. These product-agnostic integrated sets of identity tools and services provide unified identity management capabilities that span on-premises systems, multiple cloud platforms, and modern application architectures. When implemented correctly, identity fabrics provide security professionals with relief from the chaos and risk caused by the proliferation of disconnected identity solutions across diverse technology environments (IBM, 2025).

Zero Trust Architecture represents a fundamental reimagining of traditional security models. Rather than assuming that users and devices within the network perimeter can be trusted, Zero Trust operates on the principle of "never trust, always verify." Every access request, communication, and transaction is treated as potentially malicious until explicitly verified and authorized, regardless of source location or previous authentication events.

IBM's 2025 cybersecurity predictions emphasize that recognizing identity as the new security perimeter will continue to transform how enterprises think about security. As hybrid cloud adoption and application modernization initiatives accelerate, Identity-First strategies that manage and secure access to applications, critical data, and AI models will become increasingly central to organizational security postures.

Security Monitoring and Incident Response

Even the most robust preventive security measures cannot guarantee complete protection against all threats. Organizations must therefore implement comprehensive security monitoring capabilities and incident response programs that enable rapid detection of security events, effective investigation of potential compromises, and coordinated response actions that limit damage and accelerate recovery.

Security Information and Event Management (SIEM) systems collect, aggregate, and analyze log data and security events from across the IT environment. By correlating information from multiple sources, network devices, servers, applications, and security tools, SIEM platforms can identify patterns and anomalies that might indicate security incidents. Modern SIEM solutions incorporate machine learning and behavioral analytics to detect subtle indicators of compromise that might escape rule-based detection approaches.

Research indicates that organizations with IR teams and robust security testing save an average of $248,000 per year on breach costs, while those with IAM solutions save up to $223,000 annually. These cost savings reflect both the reduced likelihood of successful attacks and the improved efficiency of response when incidents do occur (IBM).

Extended Detection and Response (XDR) platforms represent an evolution beyond traditional EDR by extending visibility and response capabilities across multiple security layers, endpoints, networks, cloud workloads, and applications, through integrated platforms. Organizations that implemented XDR solutions were able to accelerate detection and containment of data breach incidents by approximately one month compared to those without XDR, with average time to containment of 275 days versus 304 days (Barracuda Networks).

Threat Intelligence provides contextual information about attackers, their tactics, techniques, and procedures (TTPs), indicators of compromise, and emerging threats. By incorporating threat intelligence into security monitoring and response processes, organizations can proactively search for signs of known threat actor activity, prioritize response efforts based on threat actor capabilities and motivations, and implement defensive measures tailored to specific threats relevant to their industry and geographic location.

Incident response planning provides organizational frameworks for managing security events. Comprehensive incident response plans document roles and responsibilities, establish communication protocols, define escalation procedures, and outline technical response actions for various incident scenarios. According to recent research, 51% of organizations now have Cybersecurity Incident Response Plans (CSIRPs) that are applied consistently across their entire enterprises, representing an increase from 46% (Ponemon Institute, 2025).

The value of well-prepared incident response capabilities is demonstrated through breach cost differentials. Organizations with high levels of incident response planning and testing experienced significantly lower breach costs compared to those with low IR preparedness or no formal IR capabilities. Regular testing and updates to IR plans, with 61% of organizations now reviewing their plans quarterly or semi-annually, ensure that response capabilities remain effective as threats, technologies, and organizational structures evolve (Ponemon Institute, 2025).

Vulnerability Management and Patch Management

No software is perfect. Vulnerabilities, security weaknesses that can be exploited by attackers, exist in virtually all complex software systems. The continuous discovery of new vulnerabilities creates an ongoing challenge for organizations that must identify, prioritize, and remediate these weaknesses before attackers can exploit them.

The volume of disclosed vulnerabilities continues to explode. Over 40,000 Common Vulnerabilities and Exposures (CVEs) were disclosed, and 2025 is on pace to hit nearly 50,000. This volume alone makes it difficult for organizations to identify which issues to patch first, especially as attacker playbooks grow more dynamic. According to the 2025 Verizon Data Breach Investigations Report, vulnerability exploitation was linked to 20% of breaches, putting it on par with stolen credentials and ahead of phishing as a breach vector (Secureframe, 2025).

More alarming is the speed at which newly disclosed vulnerabilities are being exploited. According to CISA's Known Exploited Vulnerabilities (KEV) data, over 25% of vulnerabilities exploited in Q1 2025 were attacked within 24 hours of being disclosed. This trend, sometimes called "patch gap exploitation," puts intense pressure on IT and security teams to move quickly from vulnerability disclosure to assessment to remediation, often with incomplete information or limited resources (Secureframe, 2025).

Effective vulnerability management requires several key capabilities:

Continuous Vulnerability Scanning: Automated tools regularly scan IT environments to identify known vulnerabilities in operating systems, applications, and network devices. These scans must cover all environment types: on-premises infrastructure, cloud resources, remote endpoints, and OT/ICS systems.

Risk-Based Prioritization: Not all vulnerabilities present equal risk. Prioritization considers factors such as vulnerability severity, exploitability, asset criticality, threat intelligence indicating active exploitation, and compensating controls that may reduce risk. This approach enables organizations to focus remediation efforts on the vulnerabilities that present the greatest actual risk rather than simply addressing the longest list of theoretical weaknesses.

Patch Management Processes: Formal processes for testing, approving, and deploying security patches balance the need for rapid vulnerability remediation against the risk of deploying untested patches that might cause operational disruptions. The CrowdStrike incident, where a faulty security update affected 8.5 million Windows devices globally and cost Fortune 500 companies an estimated $5.4 billion, illustrates the importance of thorough testing even during urgent security updates (CSIS, 2025).

Compensating Controls: When immediate patching is not feasible, due to testing requirements, change control windows, or vendor patch unavailability, organizations must implement compensating controls such as network segmentation, increased monitoring, or access restrictions that reduce exploitation risk while permanent remediation is prepared.

Data Protection and Encryption

At the core of most cybersecurity efforts lies the fundamental objective of protecting data, the information assets that represent value to organizations and whose loss, corruption, or unauthorized disclosure would cause harm. Data protection encompasses the policies, procedures, and technologies that safeguard data throughout its lifecycle, from creation and storage through transmission and eventual disposal.

Understanding Data States and Protection Requirements

Data exists in three primary states, each requiring specific protection approaches:

Data at Rest: Information stored in relatively stable locations such as databases, file servers, hard drives, backup tapes, or cloud storage. Data at rest is particularly vulnerable to theft through physical device compromise, unauthorized access to storage systems, or insider threats. Protection mechanisms include full disk encryption, database encryption, file-level encryption, and strong access controls that restrict who can access stored data.

Data in Transit: Information moving across networks, whether internal organizational networks or the public internet. Data in transit is vulnerable to interception through network sniffing, man-in-the-middle attacks, or compromised network infrastructure. Transport Layer Security (TLS) protocols encrypt data during transmission, ensuring that even if communications are intercepted, the content remains unreadable to unauthorized parties.

Data in Use: Information being actively processed by applications or systems, typically residing in system memory or processor caches. Data in use has traditionally been the most difficult to protect, as most operations require data to be in an unencrypted form during processing. However, emerging technologies such as homomorphic encryption, which enables computations on encrypted data without decryption, and confidential computing using specialized hardware enclaves are beginning to address this challenge (Microsoft Azure, n.d.).

Encryption: The Mathematical Foundation of Confidentiality

Encryption represents one of the most powerful tools available for protecting data confidentiality. By transforming readable plaintext into unreadable ciphertext through mathematical algorithms, encryption ensures that even if data is accessed by unauthorized parties, it remains unintelligible without the appropriate decryption keys (IBM, 2025).

According to IBM's 2025 Cost of a Data Breach Report, organizations that extensively use encryption can reduce the financial impact of data breaches by over $200,000 compared to those that don't. This cost reduction reflects both the reduced scope of data actually compromised in breaches (since encrypted data remains protected even when accessed) and the regulatory and legal benefits of demonstrating that stolen data was encrypted (IBM, 2025).

Modern encryption relies on two primary approaches:

Symmetric Encryption uses the same cryptographic key for both encryption and decryption operations. This approach is computationally efficient, making it suitable for encrypting large volumes of data. However, symmetric encryption faces the challenge of key distribution; both sender and recipient must possess the shared secret key, and that key must be transmitted securely. Common symmetric encryption algorithms include Advanced Encryption Standard (AES), which has become the de facto standard for securing data at rest and in transit in most applications (Digital Guardian, 2015).

Asymmetric Encryption (also called public-key cryptography) uses mathematically related key pairs a public key that can be freely distributed and a private key that must be kept secret. Data encrypted with the public key can only be decrypted with the corresponding private key, solving the key distribution challenge inherent in symmetric systems. The most widely used asymmetric algorithm is RSA (Rivest-Shamir-Adleman), which underpins much of internet security, including secure web browsing, email encryption, and digital signatures (Digital Guardian, 2015).

Practical encryption implementations often combine both approaches. Hybrid encryption systems use asymmetric cryptography to securely exchange symmetric keys, then use those symmetric keys for efficient bulk data encryption. This combines the security benefits of public-key cryptography with the performance advantages of symmetric algorithms.

Hash Functions complement encryption by providing one-way transformations of data into fixed-length values. Unlike encryption, hashing is intentionally irreversible given a hash value, it should be computationally infeasible to determine the original input. This makes hash functions ideal for password storage (storing hashes rather than actual passwords), data integrity verification (comparing hash values to detect modifications), and digital signatures (hashing documents before signing to improve efficiency) (IBM, 2025).

Modern hash algorithms include SHA-256 and SHA-3, which have replaced older algorithms like MD5 and SHA-1, which have been demonstrated to have cryptographic weaknesses. The security of hash functions relies on several properties: they must be deterministic (always producing the same output for the same input), must be collision-resistant (making it extremely difficult to find two inputs that produce the same hash), and must exhibit the avalanche effect (where small changes to input produce dramatically different outputs).

Key Management: The Achilles Heel of Encryption

While encryption algorithms themselves are generally mathematically sound, the security of encrypted data ultimately depends on proper key management.

Encryption keys must be generated using cryptographically secure random number generators, stored securely with access limited to authorized systems and personnel, backed up to prevent data loss if keys are corrupted or lost, rotated periodically to limit the exposure if keys are compromised, and destroyed securely when no longer needed.

Azure Key Vault and similar key management services provide centralized, hardware-backed storage for cryptographic keys and secrets. These services handle the complexity of key generation, storage, rotation, and access control while providing audit capabilities that track all key usage. The criticality of key management is reflected in best practices that emphasize soft delete and purge protection features, ensuring that keys cannot be permanently deleted immediately, as deletion of keys used for data encryption effectively results in permanent data loss (Microsoft Azure, n.d.).

Emerging Encryption Technologies

The encryption landscape continues to evolve in response to emerging threats and technological capabilities. Several developments deserve attention:

Post-Quantum Cryptography: The eventual development of practical quantum computers threatens to break many current encryption algorithms, particularly asymmetric systems like RSA and elliptic curve cryptography. Post-quantum cryptographic algorithms use mathematical problems believed to be resistant to quantum computing attacks.

Organizations must begin transitioning to quantum-resistant algorithms now, as data encrypted today with vulnerable algorithms could be stored by adversaries and decrypted once quantum computers become available (Concentric AI, 2025).

Homomorphic Encryption: This revolutionary approach enables computations on encrypted data without decryption, addressing the longstanding vulnerability of data in use. While computational overhead currently limits practical applications, ongoing research and implementation improvements suggest that homomorphic encryption may eventually enable secure cloud computing where service providers can process sensitive data without ever seeing it in unencrypted form (Concentric AI, 2025).

Biometric Encryption: As biometric authentication becomes more prevalent, techniques for securing biometric data have evolved. Biometric encryption binds cryptographic keys to biometric data such as fingerprints or facial scans in ways that neither the key nor the biometric can be retrieved from stored templates. The key can only be recreated when the original live biometric is presented for verification, providing strong authentication while protecting privacy (Concentric AI, 2025).

Regulatory Compliance and Encryption Requirements

Many regulatory frameworks now mandate encryption for specific types of sensitive data. The General Data Protection Regulation (GDPR) requires appropriate security measures, including encryption for personal data. The Health Insurance Portability and Accountability Act (HIPAA) mandates encryption for electronic protected health information (ePHI). The Payment Card Industry Data Security Standard (PCI DSS) requires encryption of cardholder data during transmission and recommends encryption of stored cardholder data.

Beyond regulatory requirements, encryption provides important legal protections. Many data breach notification laws provide safe harbor provisions for encrypted data; if stolen data was properly encrypted and keys were not compromised, organizations may be exempt from notification requirements. This reflects recognition that encrypted data, while technically accessed, remains protected and poses minimal risk to affected individuals.

The Human Element: Security Awareness and Culture

While technical security controls provide essential protection against cyber threats, the human element remains both the most vulnerable and the most valuable component of cybersecurity strategies. As evidenced by statistics showing that human error is the common root cause of 68% of data breaches, no amount of sophisticated technology can fully compensate for user behaviors that circumvent security measures, fall prey to social engineering, or simply fail to follow established security procedures (SentinelOne, 2025).

The Importance of Security Awareness Training

Security awareness training aims to transform employees from potential vulnerabilities into active participants in organizational defense. Effective programs go beyond simple compliance exercises to foster a genuine understanding of threats, consequences, and individual responsibilities. Research demonstrates that organizations with mature security awareness programs experience significantly fewer successful social engineering attacks, faster detection of security incidents by users, and greater employee buy-in for security policies and procedures.

Training must address multiple dimensions of security awareness:

Threat Recognition: Users must learn to identify common attack patterns, including phishing emails, suspicious websites, social engineering attempts, and other indicators of potential threats. This includes understanding that attackers increasingly use sophisticated techniques AI-generated content, impersonation of trusted entities, exploitation of legitimate services, that make simple heuristics like "check for spelling errors" insufficient.

Secure Behaviors: Training should instill specific security-conscious behaviors such as using strong, unique passwords; enabling multi-factor authentication; keeping software updated; being cautious about what information is shared on social media; securing physical devices; and following data handling procedures.

Reporting Procedures: Users need clear, simple processes for reporting suspected security incidents, phishing attempts, lost devices, or other security concerns. Organizations that make reporting easy and non-punitive (within reason) benefit from earlier detection and response to potential compromises.

Practical Exercises: Simulated phishing campaigns, tabletop exercises, and security scenario discussions provide hands-on experience that reinforces training concepts and reveals gaps in understanding or compliance that require additional attention.

Building a Security-Conscious Culture

Beyond formal training programs, organizations must foster security cultures where protection of information assets is recognized as everyone's responsibility rather than solely the concern of IT security teams. This cultural transformation requires several elements:

Leadership Commitment: Security culture must be championed from the top, with executive leadership demonstrating through words and actions that security is a business priority worthy of investment and attention.

Integration into Business Processes: Rather than treating security as a separate concern or obstacle to overcome, it should be integrated into how work gets done, factored into project planning, included in performance evaluations, and reflected in resource allocation decisions.

Balanced Risk Approach: Security cultures that are overly restrictive or punitive often backfire, driving users to find workarounds that create even greater risks. Effective approaches balance security requirements with usability considerations, providing secure ways for users to accomplish legitimate business objectives.

Continuous Improvement: Security culture, like technical security measures, requires ongoing attention and evolution. Regular assessment of security awareness levels, analysis of security incidents to identify human factors, and adaptation of training and policies based on changing threats and organizational needs ensure that security culture remains relevant and effective.

Conclusion: Building on Foundational Knowledge

This chapter has provided a comprehensive exploration of cybersecurity fundamentals, establishing the knowledge foundation necessary for understanding how artificial intelligence is transforming both the threat landscape and defensive capabilities explored in subsequent chapters. We have examined the CIA triad that guides security strategy development, explored common threat categories from malware and phishing to APTs and supply chain attacks, discussed essential defensive strategies including defense in depth and identity-centric security, and recognized the critical role of data protection and human factors in achieving effective security postures.

Several key themes emerge from this foundational examination. First, cybersecurity is inherently a multi-dimensional challenge requiring attention to technical, procedural, and human elements. No single control or approach provides complete protection; instead, organizations must implement layered defenses that address diverse attack vectors and failure modes. Second, the threat landscape continues to evolve rapidly, with attackers constantly developing new techniques, exploiting emerging technologies, and adapting to defensive countermeasures. This necessitates continuous learning, adaptation, and investment in security capabilities.

Third, while specific threats and technologies change, fundamental security principles endure. The CIA triad, formulated decades ago, remains relevant because it addresses timeless challenges, protecting information confidentiality, ensuring data integrity, and maintaining service availability. Even as AI transforms how these principles are implemented, the core objectives remain constant. Finally, effective cybersecurity requires a balance between security and usability, between preventive and detective controls, between centralized policy and distributed execution, and between technological solutions and human judgment.

As we progress to Chapter 3's examination of artificial intelligence fundamentals, keep in mind how AI technologies both threaten and enhance each aspect of cybersecurity discussed in this chapter. AI-powered attacks exploit the same vulnerabilities: human psychology, software weaknesses, trust relationships, but do so with unprecedented speed, scale, and sophistication. Simultaneously, AI-enhanced defenses provide capabilities for threat detection, analysis, and response that transcend human limitations. Understanding these foundational cybersecurity concepts provides the necessary context for appreciating AI's transformative impact on both offense and defense in the ongoing struggle for digital security.

References

American Public University. (2024, May 3). *Cybersecurity fundamentals: Why MFA needs to be so robust.* Retrieved from https://www.apu.apus.edu/area-of-study/security-and-global-studies/resources/cybersecurity-fundamentals-why-mfa-needs-to-be-so-robust/

Barracuda Networks. (2024, August 20). *2024 IBM breach report: More breaches, higher costs.* Retrieved from https://blog.barracuda.com/2024/08/20/2024-IBM-breach-report-more-breaches-higher-costs

Cobalt. (2025, June 24). *Top 40 AI cybersecurity statistics.* Retrieved from https://www.cobalt.io/blog/top-40-ai-cybersecurity-statistics

Concentric AI. (2025, July 3). *Exploring new encryption technology in 2025.* Retrieved from https://concentric.ai/advances-in-encryption-technology/

ConnectWise. (2025). *10 common cybersecurity threats and attacks: 2025 update.* Retrieved from https://www.connectwise.com/blog/common-threats-and-attacks

CrowdStrike. (2025, August 12). *Types of cyberattacks.* Retrieved from https://www.crowdstrike.com/en-us/cybersecurity-101/cyberattacks/common-cyberattacks/

CSIS. (2025). *Significant cyber incidents.* Strategic Technologies Program. Retrieved from https://www.csis.org/programs/strategic-technologies-program/significant-cyber-incidents

Digital Guardian. (2015, February 23). *What is data encryption?.* Retrieved from https://www.digitalguardian.com/blog/what-data-encryption

DTEX Systems. (2025, February 25). *2025 Cost of Insider Risks Global Report.* Retrieved from https://www.dtexsystems.com/newsroom/press-releases/2025-ponemon-insider-threat-report-release/

Fortinet. (2025). *What is the CIA Triad and why is it important?* Retrieved from https://www.fortinet.com/resources/cyberglossary/cia-triad

GeeksforGeeks. (2025). *What is CIA Triad?* Retrieved from https://www.geeksforgeeks.org/computer-networks/the-cia-triad-in-cryptography/

Hacker News. (2025, May 13). *Deepfake defense in the age of AI.* Retrieved from https://thehackernews.com/2025/05/deepfake-defense-in-age-of-ai.html

IBM. (2024, July 30). *IBM Report: Escalating data breach disruption pushes costs to new highs*. Retrieved from https://newsroom.ibm.com/2024-07-30-ibm-report-escalating-data-breach-disruption-pushes-costs-to-new-highs

IBM. (2025, August 8). *Cybersecurity trends: IBM's predictions for 2025.* Retrieved from https://www.ibm.com/think/insights/cybersecurity-trends-ibm-predictions-2025

IBM. (2025). *What is encryption?* Retrieved from https://www.ibm.com/think/topics/encryption

IT Governance. (2025, June 18). *What is the CIA Triad and why is it important?* Retrieved from https://www.itgovernance.co.uk/blog/what-is-the-cia-triad-and-why-is-it-important

Microsoft Azure. (n.d.). *Data security and encryption best practices.* Retrieved from https://learn.microsoft.com/en-us/azure/security/fundamentals/data-encryption-best-practices

NIST. (2020, December). *Executive Summary NIST SP 1800-26: Data integrity: Detecting and responding to ransomware and other destructive events.* Retrieved from https://www.nccoe.nist.gov/publication/1800-26/VolA/index.html

Norton. (2023, July 18). *Cybersecurity basics for beginners: 2024 guide.* Retrieved from https://us.norton.com/blog/how-to/cybersecurity-basics

Ponemon Institute. (2025, June). *The 2025 study on the state of AI in cybersecurity.* Retrieved from https://ponemonsullivanreport.com/2025/06/the-2025-study-on-the-state-of-ai-in-cybersecurity/

PT Security. (2025). *Cybersecurity threatscape: Q4 2024 – Q1 2025.* Retrieved from https://global.ptsecurity.com/analytics/cybersecurity-threatscape-q4-2024-q1-2025

SailPoint. (n.d.). *CIA triad: Confidentiality, integrity, and availability.* Retrieved from https://www.sailpoint.com/identity-library/cia-triad

Secureframe. (2025, July 14). *20 recent cyber attacks & what they tell us about the future of cybersecurity.* Retrieved from https://secureframe.com/blog/recent-cyber-attacks

SecurityScorecard. (2025, May 22). *What is the CIA Triad? Definition, importance, & examples.* Retrieved from https://securityscorecard.com/blog/what-is-the-cia-triad/

SentinelOne. (2025, July 30). *Key cyber security statistics for 2025.* Retrieved from https://www.sentinelone.com/cybersecurity-101/cybersecurity/cyber-security-statistics/

Splunk. (n.d.). *Data encryption methods & types: A beginner's guide.* Retrieved from https://www.splunk.com/en_us/blog/learn/data-encryption-methods-types.html

Tech Advisors. (2025). *AI cyber attack statistics 2025.* Retrieved from https://tech-adv.com/blog/ai-cyber-attack-statistics/

University of San Diego. (2025, August 8). *Top cybersecurity threats [2025].* Retrieved from https://onlinedegrees.sandiego.edu/top-cyber-security-threats/

University of Tulsa. (2024, January 4). *What is the CIA Triad?* Retrieved from https://online.utulsa.edu/blog/what-is-the-cia-triad/

Viking Cloud. (2025). *207 Cybersecurity stats and facts for 2025.* Retrieved from https://www.vikingcloud.com/blog/cybersecurity-statistics

VinciWorks. (2022, March 31). *What are confidentiality, integrity and availability in information security?* Retrieved from https://vinciworks.com/blog/what-are-confidentiality-integrity-and-availability-in-information-security/

Washington University. (n.d.). *Confidentiality, integrity, and availability: The CIA Triad.* Office of Information Security. Retrieved from https://informationsecurity.wustl.edu/guidance/confidentiality-integrity-and-availability-the-cia-triad/

Chapter 3: Artificial Intelligence Basics: From Algorithms to Learning Machines

Introduction: The Dawn of Machine Intelligence

Artificial Intelligence has transitioned from science fiction speculation to an omnipresent force reshaping every facet of modern society. In 2025, AI technologies have started to influence how we communicate, work, shop, travel, access healthcare, consume entertainment, and interact with the digital world.

The integration of AI into daily life has been so rapid and pervasive that many people interact with AI systems dozens or hundreds of times each day without conscious awareness from smartphone voice assistants and personalized content recommendations to fraud detection systems protecting financial transactions and diagnostic tools supporting medical decisions.

According to a survey of senior data leaders, 64% of respondents identified generative AI as having the potential to be the most transformative technology in a generation (MIT Sloan, 2025).

This assessment reflects not merely technological enthusiasm but recognition of AI's demonstrated capacity to augment human capabilities, automate complex tasks, and solve problems previously considered intractable by traditional computational approaches.

The World Economic Forum's State of Data & AI Literacy Report 2025 found that 69% of organizational leaders believe AI literacy is important for their teams' daily tasks, underscoring how AI competency has evolved from a specialized technical skill to a fundamental professional requirement across industries (DataCamp, 2025).

Professionals in fields ranging from marketing and finance to healthcare and education increasingly rely on AI tools like ChatGPT, Midjourney, and Gemini to transform their workflows, enhance productivity, and create value in ways that were impossible just years ago.

Understanding the fundamentals of artificial intelligence how machines learn from data, recognize patterns, make decisions, and improve performance through experience has become essential not only for technical practitioners but for anyone seeking to navigate and thrive in an AI-augmented world.

This chapter provides a comprehensive introduction to AI basics, exploring the core concepts, technologies, and methodologies that enable machines to exhibit intelligent behavior.

We will examine what artificial intelligence truly means, distinguishing between different types and levels of AI capabilities; explore machine learning as the primary approach through which modern AI systems acquire knowledge and skills; investigate neural networks and deep learning, the technologies driving the current AI revolution; and understand how these technologies enable machines to perform tasks that traditionally required human intelligence from visual perception and language understanding to strategic decision-making and creative content generation.

Defining Artificial Intelligence: Scope and Categories

At its most fundamental level, artificial intelligence refers to the branch of computer science focused on creating systems capable of performing tasks that would normally require human-level intelligence. These tasks include understanding natural language, recognizing patterns in data, making decisions based on complex information, solving problems in uncertain environments, and learning from experience to improve performance over time (DataCamp, 2025).

However, this broad definition encompasses a vast spectrum of capabilities, approaches, and applications. To better understand the AI landscape, it is helpful to categorize AI systems along several dimensions based on their capabilities, approaches to learning, and operational characteristics.

Levels of AI: From Narrow to General Intelligence

AI systems can be categorized into three primary levels based on the scope and generality of their capabilities:

Artificial Narrow Intelligence (ANI), also called "weak AI," represents the most common form of AI encountered in practical applications today. ANI systems are designed to excel at specific, well-defined tasks within limited domains. While these systems may demonstrate superhuman performance within their specialized areas, they cannot generalize their capabilities to tasks outside their training domain (DataCamp, 2025).

Examples of ANI include: image recognition systems that can identify objects, faces, or medical conditions in photographs with accuracy exceeding human experts; recommendation algorithms that personalize content, products, or services based on user behavior and preferences; natural language processing systems that translate between languages, answer questions, or generate text; game-playing AI that masters specific games like chess, Go, or complex video games; and autonomous driving systems that navigate vehicles through traffic while detecting obstacles and making real-time decisions.

Despite the "narrow" designation, ANI systems have achieved remarkable capabilities and created enormous economic value. The AI market, driven primarily by narrow AI applications, is experiencing exponential growth.

According to the International Data Corporation, worldwide spending on AI including AI-enabled applications, infrastructure, and related services is projected to more than double to $632 billion by 2028, with a compound annual growth rate of 29% over the 2024-2028 forecast period (TechTarget, n.d.).

Artificial General Intelligence (AGI), sometimes called "strong AI," refers to hypothetical AI systems that would possess human-like general intelligence the ability to understand, learn, and apply knowledge across a wide range of tasks and domains without requiring specific programming or training for each new challenge. AGI systems would demonstrate flexibility, transfer learning across contexts, common sense reasoning, and the capacity to solve novel problems using general principles rather than domain-specific training.

As of 2025, AGI remains a theoretical goal rather than a practical reality. While researchers continue making progress toward more flexible and generalizable AI systems, creating machines with true general intelligence comparable to humans presents profound scientific and engineering challenges that likely require fundamental breakthroughs beyond current approaches.

Artificial Superintelligence (ASI) represents a speculative further level beyond AGI, describing hypothetical AI systems that would significantly exceed human cognitive capabilities across all domains. ASI remains firmly in the realm of theoretical speculation and science fiction, though its potential implications both positive and concerning drive important discussions about AI safety, ethics, and governance.

For practical purposes and the focus of this chapter, we concentrate on the technologies and approaches underlying Artificial Narrow Intelligence the AI systems deployed today that are transforming cybersecurity, driving business value, and shaping technological progress across industries.

Approaches to Learning: Supervised, Unsupervised, and Reinforcement Learning

Beyond categorizing AI by capability level, we can distinguish AI systems based on how they learn from data. Machine learning, the predominant approach to creating modern AI systems, encompasses several fundamentally different learning paradigms:

Supervised Learning trains models on labeled datasets, where each training example includes both input features and the correct output or label. The model learns to map inputs to outputs by identifying patterns in the labeled examples, then applies this learned mapping to make predictions on new, unseen data. Supervised learning is used for both classification tasks (predicting categorical labels like "spam" vs. "not spam") and regression tasks (predicting continuous values like stock prices or temperature forecasts) (GeeksforGeeks).

Common supervised learning applications include: image classification and object detection; speech recognition and natural language understanding; medical diagnosis from symptoms or test results; credit scoring and loan approval decisions; and customer churn prediction.

Unsupervised Learning finds patterns, structures, or groups in unlabeled data without being told what to look for. These algorithms identify natural groupings, dimensionality reductions, or anomalies in datasets where correct answers aren't provided during training. Unsupervised learning is particularly valuable for exploratory data analysis, discovering hidden patterns, and reducing complex data to more manageable representations (GeeksforGeeks).

Key unsupervised learning techniques include: clustering algorithms that group similar data points together; dimensionality reduction methods that compress high-dimensional data while preserving important relationships; anomaly detection systems that identify unusual patterns potentially indicating fraud, equipment failure, or security threats; and association rule learning that discovers interesting relationships between variables in large databases.

Reinforcement Learning takes a fundamentally different approach, training agents to make sequences of decisions by learning from the consequences of their actions. Rather than learning from labeled examples or finding patterns in static data, reinforcement learning agents learn through trial and error, receiving rewards for desirable actions and penalties for undesirable ones. This paradigm is particularly powerful for sequential decision-making problems where actions have long-term consequences (GeeksforGeeks).

Reinforcement learning applications include: game-playing AI that learns optimal strategies through self-play; robotics systems that learn to manipulate objects or navigate environments; autonomous vehicle control systems; resource allocation and scheduling optimization; and personalized recommendation systems that adapt based on user engagement.

Semi-Supervised Learning combines elements of supervised and unsupervised approaches, leveraging both labeled and unlabeled data during training. This approach is valuable when labeling data is expensive or time-consuming, but unlabeled data is abundant. By using the structure discovered in unlabeled data to improve learning from limited labeled examples, semi-supervised methods can achieve performance approaching fully supervised systems while requiring significantly less labeled training data.

Machine Learning: The Foundation of Modern AI

Machine learning represents the primary methodology through which contemporary AI systems acquire capabilities and improve performance. Rather than being explicitly programmed with rules for every possible situation, machine learning systems learn from examples, identifying patterns in data that enable them to make predictions, decisions, or discoveries without being specifically programmed for each task.

The fundamental premise of machine learning, as articulated by researcher Arvind Ramakrishnan, is elegantly simple: "It's a lot easier to collect data than to collect understanding." Instead of requiring human experts to articulate explicit rules governing complex phenomena which may be impossible for tasks like image recognition or natural language understanding machine learning systems derive their own internal representations and decision rules from examples (MIT Sloan, 2025).

The Machine Learning Process: From Data to Decisions

Machine learning follows a systematic process that transforms raw data into actionable predictions or decisions:

1. Data Collection and Preparation: The foundation of any machine learning system is high-quality, relevant data. This data can take many forms numbers in spreadsheets, text documents, images, audio recordings, video files, sensor readings, or transactional records. The volume and diversity of training data significantly impact model performance; generally, more data enables more accurate and robust models (MIT Sloan, 2025).

Data preparation involves cleaning data to remove errors and inconsistencies, handling missing values through imputation or removal, transforming features into appropriate formats for modeling, normalizing or standardizing numerical features to comparable scales, encoding categorical variables into numerical representations, and splitting data into training, validation, and test sets for proper evaluation.

2. Feature Engineering and Selection: Features are the measurable properties or characteristics used as inputs to machine learning models. Effective feature engineering creating informative features from raw data often determines the difference between mediocre and excellent model performance. This process requires domain expertise to identify which aspects of the data are likely to be predictive and creativity to construct features that capture relevant patterns.

3. Model Selection and Training: Machine learning practitioners choose algorithms appropriate for their specific problem type, data characteristics, and performance requirements. During training, the model iteratively adjusts its internal parameters to minimize the difference between its predictions and actual outcomes in the training data. This optimization process typically employs variants of gradient descent mathematical techniques that incrementally adjust parameters in directions that improve model performance.

4. Model Evaluation and Validation: Trained models must be rigorously evaluated on data not used during training to assess their ability to generalize to new situations. Common evaluation metrics include accuracy, precision, recall, and F1-score for classification problems; mean squared error and R-squared for regression tasks; and task-specific metrics for specialized applications.

5. Deployment and Monitoring: Once validated, models are deployed in production environments where they make real-time predictions or decisions on new data. Continuous monitoring ensures models maintain performance as data distributions evolve over time, triggering retraining when performance degradation is detected.

Common Machine Learning Algorithms

The field of machine learning encompasses numerous algorithms, each with particular strengths, weaknesses, and appropriate application domains:

Linear Regression models the relationship between input features and continuous output variables as a linear combination. Despite its simplicity, linear regression remains widely used for prediction tasks where relationships are approximately linear, and interpretability is valued.

Logistic Regression, despite its name, performs classification rather than regression by modeling the probability that an input belongs to a particular class. It is commonly used for binary classification tasks and as a baseline against which more complex methods are compared.

Decision Trees learn hierarchical rules that partition the feature space into regions associated with different predictions. Trees are highly interpretable and can model non-linear relationships, though they tend to overfit training data without careful regularization.

Random Forests combine multiple decision trees trained on different subsets of data and features, aggregating their predictions to improve accuracy and robustness. This ensemble approach reduces overfitting while maintaining many advantages of individual trees.

Support Vector Machines (SVMs) find optimal boundaries separating different classes in high-dimensional feature spaces. SVMs excel at classification tasks, particularly when classes are well-separated, and the number of features is large relative to the number of training examples.

K-Nearest Neighbors (KNN) classifies new examples based on the majority class among their k most similar training examples. This simple yet effective approach works well for many applications but becomes computationally expensive with large datasets.

Naive Bayes classifiers apply probability theory and make simplifying independence assumptions to enable efficient classification based on feature probabilities. Despite their "naive" assumptions, these classifiers often perform surprisingly well in practice, particularly for text classification tasks.

The Role of Statistics and Probability

Machine learning is fundamentally grounded in statistics and probability theory. Understanding distributions, hypothesis testing, correlation, and uncertainty quantification enables practitioners to: select appropriate algorithms for specific data characteristics; tune model parameters to balance complexity and generalization; assess confidence in predictions and identify when models are uncertain; detect and correct bias in training data and model predictions; and validate that observed performance improvements are statistically significant rather than random variation.

The probabilistic interpretation of machine learning views models as estimating conditional probability distributions the likelihood of different outcomes given observed features. This perspective enables principled approaches to uncertainty quantification, which is critical for applications where wrong predictions carry significant consequences.

Neural Networks: Artificial Brains Inspired by Biology

Neural networks represent a class of machine learning models inspired by the structure and function of biological neural systems, particularly the human brain. While modern artificial neural networks do not accurately simulate biological brains and are not intended as faithful brain models, the biological analogy provides useful intuition for understanding how these systems process information and learn from data (GeeksforGeeks, 2025).

The Building Blocks: Artificial Neurons

The fundamental unit of a neural network is the artificial neuron, a computational element that mimics certain aspects of biological neurons. An artificial neuron receives multiple inputs, processes them mathematically, and produces an output that may serve as input to other neurons.

Mathematically, a neuron computes a weighted sum of its inputs, adds a bias term, and applies an activation function to produce its output:

$$\text{output} = \text{activation\_function}(w_1x_1 + w_2x_2 + \ldots + w_nx_n + \text{bias})$$

Where x_1 through x_n are the inputs, w_1 through w_n are learned weights determining each input's importance, bias allows the neuron to shift its activation threshold, and the activation function introduces non-linearity, enabling the network to learn complex patterns.

The **weights and biases** represent the parameters that the network learns during training. By adjusting these values, the network changes how it transforms inputs into outputs, gradually improving its performance on the training task. A typical neural network may contain millions or even billions of these parameters, collectively encoding the knowledge extracted from training data.

Activation functions introduce critical non-linearity into neural network computations. Without activation functions, stacking multiple layers of neurons would collapse into a single linear transformation, severely limiting the network's expressiveness. Common activation functions include:

- **ReLU (Rectified Linear Unit):** Returns the input if positive, zero otherwise. ReLU has become the default activation function for hidden layers due to its computational efficiency and effectiveness at mitigating gradient vanishing problems.
- **Sigmoid:** Transforms inputs to values between 0 and 1, historically popular but less common now due to gradient vanishing issues at extreme values.
- **Tanh:** Similar to sigmoid, but outputs values between -1 and 1, providing stronger gradients than sigmoid.
- **Softmax:** Used in output layers for multi-class classification, transforming raw scores into probability distributions over classes.

Network Architecture: From Inputs to Outputs

Neural networks are organized into layers of interconnected neurons:

Input Layer: Receives the raw features from data. Each neuron in the input layer corresponds to one feature in the dataset pixel values in images, word embeddings in text, or measurement values in tabular data (GeeksforGeeks, 2025).

Hidden Layers: Perform the computational work of the network, transforming inputs through successive non-linear transformations. Networks may contain one or hundreds of hidden layers, with each layer extracting progressively more abstract and complex features from the data. The depth of a network its number of hidden layers gives "deep learning" its name.

Output Layer: Produces the network's final predictions. For binary classification, the output layer typically contains a single neuron with sigmoid activation. For multi-class classification, it contains one neuron per class with softmax activation. For regression, it produces continuous values without probabilistic interpretation.

The architecture of a neural network the number of layers, number of neurons per layer, connectivity patterns between layers, and choice of activation functions represents critical design decisions that profoundly impact model performance. Architecture search, once a matter of expert intuition and trial-and-error, increasingly employs automated methods including neural architecture search (NAS) algorithms that use machine learning to design optimal network structures.

The Learning Process: Forward Propagation and Backpropagation

Neural networks learn through an iterative process involving two key phases:

Forward Propagation computes the network's predictions by passing input data through successive layers, with each layer transforming its inputs through weighted sums and activation functions until the output layer produces final predictions. This process flows in one direction from inputs to outputs, hence the name "feedforward neural network" for basic architectures.

Backpropagation, short for "backward propagation of error," represents the mathematical technique through which neural networks learn from their mistakes. After forward propagation produces predictions, backpropagation computes how much each weight and bias contributed to the prediction error, then adjusts these parameters to reduce future errors (NYIT, 2025).

The backpropagation algorithm employs calculus, specifically the chain rule for computing derivatives, to efficiently calculate gradients the rates at which small changes in each parameter would affect the overall error. These gradients point in the direction of the steepest increase in error, so moving parameters in the opposite direction (gradient descent) reduces error and improves model performance.

The learning process typically involves:

1. Initialize network weights randomly.
2. For each batch of training examples:
    - Perform forward propagation to compute predictions
    - Calculate the loss (difference between predictions and true labels)
    - Perform backpropagation to compute parameter gradients.
    - Update weights and biases using gradient descent or variants like Adam or RMSprop.
3. Repeat until the model converges to satisfactory

performance.

This seemingly simple procedure, when applied to networks with millions of parameters across thousands or millions of training examples, enables neural networks to learn remarkably sophisticated representations and achieve superhuman performance on many tasks.

Universal Approximation and the Power of Depth

A fundamental theoretical result in neural network theory is the **universal approximation theorem**, which states that feedforward neural networks with a single hidden layer containing a sufficient number of neurons can approximate any continuous function to arbitrary accuracy (Wikipedia, 2025).

This theorem provides theoretical justification for neural networks' ability to learn complex patterns, but it doesn't specify how many neurons are "sufficient" for practical problems, nor does it address how easily networks can learn appropriate approximations through gradient descent.

In practice, deeper networks those with many hidden layers rather than many neurons in a single layer prove more effective for most applications. Deep architectures enable hierarchical feature learning, where early layers detect simple patterns (edges and textures in images, phonemes in speech), middle layers combine these into intermediate concepts (object parts, words), and deep layers represent high-level abstractions (complete objects, semantic meaning).

Modern theoretical work on deep neural networks proves that networks with bounded width but unlimited depth can approximate any Lebesgue integrable function, provided the width exceeds the input dimension. Conversely, networks with a width less than or equal to the input dimension cannot serve as universal approximators regardless of depth (Wikipedia, 2025). These results help explain why depth proves so valuable in practice.

Deep Learning: The Current AI Revolution

Deep learning refers to machine learning using neural networks with multiple hidden layers typically three or more layers of transformations from input to output. The "deep" in deep learning describes these multilayered network architectures rather than any profound philosophical depth (GeeksforGeeks, 2018).

While neural networks have existed since the 1960s, deep learning's current prominence stems from convergence of several enabling factors: vastly increased computational power, particularly Graphics Processing Units (GPUs) designed for parallel computation; availability of massive datasets from internet-scale applications, social media, and sensors; algorithmic innovations including better activation functions (ReLU), initialization strategies, and optimization techniques; and software frameworks (TensorFlow, PyTorch, Keras) that make implementing complex models accessible.

Why Deep Learning Now?

The resurgence of neural networks and the emergence of deep learning as the dominant AI paradigm reflect the resolution of historical limitations. Earlier neural network research in the 1960s and 1980s generated enthusiasm followed by "AI winters" periods of reduced funding and interest when systems failed to meet inflated expectations (NYIT, 2025).

The difference between historical failures and contemporary success lies in:

Computational Resources: Training deep neural networks requires enormous computational power. Modern GPUs can perform trillions of operations per second, enabling training of networks with billions of parameters on datasets containing millions of examples orders of magnitude beyond what was possible even a decade ago.

Data Availability: The Internet, mobile devices, social media, and ubiquitous sensors generate data at unprecedented scales. Deep learning's hunger for data which increases with model size can now be satisfied in ways impossible during earlier AI eras.

Algorithmic Improvements: Techniques like batch normalization, dropout regularization, residual connections, and attention mechanisms address training difficulties that plagued earlier deep networks. Better optimization algorithms like Adam adaptively adjust learning rates for each parameter, accelerating training and improving convergence.

Software Infrastructure: Modern deep learning frameworks provide automatic differentiation, enabling researchers to design novel architectures without manually deriving backpropagation equations. These frameworks also optimize computations for GPUs and distributed systems, abstracting complex technical details.

Specialized Architectures for Specific Domains

While feedforward neural networks provide general-purpose learning capabilities, specialized architectures have been developed for particular types of data and tasks:

Convolutional Neural Networks (CNNs) dominate computer vision tasks by exploiting the spatial structure of images. CNNs use convolutional layers that slide learned filters across images, detecting visual features like edges, textures, and object parts regardless of their location in the image. This architecture dramatically reduces the number of parameters compared to fully connected networks while better capturing the hierarchical structure of visual information (GeeksforGeeks, 2018).

CNNs have achieved remarkable success in: image classification (identifying objects in photographs); object detection and segmentation (localizing objects within images); facial recognition; medical image analysis; and autonomous vehicle perception systems.

Recurrent Neural Networks (RNNs) process sequential data by maintaining hidden states that accumulate information across time steps. This makes RNNs suitable for tasks involving sequences like text, speech, or time-series data, where order matters and context from earlier elements influences the interpretation of later ones.

Key RNN applications include: natural language processing (language modeling, machine translation); speech recognition; time-series prediction (stock prices, weather, equipment maintenance); and video analysis, where temporal relationships matter.

However, basic RNNs struggle with long-term dependencies maintaining relevant information over many time steps. Advanced variants like **Long Short-Term Memory (LSTM)** networks and **Gated Recurrent Units (GRUs)** address this limitation through sophisticated gating mechanisms that selectively remember or forget information across sequences.

Transformers represent a revolutionary architecture introduced in 2017 that has largely supplanted RNNs for sequence processing tasks. Unlike RNNs that process sequences step-by-step, transformers employ attention mechanisms enabling them to consider all positions in a sequence simultaneously. This parallel processing proves much more computationally efficient and better captures long-range dependencies (Wikipedia, 2025).

Transformers underpin modern breakthrough AI systems, including: Large Language Models (GPT series, Claude, Gemini) for text generation and understanding; BERT and similar models for natural language understanding tasks; vision transformers adapting attention mechanisms for image processing; and multimodal models combining text, images, and other data types.

Generative Adversarial Networks (GANs) employ a unique two-network architecture where a generator creates synthetic data and a discriminator attempts to distinguish real from generated examples. Through this adversarial process, generators learn to create increasingly realistic outputs. GANs enable: photorealistic image generation; style transfer and image-to-image translation; data augmentation for training other models; and creative applications in art and design.
(GeeksforGeeks, 2018).

Training Deep Networks: Challenges and Solutions

Training deep neural networks presents unique challenges beyond those faced by shallow models:

Vanishing and Exploding Gradients: In very deep networks, gradients computed through backpropagation can become extremely small (vanishing) or large (exploding) as they propagate through many layers. Vanishing gradients prevent early layers from learning, while exploding gradients cause training instability. Modern activation functions (ReLU), careful initialization strategies, batch normalization, and residual connections mitigate these issues.

Overfitting: Deep networks' enormous capacity enables them to memorize training data rather than learning generalizable patterns. Regularization techniques, including dropout (randomly deactivating neurons during training), L2 weight decay, data augmentation, and early stopping, combat overfitting.

Computational Requirements: Training state-of-the-art deep learning models may require weeks of computation on clusters of GPUs, consuming megawatts of electricity. Techniques like mixed-precision training, gradient accumulation, and model parallelism make training more tractable, while transfer learning enables reusing features learned on large datasets for new tasks with limited data.

Hyperparameter Tuning: Deep networks require careful selection of learning rates, batch sizes, layer dimensions, regularization strength, and numerous other hyperparameters.
Grid search, random search, and Bayesian optimization automate this process, though it remains computationally expensive.

Practical Machine Learning with Modern Frameworks

Contemporary deep learning owes much of its accessibility to sophisticated software frameworks that abstract mathematical and computational complexities. In 2025, **PyTorch** has emerged as one of the most important libraries for training neural networks, widely adopted in both research and production applications (Towards Data Science, 2025).

PyTorch: Dynamic Computation and Automatic Differentiation

PyTorch's core innovation is **automatic differentiation** the ability to automatically compute gradients for any differentiable computation without manually deriving backpropagation equations. Researchers can focus on designing network architectures and loss functions while PyTorch handles the mathematics of training.

The fundamental PyTorch workflow involves:

1. **Define the forward pass:** Specify how inputs are transformed into outputs through a series of operations
2. **Compute the loss:** Calculate the difference between predictions and ground truth
3. **Automatic backpropagation:** PyTorch computes gradients automatically
4. **Update parameters:** Adjust weights and biases using computed gradients

This design philosophy called "define-by-run" creates computation graphs dynamically as operations execute, enabling flexible architectures including conditional logic, loops, and recursive structures. This contrasts with earlier frameworks that required defining static graphs before execution.

Building Neural Networks with PyTorch

PyTorch provides building blocks for constructing neural networks through its torch.nn module:

- **nn.Linear:** Fully connected layers that transform inputs through learned weight matrices
- **nn.Conv2d:** Convolutional layers for processing images
- **nn.LSTM/nn.GRU:** Recurrent layers for sequential data

- **nn.Transformer:** Transformer architectures for advanced sequence modeling
- **Activation functions:** nn.ReLU, nn.Sigmoid, nn.Tanh, etc.
- **Loss functions:** nn.CrossEntropyLoss, nn.MSELoss, etc.
- **Optimizers:** torch.optim.Adam, torch.optim.SGD, etc.

Researchers compose these components into custom architectures by subclassing nn.Module and defining forward methods that specify how data flows through the network. PyTorch's flexibility enables rapid experimentation with novel architectures while maintaining performance through optimized implementations.

Transfer Learning: Standing on the Shoulders of Giants

One of deep learning's most powerful techniques is **transfer learning** reusing knowledge learned on one task to bootstrap learning on related tasks. Rather than training models from scratch for each application, practitioners fine-tune pre-trained models that have learned general features from massive datasets.

For example, image classification models trained on ImageNet (millions of labeled images) learn general visual features edges, textures, object parts that transfer to specialized tasks like medical image analysis or satellite imagery classification. Similarly, language models trained on vast text corpora learn linguistic patterns useful for downstream tasks like sentiment analysis, question answering, or text classification.

Transfer learning dramatically reduces data requirements for new tasks (models can be fine-tuned with hundreds rather than millions of examples), accelerates development by starting from capable baseline models, and improves performance, especially when task-specific training data is limited.

Real-World Applications: Where AI Transforms Industries

The theoretical concepts and technical mechanisms explored in this chapter enable practical AI systems that are transforming industries and creating unprecedented value:

Computer Vision enables machines to understand visual information from the world:

- Medical imaging analysis detecting diseases from X-rays, CT scans, and MRIs
- Autonomous vehicles perceiving roads, obstacles, and traffic signs
- Quality control in manufacturing, identifying defects in products
- Facial recognition for security and authentication
- Agricultural monitoring assessing crop health from drone imagery

Natural Language Processing allows machines to understand and generate human language:

Machine translation breaking down language barriers

- Chatbots and virtual assistants providing customer service
- Content moderation detecting harmful or inappropriate material
- Document analysis extracting information from unstructured text
- Sentiment analysis understanding customer opinions and feedback

Speech Recognition and Synthesis enable voice-based interfaces:

- Virtual assistants responding to voice commands
- Transcription services converting speech to text
- Language learning applications providing pronunciation feedback
- Accessibility tools assisting people with disabilities

Recommendation Systems personalize content and products:

- E-commerce platforms suggesting relevant products
- Streaming services recommending movies and music
- Social media curating content feeds
- Job matching platforms connecting candidates with opportunities

Predictive Analytics forecasts future events and trends:

- Financial markets predicting stock prices and trading opportunities

- Healthcare anticipating patient risks and disease progression
- Weather forecasting improving accuracy and lead time
- Predictive maintenance scheduling equipment service before failures

Game Playing and Strategic Decision-Making:

- AI systems mastering complex games like chess, Go, and StarCraft
- Strategic planning in logistics and resource allocation
- Optimization of manufacturing processes and supply chains

Conclusion: The Foundation for AI-Powered Cybersecurity

This chapter has provided a comprehensive introduction to artificial intelligence fundamentals, exploring the concepts, technologies, and methodologies that enable machines to exhibit intelligent behavior. We examined how machine learning systems learn from data rather than explicit programming, investigated neural networks and their biological inspiration, explored deep learning architectures specialized for different types of data, and surveyed the real-world applications transforming industries worldwide.

Understanding these AI basics provides essential context for the subsequent chapters, which examine how these same technologies are being applied in cybersecurity both to create more sophisticated defenses and to enable more dangerous attacks. The pattern recognition capabilities that allow neural networks to classify images or understand language also enable them to detect malware, identify network intrusions, and recognize anomalous user behavior.

The same deep learning techniques powering virtual assistants and recommendation systems can generate convincing phishing emails, create deepfake videos, or automate social engineering attacks at unprecedented scale.

As we transition to Chapter 4's exploration of how AI meets cybersecurity, the foundational knowledge established here will illuminate why AI represents both cybersecurity's most powerful tool and its most formidable threat. The technologies enabling machines to learn from experience, recognize complex patterns, and make sophisticated decisions operate according to the same principles, whether deployed for protection or attack, and the race to harness AI's capabilities for security defines the contemporary digital battleground.

The machine learning algorithms, neural network architectures, and training methodologies described in this chapter are not merely academic abstractions they represent the active components of systems currently protecting critical infrastructure, defending corporate networks, and simultaneously empowering the most sophisticated cyber threats organizations face. Understanding how these systems work, what they can and cannot do, and where their strengths and limitations lie proves essential for anyone seeking to navigate the AI-transformed cybersecurity landscape.

References

DataCamp. (2025, February 28). *How to learn AI from scratch in 2025: A complete expert guide.* Retrieved from https://www.datacamp.com/blog/how-to-learn-ai

GeeksforGeeks. (2018, June 1). *Introduction to deep learning.* Retrieved from https://www.geeksforgeeks.org/deep-learning/introduction-deep-learning/

GeeksforGeeks. (2024, June 11). *Machine learning tutorial.* Retrieved from https://www.geeksforgeeks.org/machine-learning/machine-learning/

GeeksforGeeks. (2025, October 7). *What is a neural network?* Retrieved from https://www.geeksforgeeks.org/machine-learning/neural-networks-a-beginners-guide/

MIT Sloan. (2025, June 2). *Machine learning and generative AI: What are they good for in 2025?* Retrieved from https://mitsloan.mit.edu/ideas-made-to-matter/machine-learning-and-generative-ai-what-are-they-good-for

NYIT. (2025, August 1). *Deep learning and neural networks: The future of machine learning.* Retrieved from https://online.nyit.edu/blog/deep-learning-and-neural-networks-the-future-of-machine-learning

TechTarget. (n.d.). *Top 10 AI certifications and courses for 2025.* Retrieved from https://www.techtarget.com/whatis/feature/10-top-artificial-intelligence-certifications-and-courses

Towards Data Science. (2025). *PyTorch explained: From automatic differentiation to training custom neural networks*. Retrieved from https://towardsdatascience.com/the-basics-of-deep-learning-with-pytorch-in-1-hour/

Chapter 4: Where AI Meets Cybersecurity

Introduction: The Convergence of Two Powerful Forces

The intersection of artificial intelligence and cybersecurity represents one of the most significant technological convergences of our time. As we have explored in previous chapters, AI's transformative capabilities extend across numerous domains, from healthcare to finance. However, nowhere is the dual nature of AI's promise and peril more apparent than in the realm of cybersecurity. This chapter examines how artificial intelligence is fundamentally reshaping the landscape of digital defense and attack, creating both unprecedented opportunities for protection and novel vectors for exploitation.

The statistics paint a compelling picture of this transformation. According to recent industry surveys, 67% of IT and security professionals globally have already tested AI for cybersecurity applications, with 57% of organizations actively using AI for anomaly detection and 50.5% deploying it for malware detection (Fortinet). This rapid adoption reflects both the growing sophistication of cyber threats and the recognition that traditional security approaches can no longer keep pace with the volume and complexity of modern attacks.

The stakes could not be higher. With cybercrime revenues estimated at $8 trillion annually nearly five times the combined market value of the world's most valuable technology companies the economic impact of cyber threats continues to escalate (Darktrace). In this high-stakes environment, artificial intelligence emerges not merely as another tool in the security arsenal but as a fundamental force multiplier that can process vast amounts of data at machine speed, identify patterns invisible to human analysts, and respond to threats in milliseconds rather than hours or days.

AI-Driven Threat Detection: The New Frontier

The application of artificial intelligence to threat detection represents a paradigm shift from reactive to proactive security postures. Traditional security systems relied heavily on signature-based detection, requiring prior knowledge of specific threats to identify them. AI-powered systems, by contrast, excel at identifying previously unknown threats through sophisticated pattern recognition and behavioral analysis.

Machine learning algorithms now continuously analyze network traffic, user behavior, and system activities to establish baseline patterns of normal operation. Any deviation from these baselines triggers immediate investigation, enabling the detection of zero-day exploits and advanced persistent threats that would otherwise remain hidden. These systems process millions of events per second, correlating data from multiple sources to identify subtle indicators of compromise that human analysts might miss.

The real-time nature of AI-driven detection cannot be overstated. Research from energy infrastructure deployments demonstrates that AI systems can achieve 98% threat detection rates in high-risk environments while reducing incident response times by 70% (Syracuse University, 2025). This speed advantage proves critical when considering that modern cyberattacks can compromise entire networks within minutes of initial infiltration.

Behavioral analytics represents another crucial advancement in AI-driven detection. Rather than looking for known attack signatures, these systems analyze how users, applications, and devices typically behave, flagging anomalies that might indicate compromise. For instance, if an employee's account suddenly begins accessing sensitive files at unusual hours or from atypical locations, AI systems can detect and respond to this potential insider threat or compromised credential scenario before significant damage occurs.

The continuous learning capability of these systems ensures they evolve alongside the threat landscape. Unlike static rule-based systems that require manual updates, AI-powered detection platforms automatically refine their models based on new data, staying current with emerging attack techniques. This adaptive capability proves essential in an environment where threat actors constantly develop new methods to evade detection.

Automated Response Systems: Speed as a Defense

The automation of incident response represents one of AI's most immediate and tangible contributions to cybersecurity. When threats are detected, every second counts. AI-powered automated response systems can take decisive action in milliseconds, containing threats before they spread throughout the network.

These systems operate on multiple levels simultaneously. At the network level, they can automatically adjust firewall rules, isolate compromised segments, and reroute traffic away from affected areas. At the endpoint level, they can quarantine suspicious files, terminate malicious processes, and prevent lateral movement within the network. This multi-layered response capability ensures comprehensive protection across the entire attack surface.

Consider the case of Darktrace's autonomous response system, which saved one organization 264 analyst hours in less than a month by automatically responding to threats that would otherwise require manual intervention (Darktrace). The system's FACADE framework demonstrates how AI can make split-second decisions about threat severity and appropriate response measures, balancing the need for security with operational continuity.

The sophistication of these automated responses continues to grow. Modern systems can distinguish between different types of threats and calibrate their responses accordingly. A suspected ransomware attack might trigger immediate network isolation and backup activation, while a potential data exfiltration attempt could result in selective blocking of specific data transfers while maintaining business operations.

IBM Watson for Cybersecurity exemplifies this graduated response approach, automatically quarantining phishing emails while simultaneously analyzing their content to update detection models for similar future threats (IBM). This dual action immediate protection coupled with continuous learning illustrates how AI transforms incident response from a purely defensive measure into an opportunity for system improvement.

Key Applications Across the Security Spectrum

Threat Intelligence and Analysis

Artificial intelligence has revolutionized threat intelligence gathering and analysis by processing vast volumes of data from diverse sources at unprecedented speeds. Security teams now leverage AI to analyze millions of indicators of compromise (IOCs), correlating information from dark web forums, security feeds, vulnerability databases, and internal telemetry to identify emerging threats before they materialize into attacks.

The volume of data involved makes human analysis impractical. AI systems can process and contextualize threat intelligence from thousands of sources simultaneously, identifying patterns and connections that would take human analysts weeks or months to uncover. This capability enables organizations to shift from reactive to predictive security postures, anticipating and preparing for attacks based on early warning signals.

Phishing and Email Security

Email remains the primary vector for cyberattacks, with phishing campaigns growing increasingly sophisticated. AI-powered email security systems now employ natural language processing and machine learning to analyze not just the technical aspects of emails but also their content, context, and intent. These systems examine sender reputation, email headers, embedded links, attachments, and even writing style to identify potential threats.

Modern AI email security goes beyond simple filtering. These systems can detect business email compromise attempts by analyzing communication patterns and identifying when legitimate accounts may have been compromised. They recognize subtle indicators like unusual urgency in requests, atypical language patterns, or requests that deviate from normal business processes. The continuous learning aspect means these systems become more accurate over time, adapting to new phishing techniques as they emerge.

Malware Detection and Analysis

The explosion of malware variants with hundreds of thousands of new samples discovered daily has made traditional signature-based detection obsolete. AI-powered malware detection systems use behavioral analysis and machine learning to identify malicious code based on its actions rather than its appearance. This approach proves particularly effective against polymorphic malware that changes its code to evade signature-based detection.

These systems analyze multiple characteristics simultaneously: file behavior, system calls, network communications, and resource usage patterns. By examining how software behaves rather than what it looks like, AI can detect zero-day malware and advanced persistent threats that have never been seen before. Companies like Cylance have demonstrated detection rates exceeding 99% for previously unknown malware using these AI-driven approaches (Cylance).

Identity and Access Management

AI has transformed identity and access management from a static, rule-based process into a dynamic, context-aware system. Modern AI-powered identity platforms continuously analyze user behavior, device characteristics, location data, and access patterns to make real-time authentication decisions. This approach, known as adaptive authentication, adjusts security requirements based on risk levels.

For example, a user accessing systems from their regular office during normal hours might face minimal authentication requirements, while the same user attempting access from an unusual location at odd hours would trigger additional verification steps. AI systems can detect and prevent credential stuffing attacks, identify compromised accounts through behavioral anomalies, and even predict which users might be at higher risk of compromise based on their digital behavior patterns.

Real-World Tools and Platforms: AI in Action

The cybersecurity industry has witnessed an explosion of AI-powered tools and platforms, each addressing specific aspects of the security challenge. Understanding these tools and their capabilities helps illustrate the practical applications of AI in cybersecurity.

Darktrace stands as a pioneer in autonomous cyber defense, using self-learning AI to detect and respond to threats without human intervention. Its Enterprise Immune System technology creates a dynamic understanding of normal behavior for every user and device, enabling it to identify subtle deviations that indicate potential threats. The platform's Antigena module can take autonomous action to contain threats, buying crucial time for security teams to investigate and respond.

CrowdStrike Falcon leverages AI for endpoint detection and response (EDR), using behavioral analysis to identify and stop breaches. The platform's cloud-native architecture enables it to correlate threat data across millions of endpoints globally, identifying attack patterns and techniques as they emerge. Its AI-powered threat hunting capabilities have proven particularly effective against nation-state actors and sophisticated criminal groups.

Microsoft Security Copilot represents the integration of generative AI into security operations, helping analysts investigate incidents, analyze vulnerabilities, and generate response recommendations. By processing natural language queries, the system makes advanced security capabilities accessible to analysts of varying skill levels, democratizing access to sophisticated threat analysis (Microsoft, 2025).

PentestGPT demonstrates AI's application in offensive security, automating aspects of penetration testing to identify vulnerabilities before attackers can exploit them. The tool has discovered critical vulnerabilities in banking applications and enterprise systems that human testers might have missed, illustrating AI's value in proactive security testing (Radiant Security, 2025).

These platforms represent just a fraction of the AI-powered security tools available today. The market continues to expand rapidly, with the generative AI in cybersecurity market expected to grow tenfold between 2024 and 2034 (Cyble, 2025).

The Opportunities: Transforming Defense Capabilities

The integration of AI into cybersecurity offers transformative opportunities that extend far beyond incremental improvements to existing security measures. These advantages fundamentally alter the economics and effectiveness of cyber defense.

Enhanced Accuracy and Reduced False Positives represent one of AI's most immediate benefits. Traditional security systems often generate overwhelming numbers of alerts, many of which prove to be false positives. Security teams waste valuable time investigating benign activities while real threats potentially go unnoticed. AI systems learn to distinguish between genuine threats and normal variations in behavior, dramatically reducing false positive rates while maintaining high detection accuracy. This improvement alone can transform security operations from a reactive scramble to a focused, strategic function.

Scalability and Processing Power enable organizations to analyze security data at volumes impossible for human teams. A typical enterprise generates terabytes of security-relevant data daily. AI systems can process this entire data stream in real-time, identifying patterns and correlations across millions of events. This capability becomes increasingly critical as organizations expand their digital footprints through cloud adoption, IoT deployment, and remote work initiatives.

24/7 Continuous Monitoring ensures that security never sleeps. While human analysts work in shifts and can suffer from fatigue, AI systems maintain constant vigilance, never missing an indicator due to distraction or exhaustion. This round-the-clock capability proves particularly valuable for organizations operating across multiple time zones or those facing persistent threat actors who deliberately attack during off-hours.

Predictive Capabilities allow organizations to anticipate and prepare for attacks before they occur. By analyzing historical data, current threat intelligence, and environmental factors, AI systems can forecast likely attack vectors and timing. This predictive power enables proactive defense measures, such as preemptively patching vulnerable systems or increasing monitoring of high-risk assets during periods of elevated threat likelihood.

Cost Optimization through AI adoption can be substantial. IBM research indicates that organizations using AI and automation in their security operations save an average of $2.2 million per data breach compared to those without these capabilities (IBM). These savings come from faster detection and containment, reduced downtime, and more efficient use of security personnel.

The Risks: Navigating the Dark Side of AI

While AI offers tremendous advantages for defenders, it simultaneously creates new risks and empowers adversaries with sophisticated attack capabilities. Understanding these risks is essential for developing effective AI-powered security strategies.

AI-Powered Attacks represent the most direct threat. Cybercriminals now use AI to automate vulnerability scanning, generate convincing phishing content, and develop malware that adapts to evade detection. These AI-enhanced attacks operate at machine speed and scale, potentially overwhelming traditional defenses. The same machine learning techniques that power defensive systems can be turned against them, creating an arms race between AI-powered attack and defense systems.

Adversarial AI poses a particularly insidious threat. Attackers can manipulate the input data that AI systems use for training or decision-making, causing them to misclassify threats or miss attacks entirely. These adversarial attacks can be subtle slightly modified malware that AI systems classify as benign, or carefully crafted network traffic that bypasses anomaly detection. The black-box nature of many AI systems makes detecting these manipulations challenging.

Over-Reliance and Skill Atrophy present organizational risks. As AI systems become more capable, there's a danger that human analysts may lose critical skills or become overly dependent on automated systems. When AI systems fail or encounter scenarios outside their training parameters, organizations may find themselves without the human expertise needed to respond effectively. Maintaining the balance between automation and human capability remains a crucial challenge.

Data Quality Dependencies highlight a fundamental vulnerability of AI systems. These systems are only as good as the data they're trained on. Poor quality training data, whether due to incompleteness, bias, or manipulation, can result in AI systems that miss threats or generate excessive false positives. Organizations must invest significantly in data quality and curation to ensure their AI systems function effectively.

Implementation Complexity and Costs can be prohibitive for many organizations. Deploying AI-powered security requires substantial investments in infrastructure, training data, and specialized expertise. The shortage of professionals with both cybersecurity and AI expertise drives up costs and creates implementation bottlenecks. Many organizations struggle to integrate AI systems with legacy security infrastructure, creating gaps that attackers can exploit.

The AI Arms Race: A New Battlefield

The cybersecurity landscape has evolved into an AI arms race, with both defenders and attackers racing to develop and deploy increasingly sophisticated AI capabilities. This competition fundamentally changes the nature of cyber conflict, introducing new dynamics and considerations.

On the defensive side, organizations deploy AI for automated threat hunting, using machine learning to proactively search for indicators of compromise across their networks. Real-time anomaly detection systems identify deviations from normal behavior patterns, while predictive threat intelligence platforms forecast likely attack vectors. These defensive applications continue to grow more sophisticated, with multi-agent AI systems that coordinate responses across different security layers.

Attackers, meanwhile, leverage AI for equally sophisticated purposes. Automated vulnerability scanning powered by AI can identify and exploit weaknesses faster than defenders can patch them. AI-generated phishing content becomes increasingly convincing, with natural language processing creating messages tailored to specific targets. Polymorphic malware uses machine learning to continuously modify its code, evading signature-based detection. Deep learning enables the creation of deepfakes for social engineering attacks, adding a new dimension to identity-based threats.

The balance in this arms race remains precarious. Industry surveys reveal a nearly even split in expert opinion, with 45% predicting adversaries will benefit most from AI, while 43% believe defenders will gain the greater advantage (Darktrace). This uncertainty reflects the dual-use nature of AI technology and the rapid pace of development on both sides.

The speed of engagement has become a critical factor. With both attacks and defenses operating at machine speed, the window for human intervention shrinks to milliseconds. This acceleration creates new risks, as errors or false positives can cascade through systems before humans can intervene. Organizations must develop new frameworks for managing AI-powered security operations that balance speed with safety.

Implementation Considerations: Practical Challenges

Successfully implementing AI in cybersecurity requires careful consideration of numerous practical challenges. Organizations must navigate technical, organizational, and ethical considerations to realize

AI's benefits while managing its risks.

Data Quality and Availability remain fundamental challenges. AI systems require large volumes of high-quality, labeled data for training. In cybersecurity, obtaining this data can be difficult due to privacy concerns, the sensitive nature of security incidents, and the rapid evolution of threats. Organizations must develop robust data governance frameworks that balance the need for comprehensive training data with privacy and security requirements.

Integration with Existing Infrastructure poses significant technical challenges. Most organizations operate heterogeneous security environments with tools from multiple vendors, legacy systems, and varying data formats. Integrating AI systems into these complex environments requires substantial effort and may necessitate infrastructure modernization. Organizations must carefully plan integration strategies that minimize disruption while maximizing AI's value.

Skills Gap and Talent Shortage create implementation bottlenecks. The intersection of AI expertise and cybersecurity knowledge remains rare, with qualified professionals commanding premium salaries. Organizations must invest in training existing staff, partnering with educational institutions, and potentially outsourcing certain AI security functions to managed service providers.

Explainability and Trust present ongoing challenges. Many AI systems, particularly deep learning models, operate as "black boxes," making it difficult to understand how they reach specific decisions. In security contexts, where false positives can disrupt operations and false negatives can be catastrophic, this lack of explainability creates trust issues. Organizations must balance the superior performance of complex AI models with the need for interpretable, auditable security decisions.

Regulatory Compliance and Ethics add layers of complexity. As governments worldwide develop AI regulations, organizations must ensure their AI security systems comply with evolving requirements. Ethical considerations around AI use in security, including privacy implications and potential bias in threat detection, require careful attention. Organizations must develop governance frameworks that address these concerns while maintaining security effectiveness.

Future Trends: The Evolution Continues

Looking toward 2025 and beyond, several trends are shaping the future of AI in cybersecurity. These developments promise to further transform how organizations defend against cyber threats while creating new challenges and opportunities.

Multi-Agent AI Systems represent the next evolution in AI-powered security. Rather than relying on single AI models, future security platforms will deploy multiple specialized AI agents that collaborate to provide comprehensive protection. These agents will specialize in different aspects of security network analysis, endpoint protection, user behavior monitoring and coordinate their actions through sophisticated orchestration frameworks.

Adaptive AI and Real-Time Evolution will enable security systems that continuously evolve in response to new threats. Unlike current systems that require periodic retraining, adaptive AI will modify its behavior in real-time based on observed attacks and environmental changes. This capability will prove crucial as attack techniques become increasingly dynamic and personalized.

Quantum-Resistant AI Security emerges as a critical requirement as quantum computing advances threaten current cryptographic protections. AI systems must evolve to operate in a post-quantum world, developing new approaches to threat detection and response that don't rely on traditional cryptographic assumptions.

Privacy-Preserving AI Techniques, such as federated learning and homomorphic encryption, will enable organizations to benefit from collective threat intelligence without sharing sensitive data. These techniques allow AI models to learn from distributed data sources without centralizing the data, addressing privacy concerns while improving detection capabilities.

Autonomous Security Operations Centers (SOCs) represent the culmination of AI integration in cybersecurity. These next-generation SOCs will operate with minimal human intervention, automatically detecting, investigating, and responding to threats while continuously optimizing their operations. Human analysts will shift from operational roles to strategic oversight and exception handling.

Case Studies: AI Success Stories in Practice

Real-world implementations demonstrate AI's transformative impact on cybersecurity across various industries and threat scenarios.

A major utility company deployed Darktrace's AI platform and observed measurable network improvements within a month. The system identified and contained several previously undetected threats, including an advanced persistent threat that had been resident in the network for months. The autonomous response capability prevented a potential service disruption that could have affected millions of customers, while saving the equivalent of 264 analyst hours in investigation and response time (Darktrace).

In the financial sector, a banking application underwent security testing using PentestGPT, which discovered critical vulnerabilities that traditional penetration testing had missed. The AI-powered tool identified a complex chain of exploits that could have allowed unauthorized access to customer financial data. The bank's subsequent remediation prevented what could have been a catastrophic breach affecting millions of accounts (Web Asha Technologies, 2025).

A global retail organization implemented Microsoft Security Copilot to enhance its security operations. The AI assistant reduced security investigation times by 60%, allowing analysts to handle three times as many incidents while improving accuracy. The system's natural language interface enabled junior analysts to perform complex investigations that previously required senior expertise, effectively multiplying the organization's security capacity (Microsoft, 2025).

Energy infrastructure, often targeted by nation-state actors, has benefited significantly from AI adoption. One energy company achieved a 98% threat detection rate using AI-powered monitoring, while reducing incident response times by 70%. The system successfully defended against a sophisticated attack campaign that used novel techniques specifically designed to evade traditional security controls (Syracuse University, 2025).

Conclusion: Balancing Power with Responsibility

The convergence of artificial intelligence and cybersecurity represents both a tremendous opportunity and a significant challenge. AI has fundamentally transformed how organizations detect, analyze, and respond to cyber threats, offering capabilities that would have seemed like science fiction just a decade ago. The ability to process vast amounts of data in real-time, identify subtle patterns indicating compromise, and respond to threats at machine speed has shifted the advantage back toward defenders after years of playing catch-up with increasingly sophisticated attackers.

However, this same technology that empowers defenders also equips adversaries with powerful new weapons. The AI arms race in cybersecurity continues to escalate, with both sides developing increasingly sophisticated capabilities. Organizations must navigate this complex landscape carefully, leveraging AI's benefits while managing its risks and limitations.

Success in this new era requires more than just deploying AI tools. Organizations must develop comprehensive strategies that integrate AI with human expertise, maintain robust data governance, address ethical considerations, and continuously adapt to evolving threats. They must resist the temptation to view AI as a silver bullet, recognizing that it represents a powerful tool that requires skilled application and careful management.

As we look toward the future, the role of AI in cybersecurity will only grow more central. The organizations that thrive will be those that successfully balance AI's power with responsible implementation, maintaining human oversight while leveraging machine capabilities. They will build adaptive, resilient security postures that evolve continuously in response to new threats.

The journey explored in this chapter from AI-driven threat detection through automated response systems to the emerging AI arms race illustrates both the promise and complexity of AI in cybersecurity. As we prepare to delve deeper into specific applications in Chapter 5, focusing on AI for threat detection, we carry forward the understanding that AI represents not just a technological advancement but a fundamental shift in how we conceptualize and implement cybersecurity.

The convergence of AI and cybersecurity is not merely about replacing human analysts with machines or automating existing processes. It represents a transformation in how we think about security, moving from reactive responses to predictive prevention, from isolated tools to integrated ecosystems, and from static defenses to adaptive, learning systems. Organizations that embrace this transformation while maintaining appropriate caution and control will be best positioned to defend against the cyber threats of tomorrow.

In this ongoing battle between attackers and defenders, AI has emerged as the decisive factor that will shape the future of cybersecurity. The question is not whether to adopt AI for security that decision has been made by the inexorable advance of AI-powered threats. The question is how to implement AI effectively, responsibly, and sustainably in a way that enhances security while managing new risks. This challenge defines the current era of cybersecurity and will continue to shape its evolution for years to come.

References

Cloud Security Alliance. (2025, March 14). *AI in cybersecurity: Revolutionizing threat detection.* https://cloudsecurityalliance.org/blog/2025/03/14/a-i-in-cybersecurity-revolutionizing-threat-detection-and-response

Cylance. (2024). *AI-driven endpoint protection: Annual threat report 2024.* Cylance Press.

Cyble. (2025, July 8). *The ultimate guide to AI agents in cybersecurity 2025.* https://cyble.com/knowledge-hub/guide-to-ai-agents-in-cybersecurity/

Darktrace. (2024, November 3). *AI and cybersecurity: Predictions for 2025.* https://www.darktrace.com/blog/ai-and-cybersecurity-predictions-for-2025

Fortinet. (2024). *Artificial Intelligence (AI) in cybersecurity: The future of threat defense.* https://www.fortinet.com/resources/cyberglossary/artificial-intelligence-in-cybersecurity

IBM. (2024). *Cost of a data breach report 2024.* IBM Security.

Infosecurity Magazine. (2025, August 27). *2025 to be a year of reckoning for AI in cybersecurity.* https://www.infosecurity-magazine.com/opinions/2025-reckoning-ai-cybersecurity/

Microsoft. (2025). *Microsoft Security Copilot: Revolutionizing security operations with AI.* Microsoft Press.

Radiant Security. (2025, June 4). *What is AI-driven threat detection and response?* https://radiantsecurity.ai/learn/ai-driven-threat-detection-and-response/

Springer. (2024). *AI-driven cybersecurity and threat intelligence.* https://link.springer.com/book/10.1007/978-3-031-54497-2

Syracuse University. (2025, July 20). *AI in cybersecurity: How AI is changing threat defense.* https://ischool.syracuse.edu/ai-in-cybersecurity/

Terralogic. (2025, April 14). *AI in cybersecurity: Redefining threat defense 2024.* https://terralogic.com/ai-in-cybersecurity/

Web Asha Technologies. (2025, February 25). *Top AI cybersecurity tools in 2025.* https://www.webasha.com/blog/top-ai-cybersecurity-tools-in-2025

Chapter 5: AI for Threat Detection

Introduction: When Every Second Counts

On a Tuesday morning, the cybersecurity team at a major financial institution in New York received an alert that would have been invisible to traditional security systems just months earlier. An AI-powered threat detection platform had identified an anomalous pattern in network traffic, a subtle deviation in data flow that human analysts would have taken days to notice, if they spotted it at all. Within two seconds, the AI system had isolated the compromised endpoint, blocked lateral movement across the network, and prevented what would have been a devastating ransomware attack affecting millions of customer accounts (CyberPro Magazine, 2025).

This incident represents the new reality of cybersecurity in 2025, where artificial intelligence has transformed threat detection from a reactive, human-limited process into a proactive, machine-speed defense system operating 24/7 at scales impossible for traditional approaches. The transformation could not come at a more critical time. Cybersecurity systems now detect approximately 560,000 new malware threats daily, roughly 6.2 billion infections annually, with AI-generated malware and sophisticated phishing campaigns driving an unprecedented surge in attack volume and complexity (DeepStrike, 2025).

The financial stakes are staggering. Global cybercrime costs are projected to exceed $10.5 trillion annually by the end of 2025, with every day bringing approximately 190,000 malware attacks per second (DeepStrike,

2025; AVG Signal). In this hostile environment, the average time to identify and contain a data breach reached 292 days for organizations using traditional methods, while those deploying AI-driven detection systems reduced this timeline to just 10 minutes, a 99% improvement that can mean the difference between a minor incident and a catastrophic compromise (Vectra AI, 2025).

This chapter examines how artificial intelligence has revolutionized threat detection across multiple dimensions of cybersecurity. We explore the technologies enabling AI systems to identify malware with unprecedented accuracy, detect sophisticated phishing campaigns that bypass human scrutiny, monitor network traffic for subtle anomalies, analyze user behavior for insider threats, and predict zero-day exploits before they materialize into attacks. Understanding these AI-powered detection capabilities is essential for comprehending both the current state of cybersecurity defense and the evolving challenges organizations face as attackers increasingly weaponize AI for offensive purposes.

The Evolution of Threat Detection: From Signatures to Intelligence

Traditional threat detection systems operated on a fundamentally reactive model, relying on signature-based identification to recognize known threats. These systems maintained databases of attack signatures, unique patterns or "fingerprints" associated with specific malware variants, viruses, or attack techniques, and compared incoming data against these known patterns. When a match was found, the system would flag the threat and take predetermined action. This approach worked reasonably well in an earlier era when new threats emerged relatively slowly, and malware development required significant technical expertise and resources (Wiley Online Library).

However, the explosion of AI-enabled cybercrime has rendered signature-based detection increasingly obsolete. Modern malware employs polymorphic techniques that continuously modify code to evade signature detection, with estimates suggesting that by Q4, 86% of new malware featured “evasion by design” capabilities specifically engineered to bypass traditional signature-based antivirus systems (Control D, 2025). The sheer volume of new threats has overwhelmed signature-based approaches, with over 40,000 Common Vulnerabilities and Exposures (CVEs) disclosed alone; maintaining current signature databases has become a losing battle (DeepStrike, 2025).

The limitations of traditional detection methods became painfully apparent as adversaries developed more sophisticated attack techniques. Advanced persistent threats (APTs) could operate within compromised networks for months before detection, with the average dwell time, the period from initial infection to discovery, reaching 16 days even as organizations invested heavily in conventional security measures (Control D, 2025). Zero-day exploits, targeting previously unknown vulnerabilities, bypassed signature-based detection entirely since no signatures existed for threats that had never been documented.

Artificial intelligence fundamentally transforms this paradigm by shifting from signature-based pattern matching to behavioral analysis and anomaly detection. Rather than asking "Does this match a known threat signature?" AI systems ask, "Does this behavior deviate from normal patterns in ways that suggest malicious intent?" This distinction proves crucial because AI can detect novel attacks, polymorphic malware, and zero-day exploits that have never been seen before, identifying threats based on their actions rather than their appearance (Fortinet, 2025).

The technical foundation of AI-driven threat detection rests on several key machine learning approaches. Supervised learning models are trained on labeled datasets containing examples of both malicious and benign activities, enabling them to classify new, unseen activities based on learned patterns. Unsupervised learning algorithms identify inherent patterns and structures within data, flagging anomalies that do not fit established norms, a capability particularly valuable for detecting zero-day attacks where no prior examples exist. Deep learning employs neural networks with multiple layers to process complex, high-dimensional data, recognizing subtle patterns that might elude traditional machine learning models (Cybersecurity Threat AI Magazine, 2025).

According to recent industry research, AI-powered threat detection has achieved remarkable performance metrics across multiple threat categories. Machine learning models can analyze vast datasets and achieve detection rates exceeding 95% even for real-time analysis, while AI excels in identifying malicious scripts, particularly obfuscated ones, achieving up to 70% better detection rates compared to traditional methods alone (MDPI; VirusTotal, 2023).

Organizations implementing AI-driven security platforms report detecting threats up to 60% faster than those using traditional methods, with some systems identifying and responding to threats in under 2 seconds compared to 5 seconds for traditional approaches (Tech Advisors, 2025; IJFMR, 2024).

AI-Powered Malware Detection: Seeing Beyond Signatures

The transformation of malware detection through artificial intelligence represents one of the most significant advances in cybersecurity's ongoing arms race.

Traditional antivirus solutions, which dominated the security landscape for decades, relied almost exclusively on signature-based detection, maintaining databases of known malware patterns and comparing files against these signatures to identify threats. This approach, while effective against known malware, proved increasingly inadequate as cybercriminals developed sophisticated evasion techniques.

Modern malware employs multiple strategies to evade signature-based detection. Polymorphic malware continuously modifies its code with each infection, creating functionally identical variants that appear different to signature-based scanners. Metamorphic malware goes further, rewriting its entire code base while maintaining malicious functionality. Encrypted malware conceals its payload within legitimate-looking files, decrypting only at execution. These techniques have proliferated rapidly, with fileless malware, which operates entirely in memory without writing to disk, projected to represent 70% of all serious malware incidents by late (Control D, 2025).

The numbers paint a stark picture of the challenge. Approximately 6.2 billion malware infections were detected globally, fueled by the proliferation of AI-generated malware and sophisticated distribution campaigns (DeepStrike, 2025). Organizations faced an average of 1,920 cyberattacks per week in Q3 2023, a 72% increase from Q3 2022, with malware implicated in the majority of these incidents (Control D, 2025).

The average monthly number of zero-day exploits used in malware campaigns reached 5.5 in 2023, nearly double the 2.8 recorded in early 2022, demonstrating how rapidly threat actors are discovering and weaponizing new vulnerabilities (Control D, 2025).

Artificial intelligence transforms malware detection by analyzing behavior rather than appearance. Machine learning models are trained on massive datasets containing examples of malware and benign software, learning to recognize the characteristics that distinguish malicious code from legitimate applications. These models examine multiple dimensions simultaneously: file properties and metadata, system calls and API usage, network communication patterns, resource consumption behaviors, and process interactions with operating system components (Web Asha Technologies, 2025).

Behavioral analysis enables AI systems to detect malware based on what it does rather than what it looks like. A machine learning model can recognize patterns such as unusual system calls made by a process, attempts to access sensitive registry keys or system files, unexpected network connections to suspicious domains, rapid encryption of multiple files (indicative of ransomware), or attempts to disable security software or logging mechanisms (Web Asha Technologies, 2025). These behavioral indicators remain consistent even when malware code changes, allowing AI to identify polymorphic and metamorphic threats that would evade signature-based detection.

The effectiveness of AI-powered malware detection is demonstrated by real-world deployment results. Companies like Cylance have achieved detection rates exceeding 99% for previously unknown malware using AI-driven approaches, while research indicates that AI-enhanced systems demonstrate up to 300% improvement in exploit identification compared to traditional tools working alone (VirusTotal, 2023). In practical applications, AI-driven endpoint detection and response (EDR) systems stopped novel fileless attacks that would have evaded all signature-based antivirus solutions by recognizing the sequence of actions, such as PowerShell spawned by a Word document, then dumping credentials, as malicious, even though the exact malware variant was completely new (Northern Technologies Group, 2025).

Deep learning architectures have proven particularly powerful for malware analysis. Convolutional neural networks (CNNs) can analyze file structures or memory dumps to detect embedded malicious code or indicators of compromise.

Recurrent neural networks (RNNs) excel at analyzing sequential data like network logs, identifying time-based attack patterns that reveal the progression of an exploit. These neural network approaches can process complex, high-dimensional data to recognize subtle patterns that traditional machine learning models might miss (Cybersecurity Threat AI Magazine, 2025).

Modern AI malware detection systems also incorporate automated sandboxing, executing suspicious files in isolated virtual environments while AI monitors their behavior. If the file exhibits malicious behaviors such as attempting to encrypt files, establishing persistence mechanisms, or communicating with command-and-control servers, it is flagged and blocked before it can infect production systems. AI enhances traditional sandboxing by analyzing behavioral patterns more effectively, identifying sophisticated malware that attempts to detect sandbox environments and modify its behavior to appear benign during analysis (Web Asha Technologies, 2025).

The emergence of AI-generated malware has created a new category of threats that traditional defenses struggle to address. In 2025, AI-crafted malware variants demonstrated an 18% higher success rate in bypassing endpoint detection systems compared to traditional malware. More concerning, malware using reinforcement learning adapted to sandbox environments in just 11 seconds, down from 22 seconds the previous year, demonstrating how rapidly AI-powered threats evolve to evade detection (SQ Magazine, 2025). Autonomous ransomware capable of lateral movement without human oversight was present in 19% of breaches in 2025, while ransomware-as-a-service providers offering AI-driven encryption tools grew by 34% in underground markets (SQ Magazine, 2025).

Despite these impressive capabilities, AI-powered malware detection faces important challenges. False positive rates remain a concern. AI models may misclassify benign applications as malware, disrupting business operations and eroding user trust in the system.

The adversarial nature of cybersecurity means attackers actively work to evade AI detection systems, developing techniques to manipulate the features AI models rely upon. Data quality and quantity requirements are substantial; effective AI models require large, high-quality training datasets that can be expensive and time-consuming to create and maintain (Web Asha Technologies, 2025).

Nevertheless, the trend is clear: AI has become indispensable for malware detection in modern cybersecurity environments. The ability to detect novel, polymorphic, and zero-day malware based on behavioral analysis rather than signatures provides organizations with capabilities that were impossible with traditional approaches. As malware continues to evolve in sophistication and volume, AI-powered detection represents not just an enhancement to existing defenses but a fundamental requirement for maintaining effective security postures.

Phishing and Social Engineering Detection: AI as the New Human Firewall

If malware represents the direct technical assault on cybersecurity defenses, phishing and social engineering represent the psychological manipulation that bypasses technical controls entirely by targeting the human element. These attacks have evolved from crude, easily spotted scams into sophisticated psychological operations powered by artificial intelligence that can fool even security-aware professionals. The numbers are sobering: phishing-based malware distribution spiked by 32% in Q2 2023, while credential phishing attacks increased by an astounding 703% in the second half (Control D, 2025; Tech Advisors, 2025).

The integration of artificial intelligence into phishing operations has created what security researchers describe as the top enterprise threat of 2025 (StrongestLayer, 2025). AI-generated phishing emails now account for 82.6% of all phishing attempts, achieving dramatically higher success rates than traditional manually-crafted attacks, 78% of recipients open AI-generated phishing emails, and 21% click on malicious content within them (Tech Advisors, 2025).

The productivity gains for attackers are equally alarming: generative AI tools enable threat actors to compose phishing emails up to 40% faster than traditional methods while simultaneously enabling mass personalization and localization that makes detection far more difficult (Tech Advisors, 2025).

The sophistication of AI-generated phishing was dramatically illustrated when criminals used deepfake video technology to impersonate a company CFO, duping a finance officer into authorizing a $25 million funds transfer. In another incident, a LastPass employee was targeted by an AI voice-cloning scam that impersonated the company's CEO with such fidelity that only the employee's security awareness prevented a successful compromise (Tech Advisors, 2025). These cases demonstrate how AI has elevated social engineering attacks from mass-distributed spam to highly targeted, individualized campaigns that exploit a deep understanding of organizational structures, communication patterns, and psychological triggers.

The challenge of AI-generated phishing extends beyond individual emails to encompass entire attack campaigns. In an experiment conducted by IBM security researchers, AI was pitted against human experts to create phishing campaigns. The AI system needed only five prompts and 5 minutes to build an attack as effective as one that took human experts 16 hours to develop (StrongestLayer, 2025). This explosive productivity enables attackers to send polymorphic campaigns, slightly varied messages at a massive scale, making detection nearly impossible for traditional rule-based email filters.

Traditional email security relied on several detection methods that AI-powered phishing increasingly defeats. Signature-based filters matched emails against known phishing patterns, but AI-generated content creates unique messages that don't match existing signatures. Reputation systems blocked emails from known malicious domains, but attackers now leverage legitimate file-hosting services like SharePoint, OneDrive, and Dropbox to host malicious content, exploiting the inherent trust users place in these platforms (ConnectWise, 2025). Simple heuristics like checking for spelling errors or unusual grammar, once reliable indicators of phishing, became obsolete as large language models generate perfectly crafted messages in any language with native-level fluency.

Artificial intelligence counters AI-powered phishing through multiple complementary approaches. Natural language processing (NLP) analyzes email content, examining not just technical headers and metadata but the actual text, tone, and intent of messages. Machine learning models trained on millions of legitimate and malicious emails can identify subtle linguistic patterns, urgency cues, and psychological manipulation tactics that indicate phishing attempts. These models recognize that phishing emails often create artificial urgency ("your account will be suspended unless you act immediately"), invoke authority ("this request comes from the CEO"), or exploit fear, greed, or curiosity to motivate hasty action (Syracuse University, 2025).

Behavioral analysis extends AI's phishing detection capabilities beyond individual messages to examine broader patterns. AI systems analyze sender reputation by examining historical communication patterns, domain age, and email authentication records.

They evaluate whether an email matches typical communication patterns for the purported sender. If the CEO normally sends brief, informal emails but a message arrives with lengthy, formal language and unusual attachments, AI flags the anomaly. Link and attachment analysis examines URLs for typosquatting, suspicious redirects, or recently registered domains that might indicate phishing infrastructure (Fortinet, 2025).

Context-aware detection represents an advanced AI capability that evaluates emails within broader organizational and temporal contexts. If multiple employees suddenly receive similar emails requesting password resets or financial transactions, AI systems recognize this as a coordinated campaign rather than isolated incidents. Temporal analysis identifies suspicious timing, such as urgent requests arriving outside normal business hours when verification is difficult.

Organizational structure awareness enables AI to detect when emails claim authority relationships that don't exist in the actual organizational hierarchy (Syracuse University, 2025).

Real-time adaptation gives AI-powered phishing detection a crucial advantage over static rule-based systems. As new phishing techniques emerge, machine learning models automatically update their detection algorithms based on observed attacks and analyst feedback.

This continuous learning ensures that defenses evolve at machine speed to match the rapid innovation cycles of AI-powered phishing campaigns. According to recent surveys, 53% of cybersecurity professionals report that AI proves effective in identifying spam and phishing emails, reducing the risk of social engineering attacks that bypass technical controls (SQ Magazine, 2025).

The battle against phishing has also extended into voice and messaging channels. Voice phishing (vishing) attacks increased by 442% between the first and second halves, driven by AI-generated phishing and impersonation tactics (Hacker News, 2025). AI voice cloning technology now requires just 20 to 30 seconds of target audio to create convincing vocal replicas, enabling attackers to impersonate executives, IT support staff, or trusted contacts over phone calls. AI detection systems counter these threats by analyzing voice characteristics, including speech patterns, emotional affect, and linguistic markers that might indicate synthetic generation.

Deepfake detection has emerged as a critical frontier in phishing defense. According to industry research, 63% of cybersecurity leaders express concern about AI and the potential creation of deepfakes, yet deepfake awareness remains alarmingly low; 71% of people globally don't know what a deepfake is, and only 0.1% can consistently identify them (Tech Advisors, 2025).

The financial industry has become a primary target, with 53% of financial professionals experiencing attempted deepfake scams. More concerning, the first quarter of 2025 saw 19% more deepfake incidents than occurred, indicating exponential growth in this attack vector (Tech Advisors, 2025).

AI-powered deepfake detection analyzes multiple dimensions of video and audio content to identify synthetic media. Computer vision algorithms examine video for inconsistencies in facial movements, lighting, shadows, and reflections that betray digital manipulation. Audio analysis detects artifacts in voice synthesis, unnatural breathing patterns, or subtle glitches in speech generation. Metadata analysis examines file properties and creation timestamps for indicators of manipulation. Behavioral analysis flags unusual communication patterns, such as video calls where the camera conveniently malfunctions or unusual requests for financial transactions via video rather than established channels (Virtual Guardian, 2025).

The effectiveness of AI in combating phishing is demonstrated by deployment results from leading organizations. According to research from Egress (a KnowBe4 company), 74.8% of phishing toolkits examined by threat intelligence analysts referenced AI capabilities, while 82.0% mentioned deepfakes being used in attacks (Virtual Guardian, 2025). Organizations implementing AI-powered email security report significant reductions in successful phishing attacks, with some platforms achieving detection rates exceeding 90% for sophisticated AI-generated phishing campaigns while maintaining false positive rates below 1%.

However, challenges remain. The arms race between AI-powered phishing and AI-powered detection continues to escalate, with attackers constantly developing new techniques to evade detection. Privacy concerns arise when AI systems analyze email content in detail to detect threats. User training remains essential despite technological advances; even the most sophisticated AI cannot protect against users who are trained to recognize and report suspicious communications. The most effective defense combines AI-powered technical controls with ongoing security awareness training that helps employees recognize social engineering tactics and verify unusual requests through independent channels.

Network Traffic: Analysis and Anomaly Detection: The AI Sentinel

Network traffic analysis represents one of the most data-intensive challenges in cybersecurity. Modern enterprise networks generate enormous volumes of traffic, millions of packets per second flowing between countless endpoints, servers, and cloud services. Traditional network monitoring tools operated on predefined rules and signatures, flagging traffic that matched known attack patterns while struggling to identify novel threats hidden within the massive data flows. Artificial intelligence has revolutionized this domain by enabling systems to process and analyze network traffic at scale, identifying subtle anomalies that might indicate compromise.

The challenge of network security in 2025 is magnified by the expanding attack surface. Organizations must protect increasingly complex hybrid environments spanning on-premises infrastructure, multiple cloud platforms, remote endpoints, and Internet of Things (IoT) devices.

According to recent estimates, more than 5.52 billion people have internet access globally, with an estimated 18.8 billion connected devices creating unprecedented opportunities for attack (Darktrace). Encrypted threats, malware hidden in SSL/TLS traffic, increased by 45% in the first half of 2023, exploiting the fact that many traditional security tools cannot inspect encrypted communications (Control D, 2025).

Intrusion Detection Systems (IDS) and Intrusion Prevention Systems (IPS) form the foundational technologies for network security monitoring. Network-based Intrusion Detection Systems (NIDS) monitor network traffic at strategic points, analyzing protocol packets and comparing them against predefined rules or learned behavioral models. Host-based Intrusion Detection Systems (HIDS) operate on individual devices, analyzing logs, application behavior, and system calls for malicious activities. Together, NIDS and HIDS provide complementary defense strategies addressing threats at both network and endpoint levels (Frontiers, 2025).

The integration of artificial intelligence transforms these traditional IDS/IPS systems from reactive signature-matching tools into proactive threat detection platforms. AI-driven network security operates on several key principles. Baseline establishment involves machine learning algorithms that analyze normal network traffic patterns over time, building comprehensive profiles of typical behavior for different times of day, user groups, applications, and network segments.

Anomaly detection compares real-time traffic against these baselines, flagging deviations that might indicate malicious activity. Pattern recognition identifies complex attack patterns across multiple network segments and time periods that would be invisible to human analysts reviewing individual events (Vectra AI, 2025).

Modern AI-powered network detection systems employ sophisticated architectures to handle the volume and complexity of network data. According to research on AI-driven intrusion detection systems for Industry 4.0 environments, properly designed systems can manage more than 500,000 inputs in approximately 10 seconds while achieving accuracy scores of up to 90% (MDPI, 2024).

This performance is made possible through several technical innovations: federated learning methodologies that enable distributed processing, advanced preprocessing techniques using adaptive algorithms, and optimized neural network architectures designed specifically for real-time network analysis.

Machine learning approaches for network intrusion detection encompass multiple techniques, each with particular strengths. Supervised learning models are trained on labeled network traffic data containing examples of both normal and attack traffic, enabling them to classify new connections as benign or malicious. Unsupervised learning algorithms identify unusual patterns in unlabeled data, detecting previously unknown attack types that supervised models might miss. Deep learning models, particularly recurrent neural networks (RNNs) and long short-term memory (LSTM) networks, excel at analyzing sequential network data to recognize temporal attack patterns that unfold over time (Wiley Online Library, 2024).

The practical deployment of AI-powered network detection has produced impressive results. Vectra AI, named a leader in the 2025 Gartner Magic Quadrant for Network Detection and Response (NDR), reports that its platform catches threats up to 99% faster than traditional methods by following attackers across network, identity, and cloud environments.

Where traditional approaches took an average of 292 days to identify and contain breaches involving stolen credentials, Vectra AI's systems accomplish this in approximately 10 minutes, stopping identity attacks within 24 hours, which represents a 99% reduction in response time (Vectra AI, 2025).

Behavioral analytics forms a crucial component of AI network security. User and Entity Behavior Analytics (UEBA) systems build profiles of normal behavior for each user, device, and application on the network. These profiles consider factors such as typical access times, data volumes transferred, applications used, geographic locations accessed from, and communication patterns with other network entities. When behavior deviates significantly from established norms, such as a user account accessing sensitive files at 3 AM, downloading far more data than usual, or logging in from an unusual geographic location, AI systems generate alerts for investigation (Northern Technologies Group, 2025).

Real-time threat detection capabilities distinguish AI-powered network security from batch-processing approaches. Rather than analyzing network logs periodically, AI systems monitor traffic continuously, identifying and responding to threats as they occur. This real-time capability proves essential for stopping fast-moving attacks like ransomware, which can encrypt nearly 100,000 files totaling 53.93 gigabytes in just 42 minutes and 52 seconds, according to research (Splunk, n.d.). Immediate detection and automated response can contain such attacks before they spread throughout the network.

Extended Detection and Response (XDR) platforms represent the evolution of network security beyond traditional boundaries. XDR solutions unify endpoint, network, cloud, and email security data into integrated platforms, using AI to correlate signals across multiple domains.

This holistic approach enables AI to piece together attack narratives that would appear benign if examined in isolation. For example, a single login failure on an endpoint might not raise concerns, but AI can correlate it with a pattern of network scans and privilege escalation attempts on a server, concluding it represents an active attack (Northern Technologies Group, 2025).

The challenges facing AI-powered network detection mirror those in other domains. False positive rates remain a concern; overly sensitive systems generate excessive alerts that overwhelm security teams and lead to alert fatigue.

Encrypted traffic presents ongoing challenges since many AI analysis techniques require inspecting packet contents. Adversarial attacks specifically target AI detection systems, with attackers developing techniques to evade machine learning models. Scalability requirements are substantial; processing and analyzing network traffic for large organizations requires significant computational resources and sophisticated distributed architectures (Fortinet, 2025).

Nevertheless, the trend toward AI-powered network detection is unmistakable. Leading vendors, including Darktrace, Vectra AI, and Cisco, have developed sophisticated platforms that demonstrate superior accuracy in identifying hidden attackers through behavioral analysis (Cybersecurity News, 2025). Organizations implementing these systems report substantial improvements in threat detection speed and accuracy while reducing the burden on security teams, who can focus on investigating genuine threats rather than sifting through false positives.

The future of AI network security points toward even greater automation and intelligence. Detection-as-Code (DaC) initiatives are enabling Security Operations Centers (SOCs) to rapidly respond to evolving threats through automated and continuous updates to detection rules aligned with the latest threat intelligence. Integration of continuous integration/continuous deployment (CI/CD) principles allows for continuous testing of detection logic, reducing false positives and enhancing detection accuracy while fostering collaboration between security engineers and developers (Digitalisation World, 2025).

Behavioral Analytics and Insider Threat Detection: When Trust Becomes Risk

While external threats dominate cybersecurity headlines, insider threats, risks posed by individuals with legitimate access to organizational resources, represent a uniquely challenging security problem.

According to comprehensive research, 83% of organizations reported at least one insider attack in the past year, with approximately 51% experiencing six or more attacks. The average cost of insider incidents reached $17.4 million in 2025, with organizations dedicating 16.5% of their annual IT security budgets to insider risk management, more than double the 8.2% allocated in 2023 (DTEX Systems, 2025).

Insider threats manifest in three primary categories that require different detection approaches. Malicious insiders deliberately abuse their access privileges for personal gain, revenge, or ideological motivations, potentially stealing sensitive data, sabotaging systems, or facilitating external attacks.

Negligent insiders inadvertently compromise security through careless behavior, poor security hygiene, or failure to follow established procedures, such as falling victim to phishing attacks or mishandling sensitive information. Compromised insiders have had their legitimate credentials stolen by external attackers who then operate under the guise of authorized users, making their malicious activities difficult to distinguish from normal operations (ConnectWise, 2025).

The challenge of detecting insider threats stems from fundamental asymmetries between insider and external attacks. Insiders possess legitimate access credentials, making their activities appear authorized in access logs and authentication systems. They understand organizational systems, security controls, and valuable data locations, enabling more targeted and effective attacks. Traditional perimeter security measures designed to keep external attackers out provide no defense against insiders who already have access. Detection often requires sophisticated behavioral analytics capable of identifying subtle deviations from normal patterns rather than obvious policy violations.

Artificial intelligence transforms insider threat detection by enabling continuous behavioral monitoring and anomaly detection at scales impossible for manual approaches. Machine learning models establish baseline behavioral profiles for each user and entity within the organization, analyzing factors including data access patterns (which files and systems are typically accessed), work hours and schedules (when access normally occurs), geographic locations (where access requests originate), data transfer volumes (how much data is typically moved), and application usage (which tools and services are used for specific tasks) (Syracuse University, 2025).

User and Entity Behavior Analytics (UEBA) represents the cornerstone of AI-powered insider threat detection. UEBA systems build comprehensive profiles of normal behavior for users, devices, servers, and applications through continuous analysis of multiple data sources: authentication logs tracking login times and locations, file access records documenting which resources are accessed, network traffic showing communication patterns, application usage indicating which tools are employed, and privilege escalations noting changes in access levels. By synthesizing information from these diverse sources, UEBA creates holistic behavioral signatures that capture the full context of user activities (Fortinet, 2025).

The detection of insider threats relies on identifying anomalies that deviate from established behavioral baselines. AI systems flag various suspicious patterns including unusual access times (accessing sensitive systems at 3 AM when normal work hours are 9-5), geographic anomalies (login attempts from foreign countries when the user is known to be local), privilege escalation (sudden increases in access permissions or attempts to access resources beyond normal job requirements), data exfiltration indicators (large data downloads or transfers to external storage), and lateral movement (accessing systems or data outside normal job responsibilities) (Davis Powers, 2025).

Real-world applications demonstrate the effectiveness of AI in detecting insider threats that traditional security controls miss. Consider a scenario where an employee planning to leave for a competitor begins systematically accessing and downloading sensitive proprietary information. The employee's access is legitimate, their credentials are valid, and they have authorized access to the files. However, the pattern is anomalous: they're accessing far more documents than usual, focusing on strategic information outside their normal job responsibilities, and transferring data during off-hours when fewer colleagues are online. AI behavioral analytics detect these subtle deviations from the employee's historical patterns, generating alerts that enable intervention before data theft is completed (Zscaler, 2025).

The challenge of shadow AI, employees using unauthorized AI tools and services, has created new insider threat vectors that require AI detection. IBM research found that 63% of organizations lack AI governance policies to manage AI systems or prevent the proliferation of unauthorized AI tools, while organizations with high levels of shadow AI usage experienced an average of $670,000 in additional breach costs (IBM, 2025). AI behavioral analytics can detect shadow AI usage by monitoring for unusual data transfers to external AI services, unexpected API calls to large language model endpoints, or anomalous patterns in how users interact with cloud-based applications.

Advanced AI systems employ multiple analytical techniques for insider threat detection. Peer group analysis compares an individual's behavior against colleagues in similar roles, identifying outliers whose activities differ from departmental norms. Time-series analysis examines behavioral changes over time, detecting gradual shifts that might indicate slowly developing threats. Risk scoring assigns numerical risk values to users based on multiple factors, enabling security teams to prioritize investigations of the highest-risk individuals.

Contextual analysis considers business context, such as project deadlines, organizational changes, or personal circumstances, to distinguish benign anomalies from genuine threats (Radiant Security, 2025).

Importantly, AI-powered insider threat detection must balance security with privacy and employee trust. Organizations must implement these systems transparently, with clear policies about what is monitored and how data is used. Effective programs focus on detecting genuine risks rather than invasive monitoring of all employee activities. Privacy-preserving techniques such as aggregated behavioral analytics and automated anonymization can provide security benefits while respecting employee privacy.

The integration of AI with zero-trust security architectures enhances insider threat detection capabilities. Zero trust operates on the principle of "never trust, always verify," requiring continuous authentication and authorization for all access requests regardless of source.

AI enhances zero trust by providing real-time risk assessment based on behavioral analytics, enabling dynamic adjustment of access controls based on current risk levels. As Darktrace researchers note, zero trust approaches must evolve to "never trust, always verify, and continuously monitor" with AI providing the continuous monitoring and behavioral understanding necessary to identify insider threats in real-time (Darktrace, 2024).

Zero-Day Vulnerability Detection: Predicting the Unpredictable

Zero-day vulnerabilities, security flaws unknown to software vendors and for which no patches exist, represent one of cybersecurity's most challenging problems. By definition, these vulnerabilities cannot be detected using signature-based methods since no signatures exist for threats that have never been documented.

The threat landscape in 2025 demonstrates the critical nature of this challenge: the average monthly number of zero-day exploits used in malware campaigns reached 5.5 in 2023, nearly double the 2.8 recorded in early 2022 (Control D, 2025). More concerning, threat actors exploited over 25% of vulnerabilities within 24 hours of disclosure in Q1 2025, leaving organizations with minimal time to respond (Secureframe, 2025).

The economic impact of zero-day vulnerabilities is substantial. Global cybercrime costs projected to reach $10.5 trillion annually by 2025 are significantly driven by zero-day exploits, with these vulnerabilities fetching high prices on underground markets and incentivizing cybercriminals to invest heavily in their discovery and weaponization (IJFMR, 2024). Traditional cybersecurity approaches struggle with zero-day threats because they rely on prior knowledge, signatures of known attacks, documented vulnerabilities, or established attack patterns, none of which exist for zero-day exploits until after they've been discovered and analyzed.

Artificial intelligence fundamentally changes the equation by enabling behavioral analysis and predictive threat detection that can identify zero-day exploits based on how they behave rather than what they look like. AI systems monitor applications and networks for behavioral patterns that deviate from normal activity, flagging security risks even when the specific exploit is brand new and has never been seen before. This capability proves particularly crucial given that AI-enhanced honeypots achieved detection rates of 92% for zero-day exploits, significantly outperforming traditional systems, which managed only 75% detection rates (IJFMR, 2024).

Machine learning approaches to zero-day detection employ multiple complementary techniques. Unsupervised learning algorithms identify inherent patterns and structures within data without requiring labeled examples of zero-day attacks. When presented with anomalous data that doesn't fit any established pattern, these algorithms flag it as potentially malicious, a capability that proves essential since, by definition, zero-day attacks lack prior examples for supervised training (Cybersecurity Threat AI Magazine, 2025). Supervised learning models, while unable to directly identify novel zero-days, contribute by accurately categorizing known attack vectors and freeing resources for the detection of truly unknown threats.

Deep learning architectures provide sophisticated capabilities for recognizing the subtle, complex patterns that characterize zero-day exploits. Recurrent neural networks (RNNs) excel at analyzing sequential data like network logs and system calls, identifying time-based attack patterns that reveal the progression of an exploit.

Convolutional neural networks (CNNs) analyze file structures, memory dumps, and binary code to detect embedded malicious code or indicators of compromise that might indicate zero-day malware. These deep learning approaches can process complex, high-dimensional data to recognize patterns that elude traditional machine learning models (Cybersecurity Threat AI Magazine, 2025).

Reinforcement learning enables security systems to learn and adapt in dynamic environments, continuously refining their understanding of threats based on new attack patterns they encounter. This adaptive capability proves particularly valuable for zero-day detection since threat actors constantly evolve their techniques to evade detection.

Reinforcement learning models adjust their detection strategies in real-time based on the effectiveness of different approaches, creating security systems that become more effective over time without requiring manual updates (Cybersecurity Threat AI Magazine, 2025).

Behavioral analytics forms the foundation of AI-powered zero-day detection. Rather than looking for known exploit signatures, AI systems establish baselines of normal system behavior and flag deviations that might indicate exploitation attempts.

These systems analyze multiple behavioral dimensions simultaneously: unusual system calls made by processes that typically don't require such privileges, attempts to access sensitive registry keys or system files outside normal application behavior, unexpected network connections to suspicious or newly-registered domains, rapid file encryption patterns characteristic of ransomware, memory manipulation techniques used by exploit kits, and privilege escalation attempts that suggest attackers trying to gain elevated system access (Zscaler, 2025).

Anomaly detection represents a core AI capability for identifying zero-day exploits. Machine learning models trained on large datasets of normal network traffic, system logs, and application behaviors can identify patterns that deviate significantly from established norms. For example, if a web application server suddenly begins sending outbound packets that don't match its usual behavior patterns, this anomaly could indicate a zero-day attack exploiting a previously unknown vulnerability.

AI algorithms learn from historical data to establish baseline behaviors and flag anomalies in real-time, enabling detection of zero-day threats based on behavioral deviations rather than signature matches (Securify AI, 2025).

User behavior analytics extends zero-day detection beyond technical systems to human activity patterns. AI systems monitor and analyze user behavior to identify deviations that might indicate account compromise through zero-day exploits.

If a user account suddenly exhibits unusual access patterns, such as accessing files they've never touched before, logging in from atypical locations, or performing actions outside their normal job responsibilities, AI flags these anomalies for investigation. This proves particularly valuable for detecting zero-day attacks that compromise user credentials and then leverage legitimate access to exfiltrate data or spread laterally through networks (Securify AI, 2025).

Predictive analysis represents one of AI's most powerful capabilities for zero-day threat mitigation.

By analyzing historical vulnerability data, current threat intelligence from multiple sources, and patterns in how attackers discover and exploit vulnerabilities, AI systems can predict which systems or applications might be targeted next. Machine learning models identify patterns that indicate future cyberattacks, enabling security teams to take preemptive steps to strengthen defenses in high-risk areas before zero-day exploits materialize (Securify AI, 2025).

Threat intelligence platforms (TIPs) enhanced with AI capabilities play crucial roles in zero-day detection and response. These platforms aggregate and analyze threat data from diverse sources, including dark web forums, hacker communications, vulnerability databases, security research publications, and telemetry from deployed security systems across multiple organizations.

AI processes this vast threat intelligence to identify anomalies in traffic patterns, rare file behaviors, or unexpected system calls that could signal exploitation attempts. Advanced analytics correlate multiple data points, such as email phishing attacks, network scanning activities, and dark web chatter, indicating that a zero-day exploit may be in progress (TrustCloud AI, 2025).

The integration of AI with Attack Surface Management (ASM) tools provides additional zero-day detection capabilities. ASM tools use AI to assess networks from a hacker's perspective, identifying potential entry points and vulnerabilities that might be exploited.

By simulating how threat actors might exploit assets to gain access, these tools can help uncover zero-day vulnerabilities before attackers discover them. This proactive approach reduces the attack surface and minimizes opportunities for zero-day exploitation (Zscaler, 2025).

Real-world deployments demonstrate AI's effectiveness in zero-day detection. Advanced systems achieved average response times for identifying and mitigating zero-day threats of just 2 seconds with AI-enhanced platforms, compared to 5 seconds with traditional systems: a 60% improvement in response time that can be critical for containing fast-moving exploits (IJFMR, 2024).

Organizations using AI-driven security solutions report 50% reductions in the time taken to detect and respond to threats, demonstrating AI's potential to transform zero-day defense from reactive to proactive (IJFMR, 2024).

However, zero-day detection faces unique challenges that even sophisticated AI struggles to fully address. The inherent unpredictability of zero-day vulnerabilities means no detection system can guarantee 100% coverage. Determined attackers with sufficient resources may discover and exploit vulnerabilities that evade even advanced AI detection.

Adversarial attacks specifically target AI detection systems, with attackers developing techniques to evade machine learning models through carefully crafted inputs that appear benign. Data quality requirements are substantial; effective AI models require diverse, high-quality training data that represents the full range of normal and anomalous behaviors.

The sophistication of modern zero-day exploits continues to increase. Research from 2025 reveals alarming trends: malware using reinforcement learning adapted to sandbox environments in just 11 seconds, AI-embedded steganography was used to conceal payloads in images and video files in 13% of malware campaigns, and code mutation using AI led to an average of 21 unique variants per malware family detected (SQ Magazine, 2025). These statistics illustrate how attackers leverage AI to create zero-day exploits that adapt in real-time to detection attempts.

Future directions in AI-powered zero-day detection point toward even more sophisticated capabilities. Federated learning will enable multiple organizations to share AI models and threat intelligence without exposing sensitive data, improving collaborative threat detection while maintaining privacy.

Self-healing networks will autonomously detect, isolate, and remediate zero-day vulnerabilities without human intervention. Predictive cybersecurity will shift from reactive detection to preventive blocking, stopping threats before they materialize based on AI analysis of vulnerability patterns and attacker behaviors (Zscaler, 2025).

The role of continuous learning cannot be overstated in zero-day defense. AI systems must continuously evolve and adapt to remain effective against emerging threats. Reinforcement learning approaches train algorithms to optimize their performance based on environmental feedback, ensuring that AI-powered cybersecurity solutions adapt to new zero-day vulnerabilities as they emerge. This continuous learning capability distinguishes AI from static security measures and provides the adaptability necessary to combat the ever-changing zero-day threat landscape (Securify AI, 2025).

Real-Time Threat Intelligence and Pattern Recognition: The Collective Defense

Individual organizations, regardless of their size or security sophistication, cannot effectively defend against the global threat landscape in isolation. The volume, velocity, and variety of cyber threats require collaborative intelligence sharing and pattern recognition across organizational boundaries. Artificial intelligence has transformed threat intelligence from periodic manual reports into real-time, automated systems that continuously collect, analyze, and distribute actionable security information at machine speed.

Threat intelligence encompasses the systematic collection, analysis, and dissemination of data regarding potential and active threats. In traditional cybersecurity frameworks, threat intelligence involved human analysts reading security reports, monitoring underground forums, analyzing malware samples, and compiling threat assessments; a labor-intensive process that struggled to keep pace with rapidly evolving threats. AI fundamentally transforms this paradigm by automating intelligence gathering from thousands of sources simultaneously, analyzing patterns across billions of data points, correlating seemingly unrelated indicators to identify coordinated campaigns, and distributing actionable intelligence in real-time to defensive systems.

The scale of AI-powered threat intelligence operations is staggering. Leading platforms process threat data from millions of endpoints globally, analyzing petabytes of security telemetry daily to identify emerging attack patterns and techniques. This collective intelligence enables the detection of global attack campaigns that would be invisible to individual organizations examining only their local environment.

When a new threat is identified in one organization, AI systems can immediately share indicators and detection signatures with all participating organizations, enabling preemptive defense before the threat spreads (Radiant Security, 2025).

Natural language processing plays a crucial role in AI-powered threat intelligence by enabling automated analysis of textual information from diverse sources.

NLP algorithms scan threat intelligence reports, security advisories, dark web forums, hacker communications, social media discussions, vulnerability databases, and security research publications to identify trends and emerging vulnerabilities before they are widely exploited. This automated analysis processes volumes of information that would be impossible for human analysts to review manually, extracting structured intelligence from unstructured text sources (Zscaler, 2025).

Machine learning models identify subtle correlations across multiple data sources that reveal coordinated attack campaigns. For example, an increase in reconnaissance scanning targeting specific software versions, combined with dark web discussions about exploiting particular vulnerabilities and a spike in domain registrations using typosquatting techniques, might collectively indicate an imminent attack campaign. AI systems correlate these disparate indicators to provide early warning of coordinated threats, enabling organizations to strengthen defenses before attacks materialize (TrustCloud AI, 2025).

Predictive threat intelligence represents one of AI's most valuable contributions to cybersecurity. By analyzing historical attack data, current threat actor activities, geopolitical events, software vulnerability disclosures, and seasonal patterns in attack frequency, machine learning models can forecast likely attack vectors and timing.

This predictive capability enables proactive defense measures, such as preemptively patching vulnerable systems, increasing monitoring of high-risk assets during periods of elevated threat likelihood, or adjusting security controls based on predicted attack techniques (Digitalisation World, 2025).

The integration of threat intelligence with automated response systems creates powerful defensive capabilities. When AI identifies a new threat through threat intelligence analysis, this information automatically updates detection rules across all defensive systems. Security Information and Event Management (SIEM) platforms incorporate new indicators of compromise into correlation rules. Intrusion prevention systems update blocking rules to prevent known attack techniques. Endpoint detection systems receive updated behavioral signatures for emerging malware families. This automation ensures that defenses evolve at machine speed to match the rapid innovation cycles of threat actors (Northern Technologies Group, 2025).

Adversary profiling enables AI to understand not just individual threats but the tactics, techniques, and procedures (TTPs) of specific threat actor groups. By analyzing attack patterns, tool preferences, infrastructure usage, and targeting selection across multiple incidents, AI systems build comprehensive profiles of adversary behaviors.

This profiling enables more accurate attribution of attacks to specific groups and more effective prediction of future activities based on known TTPs. Organizations can tailor their defenses based on which adversary groups are most likely to target their industry or region (Radiant Security, 2025).

The democratization of advanced threat intelligence through AI benefits organizations of all sizes. Previously, only large enterprises with dedicated threat intelligence teams could effectively leverage strategic threat information. AI-powered platforms now provide small and medium organizations with access to enterprise-grade threat intelligence through automated collection, analysis, and integration with existing security tools. This democratization helps level the playing field, enabling smaller organizations to benefit from collective intelligence about global threat campaigns (Northern Technologies Group, 2025).

However, challenges persist in AI-powered threat intelligence. Information overload remains a concern, even with AI filtering; the volume of threat intelligence can overwhelm security teams if not properly prioritized and contextualized.

False positives in threat intelligence can lead to unnecessary defensive actions that disrupt business operations. Data quality and source reliability require careful vetting; not all threat intelligence sources provide accurate or timely information. Privacy and sharing restrictions limit the types of information organizations can contribute to collective intelligence platforms, potentially creating blind spots in threat coverage.

The future of AI-powered threat intelligence points toward even greater integration and automation. Gartner predicts that 70% of organizations will have integrated AI-driven threat intelligence systems by 2025, enhancing their ability to identify and mitigate threats before they manifest into major incidents (Digitalisation World, 2025). Advanced platforms will employ multi-agent AI systems where specialized agents focus on different threat categories: malware, phishing, network intrusions, and insider threats, and coordinate their findings to provide comprehensive threat awareness.

Synthetic data will play an increasing role in training AI threat intelligence systems. With concerns about data privacy and regulatory constraints, organizations are turning to synthetic data generation for training AI models without exposing sensitive information. This approach enables more robust model training while maintaining compliance with privacy regulations and protecting sensitive organizational data (Darktrace, 2024).

Integration and Orchestration: Building Comprehensive AI-Driven Detection

While individual AI-powered detection capabilities, malware analysis, phishing detection, network monitoring, behavioral analytics, and zero-day prediction each provide valuable security benefits, their true power emerges through integration and orchestration. Modern cybersecurity requires coordinated detection across multiple layers and domains, with AI serving as the connective tissue that enables disparate security systems to function as unified defensive platforms.

Security Information and Event Management (SIEM) systems enhanced with AI capabilities form the central nervous system of integrated threat detection. Modern SIEM platforms use AI and machine learning models to analyze mountains of log data and network traffic in real-time, correlating events across endpoints, networks, applications, and cloud services to identify attack patterns that would be invisible when examining individual systems in isolation.

According to industry research, AI-based analytics can learn the normal behavior of each user and device in organizational environments through User and Entity Behavior Analytics, then raise alarms when activities deviate significantly from established baselines (Northern Technologies

Group, 2025).

Extended Detection and Response (XDR) platforms represent the evolution beyond traditional SIEM by unifying endpoint, network, cloud, and email security data into integrated architectures. XDR solutions heavily enabled by AI correlate signals across multiple domains to piece together attack narratives. A single event might appear benign in isolation: a login failure, a network scan, a file access, but AI correlation reveals these as stages in a coordinated attack campaign.

According to research, organizations implementing XDR solutions accelerated detection and containment of data breach incidents by approximately one month compared to those without XDR, reducing average containment time from 304 days to 275 days (Barracuda Networks, 2024).

Security Orchestration, Automation, and Response (SOAR) platforms integrate AI to automate complex threat detection, analysis, and response processes with unprecedented efficiency. By utilizing AI for dynamic and adaptive defense strategies, SOAR achieves faster mean time to detect (MTTD) and mean time to respond (MTTR), streamlining incident response processes and bolstering overall threat management. With AI-driven reasoning, organizations can coordinate responses across multiple security tools and systems without requiring constant human intervention for routine decisions (Digitalisation World, 2025).

The integration of AI across security layers creates force multiplication effects. When AI-powered email security identifies a phishing campaign, this intelligence automatically feeds to network monitoring systems that watch for command-and-control communications. Endpoint detection systems receive updated behavioral signatures for associated malware.

Identity and access management platforms increase authentication requirements for targeted user groups. This coordinated response across all security layers creates defense in depth that adapts in real-time to emerging threats.

Continuous monitoring forms the foundation of integrated AI detection. Unlike periodic security assessments that provide snapshots of security posture, AI-enabled systems maintain constant vigilance across all monitored environments. This 24/7 monitoring ensures that threats are detected regardless of when they occur, including during off-hours when human analysts may be unavailable and attackers often strike. The combination of continuous monitoring with automated response enables security operations that never sleep, maintaining constant protection against persistent adversaries (HC Robotics, 2025).

However, integration presents technical and organizational challenges. Legacy systems may lack the APIs or data formats necessary for seamless integration with modern AI platforms. Vendor fragmentation creates silos where security tools from different vendors cannot easily share data or coordinate responses.

Skill gaps persist; organizations need personnel who understand both AI technologies and cybersecurity operations to effectively deploy and manage integrated platforms. Alert fatigue remains a concern even with

AI filtering when poorly tuned systems generate excessive notifications.

Best practices for integrated AI detection emphasize several key principles. Start with high-quality data; AI systems are only as effective as the data they analyze, requiring clean, normalized, and comprehensive data feeds from all security layers. Maintain human oversight, while AI provides powerful automation, human judgment remains essential for complex decisions, policy setting, and handling edge cases that fall outside AI training parameters. Ensure transparency through explainable AI approaches that provide insight into why systems make specific decisions, building trust and enabling verification. Foster collaboration between AI systems and human analysts, combining machine processing power with human creativity and contextual understanding (Fortinet, 2025).

Challenges, Limitations, and the Path Forward

Despite remarkable advances, AI-powered threat detection faces significant challenges and limitations that organizations must understand and address. The adversarial nature of cybersecurity means that as defensive AI improves, attackers develop countermeasures specifically designed to evade AI detection systems. This creates an endless arms race where both offense and defense continuously evolve, with neither side gaining a permanent advantage.

Adversarial machine learning represents one of the most concerning challenges. Attackers can manipulate inputs to AI systems in ways that cause misclassification or evasion.

For example, malware can be crafted with subtle modifications that cause AI classifiers to incorrectly label it as benign, or network traffic can be carefully shaped to appear within normal behavioral baselines while conducting malicious activities. Research indicates that 26% of security vendors in 2025 acknowledged difficulty keeping pace with AI-driven threat innovation cycles, suggesting that defensive AI development struggles to match the pace of offensive innovation (SQ Magazine, 2025).

Data quality and bias present ongoing challenges for AI detection systems. Machine learning models trained on biased or incomplete datasets may produce skewed results, potentially missing threats in underrepresented categories while generating excessive false positives for over represented patterns.

The need for large, diverse, high-quality training datasets creates barriers for many organizations, particularly smaller entities that may lack the resources to develop comprehensive training corpora. Privacy concerns and regulatory restrictions limit the types of data that can be collected and used for AI training, potentially creating blind spots in detection capabilities.

False positives and false negatives represent fundamental tradeoffs in any detection system. AI systems tuned for high sensitivity detect more threats but generate more false positives that waste analyst time and potentially cause alert fatigue. Systems tuned for high specificity reduce false positives but risk missing genuine threats through false negatives. Finding the optimal balance requires careful tuning based on organizational risk tolerance, available analyst resources, and specific threat profiles.

Explainability remains a significant challenge, particularly for deep learning models that operate as "black boxes" with opaque decision-making processes. When AI systems flag potential threats, security analysts need to understand why the system made that determination to validate the finding and take appropriate action.

The inability to interpret AI decisions creates trust issues and complicates incident investigation. Efforts to develop explainable AI (XAI) approaches specifically for cybersecurity are ongoing but have not yet fully addressed this challenge (Frontiers, 2025).

Resource requirements for AI-powered detection can be substantial. Training sophisticated models requires significant computational power, often necessitating specialized hardware like GPUs. Processing real-time threat data at scale demands high-performance infrastructure. Organizations must invest in data storage, processing capabilities, and specialized expertise to deploy and maintain AI detection systems effectively. These resource requirements can create barriers to adoption, particularly for resource-constrained organizations.

The evolution of AI-powered attacks creates moving targets for defensive AI. As discussed throughout this chapter, attackers increasingly leverage AI to generate malware, craft phishing campaigns, and develop evasion techniques.

The sophistication of AI-generated threats continues to increase, with malware adapting to sandbox environments in seconds, polymorphic code generating unique variants to evade signature detection, and deepfakes becoming increasingly difficult to distinguish from authentic content. Defensive AI must continuously evolve to counter these advancing threats.

Despite these challenges, the path forward for AI threat detection is clear. Organizations cannot afford to rely solely on traditional detection methods given the scale, speed, and sophistication of modern threats.

The statistics presented throughout this chapter demonstrate that AI-powered detection provides substantial benefits: detecting threats 60% faster than traditional methods, reducing breach containment times from months to minutes, achieving detection rates exceeding 90% for sophisticated attacks, and enabling security operations at scales impossible for purely human teams.

Success requires balanced approaches that combine AI capabilities with human expertise. AI excels at processing vast data volumes, identifying subtle patterns, and operating at machine speed: capabilities that complement rather than replace human judgment, creativity, and contextual understanding. The most effective security operations employ AI to handle routine detection and initial triage, freeing human analysts to focus on complex investigations, strategic planning, and handling sophisticated threats that require nuanced judgment.

Continuous improvement through feedback loops ensures AI detection systems evolve alongside threats. When analysts investigate AI-generated alerts, their findings should feed back into model training, improving future detection accuracy. Regular model updates incorporating new threat intelligence, attack patterns, and environmental changes maintain detection effectiveness as the threat landscape shifts. Organizations must treat AI detection as continuous programs requiring ongoing investment rather than one-time implementations.

Conclusion: The New Paradigm of Threat Detection

The transformation of threat detection through artificial intelligence represents not merely an incremental improvement to existing capabilities but a fundamental paradigm shift in how organizations identify and respond to cyber threats. The statistics and real-world examples presented throughout this chapter illustrate the magnitude of this transformation: from 560,000 new malware threats detected daily to AI systems that respond to attacks in 2 seconds rather than hours, from 99% detection rates for zero-day exploits to threat intelligence platforms processing billions of security events in real-time.

The evolution from signature-based detection to behavioral analysis and anomaly detection has created capabilities that were impossible just years ago. AI systems now detect threats based on subtle behavioral patterns rather than known signatures, identify zero-day exploits before patches exist, recognize AI-generated phishing campaigns that fool human recipients, monitor network traffic at scales exceeding human comprehension, and predict future attacks based on threat intelligence and historical patterns. These capabilities have shifted cybersecurity from reactive incident response to proactive threat hunting and predictive defense.

Yet the chapter has also highlighted important limitations and challenges. AI detection is not a silver bullet; it faces adversarial manipulation, requires substantial data and computational resources, struggles with explainability, and operates within an adversarial environment where attackers continuously develop countermeasures. The 26% of security vendors acknowledging difficulty keeping pace with AI-driven threats, the persistent challenges with false positives, and the substantial investment required for effective implementation all underscore that AI enhances rather than replaces comprehensive security programs.

The dual nature of AI, serving as both the most powerful defensive tool and an increasingly sophisticated weapon for attackers, creates an ongoing arms race that will define cybersecurity for years to come. Organizations face attackers who leverage AI to generate malware at unprecedented scales, craft convincing phishing campaigns in minutes, and develop evasion techniques specifically designed to fool AI detection systems. The only viable response is defensive AI that evolves at comparable speeds, learning from each encounter and sharing intelligence across organizational boundaries to create collective defenses greater than the sum of individual efforts.

As we transition to Chapter 6's examination of AI in network security, the foundation established here provides essential context. The threat detection capabilities explored in this chapter, which are malware analysis, phishing detection, behavioral analytics, zero-day prediction, and threat intelligence, all operate within network environments. Understanding how AI detects threats at the individual system and application level enables a deeper appreciation for how these capabilities extend to protecting entire network infrastructures, securing cloud environments, and defending the expanding attack surfaces created by Internet of Things deployments.

The future of threat detection lies in the continued evolution and integration of AI capabilities. Machine learning models will become more sophisticated, requiring less training data and providing better explainability. Federated learning will enable threat intelligence sharing while preserving privacy. Autonomous security operations will handle routine threats without human intervention, allowing analysts to focus on strategic challenges. Yet amid all this technological advancement, the fundamental principle remains constant: effective cybersecurity requires combining AI's processing power and pattern recognition capabilities with human judgment, creativity, and strategic thinking.

Organizations that successfully navigate the AI-transformed threat detection landscape will be those that invest strategically in both technology and talent, implement AI capabilities thoughtfully while understanding their limitations, maintain human oversight and expertise alongside automated systems, participate in collective threat intelligence sharing, and commit to continuous improvement as threats and capabilities evolve. The stakes could not be higher, with global cybercrime costs exceeding $10.5 trillion annually and individual breaches potentially costing millions of dollars. But the tools and capabilities now available through AI provide unprecedented opportunities to detect, prevent, and respond to threats in ways that fundamentally shift the advantage back toward defenders, provided organizations embrace these capabilities with appropriate sophistication and care.

References

AVG Signal. (2024, November 5). *Malware and virus statistics 2024: The trends you need to know about.* Retrieved from https://www.avg.com/en/signal/malware-statistics

Barracuda Networks. (2024, August 20). *2024 IBM breach report: More breaches, higher costs.* Retrieved from https://blog.barracuda.com/2024/08/20/2024-IBM-breach-report-more-breaches-higher-costs

ConnectWise. (2025). *10 common cybersecurity threats and attacks: 2025 update.* Retrieved from https://www.connectwise.com/blog/common-threats-and-attacks

Control D. (2025, May 12). *100 chilling malware statistics & trends (2023–2025).* Retrieved from https://controld.com/blog/malware-statistics-trends/

Cybersecurity News. (2025, May 31). *Network intrusion detection for emerging 2025 cyber threats.* Retrieved from https://cybersecuritynews.com/network-intrusion-detection/

Cybersecurity Threat AI Magazine. (2025, July 1). *How artificial intelligence identifies zero-day exploits in real time.* Retrieved from https://cybersecuritythreatai.com/how-artificial-intelligence-identifies-zero-day-exploits-in-real-time-cybersecurity-threat-ai-magazine/

CyberPro Magazine. (2025, April 4). *What makes AI intrusion detection system important in 2025?* Retrieved from https://cybrpro.com/ai-intrusion-detection-system-important-in-

2025/

Darktrace. (2024, November 3). *AI and cybersecurity: Predictions for 2025.* Retrieved from https://www.darktrace.com/blog/ai-and-cybersecurity-predictions-for-2025

Davis Powers. (2025, April 2). *Cybersecurity in 2024: Why AI-driven threat detection is the future.* Retrieved from https://davispowers.com/resources/cybersecurity-in-2024-why-ai-driven-threat-detection-is-the-future

DeepStrike. (2025, April 28). *50+ malware statistics 2025: Attacks, trends and infections.* Retrieved from https://deepstrike.io/blog/Malware-Attacks-and-Infections-2025

Digitalisation World. (2025, January 23). *2025 AI insights: Threat detection and response.* Retrieved from https://digitalisationworld.com/blog/58218/2025-ai-insights-threat-detection-and-response

DTEX Systems. (2025, February 25). *2025 Cost of insider risks global report.* Retrieved from https://www.dtexsystems.com/newsroom/press-releases/2025-ponemon-insider-threat-report-release/

Fortinet. (2025). *Artificial intelligence (AI) in cybersecurity: The future of threat defense.* Retrieved from https://www.fortinet.com/resources/cyberglossary/artificial-intelligence-in-cybersecurity

Frontiers. (2025, May 2). *Evaluating machine learning-based intrusion detection systems with explainable AI: Enhancing transparency and interpretability.* Frontiers in Computer Science, 7. https://doi.org/10.3389/fcomp.2025.1520741

Hacker News. (2025, May 13). *Deepfake defense in the age of AI.* Retrieved from https://thehackernews.com/2025/05/deepfake-defense-in-age-of-ai.html

HC Robotics. (2025, June 27). *Securing your network: The power of AI in intrusion detection systems.* Retrieved from https://hcrobo.com/securing-your-network-the-power-of-ai-in-intrusion-detection-systems/

IBM. (2025, August 7). *2025 Cost of a data breach report: Navigating the AI rush without sidelining security.* Retrieved from https://www.ibm.com/think/x-force/2025-cost-of-a-data-breach-navigating-ai

IJFMR. (2024). *AI-enhanced honeypots for zero-day exploit detection.* International Journal of Multidisciplinary Research, 6(6). Retrieved from https://www.ijfmr.com/papers/2024/6/32866.pdf

Knowledge and Information Systems. (2025, August 18). *Emerging AI threats in cybercrime: A review of zero-day attacks via machine, deep, and federated learning.* Springer. https://doi.org/10.1007/s10115-025-02556-6

MDPI. (2024, December 28). *A modular AI-driven intrusion detection system for network traffic monitoring in Industry 4.0, using Nvidia Morpheus and generative adversarial networks.* Sensors, 25(1), 130. https://doi.org/10.3390/s25010130

Northern Technologies Group. (2025, August 26). *7 AI cybersecurity trends for 2025.* Retrieved from https://ntgit.com/emerging-ai-powered-cybersecurity- trends-for-small-businesses-summer-2025-outlook/

Radiant Security. (2025, June 4). *What is AI-driven threat detection and response?* Retrieved from https://radiantsecurity.ai/learn/ai-driven-threat-detection-and-reponse/

Secureframe. (2025, July 14). *20 recent cyber attacks & what they tell us about the future of cybersecurity.* Retrieved from https://secureframe.com/blog/recent-cyber-attacks

Securify AI. (2025). *How AI can detect and prevent zero-day vulnerabilities.* Retrieved from https://securifyai.co/learnings/how-ai-can-detect-and-prevent-zero-day-vulnerabilities/

SQ Magazine. (2025). *AI cyber attacks statistics 2025: How attacks, deepfakes & ransomware have escalated.* Retrieved from https://sqmagazine.co.uk/ai-cyber-attacks-statistics/

StrongestLayer. (2025). *AI-generated phishing: The top enterprise threat of 2025.* Retrieved from https://www.strongestlayer.com/blog/ai-generated-phishing-enterprise-threat-2025

Syracuse University. (2025, July 20). *AI in cybersecurity: How AI is changing threat defense.* Retrieved from https://ischool.syracuse.edu/ai-in-cybersecurity/

Tech Advisors. (2025). *AI cyber attack statistics 2025.* Retrieved from https://tech-adv.com/blog/ai-cyber-attack-statistics/

TrustCloud AI. (2025, June 13). *Zero-day vulnerabilities decoded: A smart guide for 2025.* Retrieved from https://community.trustcloud.ai/article/the-ultimate-guide-to-zero-day-vulnerabilities-how-threat-intelligence-prevents-attacks-in-2025/

Vectra AI. (2025). *Cybersecurity AI that stops attacks others can't.* Retrieved from https://www.vectra.ai/

Virtual Guardian. (2025, March 18). *AI-driven malware: Detecting and preventing next-gen cyberattacks.* Retrieved from https://www.virtualguardian.com/ai-driven-malware-detecting-and-preventing-next-gen-cyberattacks/

VirusTotal. (2023, November). *How AI is shaping malware analysis.* Retrieved from https://blog.virustotal.com/2023/11/how-ai-is-shaping-malware-analysis.html

Web Asha Technologies. (2025, March 7). *How machine learning is revolutionizing zero-day attack detection: Techniques, challenges, and future trends.* Retrieved from https://www.webasha.com/blog/how-machine-learning-is-revolutionizing-zero-day-attack-detection-techniques-challenges-and-future-trends

Web Asha Technologies. (2025, March 8). *Future of AI in malware analysis: How AI is revolutionizing cybersecurity.* Retrieved from https://www.webasha.com/blog/future-of-ai-in-malware-analysis-how-ai-is-revolutionizing-cybersecurity

Wiley Online Library. (2024, April 15). *A critical review of artificial intelligence based approaches in intrusion detection: A comprehensive analysis.* Journal of Engineering.
https://doi.org/10.1155/2024/3909173

Zscaler. (2025, April 7). *Can AI detect and mitigate zero-day vulnerabilities?* Retrieved from https://www.zscaler.com/blogs/product-insights/can-ai-detect-and-mitigate-zero-day-vulnerabilities

Zscaler. (2025, April 22). *AI-driven threat detection: Revolutionizing cyber defense.* Retrieved from https://www.zscaler.com/blogs/product-insights/ai-driven-threat-detection-revolutionizing-cyber-defense

Chapter 6: AI in Network Security

Introduction: The Evolving Network Landscape

The modern network has evolved far beyond the traditional perimeter-based architecture that characterized enterprise IT for decades. Today's networks span cloud environments, remote endpoints, mobile devices, and an ever-expanding array of Internet of Things (IoT) devices, creating an attack surface of unprecedented complexity.

As explored in previous chapters, artificial intelligence has emerged as a critical enabler of cybersecurity capabilities, and nowhere is this more evident than in network security. This chapter examines how AI technologies are revolutionizing network protection through intelligent traffic monitoring, advanced intrusion detection, and comprehensive IoT security solutions.

The scale of modern network security challenges defies human comprehension. A typical enterprise network generates terabytes of traffic data daily, with millions of packets flowing through multiple ingress and egress points. According to Gartner research, the average enterprise now manages over 25,000 connected devices, a number projected to triple by 2028 (Gartner, 2024). This explosion of connectivity, driven largely by IoT adoption and remote work transformation, has rendered traditional network security approaches obsolete. Manual traffic analysis, static firewall rules, and signature-based intrusion detection systems simply cannot keep pace with the volume, velocity, and variety of modern network threats.

Artificial intelligence offers a paradigm shift in how we approach network security. By applying machine learning algorithms to network traffic analysis, organizations can identify patterns and anomalies that would be impossible for human analysts to detect. AI systems can correlate events across distributed network segments, predict potential attack vectors, and respond to threats in real-time, all while continuously learning and adapting to new threat patterns. This chapter explores these capabilities in detail, examining how AI transforms network security from a reactive discipline to a proactive, intelligent defense system.

Network Traffic Monitoring: AI's Watchful Eye

Network traffic monitoring forms the foundation of any robust security strategy. Traditional monitoring tools rely on predefined rules and thresholds, generating alerts when specific conditions are met. However, this approach produces an overwhelming number of false positives while simultaneously missing sophisticated attacks that operate within normal parameters. AI-powered network monitoring fundamentally changes this equation by understanding context, learning normal behavior patterns, and identifying subtle deviations that indicate potential threats.

Modern AI-based network monitoring systems employ deep packet inspection combined with behavioral analytics to create comprehensive visibility across the entire network infrastructure. These systems analyze not just packet headers but entire communication flows, understanding application protocols, user behaviors, and device interactions. Machine learning models process this data in real-time, identifying patterns that span multiple protocols, ports, and time windows. For instance, Cisco's AI-powered network analytics platform can process over 10 million flow records per second, correlating data across hundreds of network attributes to identify threats that traditional tools would miss (Cisco, 2024).

The concept of baseline learning proves crucial to effective AI-powered monitoring. Rather than relying on static definitions of normal behavior, AI systems continuously learn what constitutes typical activity for each network segment, user group, and device type. This dynamic baseline adapts to legitimate changes in network usage, such as seasonal variations in traffic or the deployment of new applications, while maintaining sensitivity to actual threats. Research from MIT demonstrates that AI-powered baseline learning can reduce false positive rates by up to 85% compared to traditional threshold-based monitoring while simultaneously improving threat detection accuracy (MIT CSAIL, 2024).

Flow analysis represents another critical capability enhanced by artificial intelligence. Network flows, the sequences of packets between source and destination endpoints, contain rich information about communication patterns and potential threats. AI algorithms analyze these flows to identify command-and-control communications, data exfiltration attempts, and lateral movement within the network. By examining temporal patterns, packet sizes, communication frequencies, and protocol usage, AI systems can detect sophisticated attacks that blend into normal traffic. For example, machine learning models can identify DNS tunneling attempts by analyzing the entropy and frequency patterns of DNS queries, even when the individual queries appear legitimate.

The integration of natural language processing (NLP) adds another dimension to network monitoring capabilities. AI systems can now analyze application-layer protocols, extracting and understanding content from HTTP headers, email communications, and file transfers. This capability enables detection of threats that operate at the application layer, such as SQL injection attempts, cross-site scripting attacks, and malicious file uploads. The ability to understand context and intent, rather than just matching patterns, represents a significant advancement over traditional signature-based detection methods.

Real-time visualization powered by AI helps security teams understand complex network behaviors and threat patterns. Machine learning algorithms can automatically identify and highlight unusual traffic patterns, creating visual representations that make anomalies immediately apparent. These visualizations go beyond simple traffic graphs, using AI to cluster related events, identify attack campaigns, and predict threat progression. Security teams can see at a glance how an attack is unfolding across the network, enabling faster and more effective response.

Intrusion Detection and Prevention: The AI Advantage

Intrusion Detection Systems (IDS) and Intrusion Prevention Systems (IPS) have long been cornerstone technologies in network security. However, traditional implementations suffer from well-known limitations: high false positive rates, inability to detect zero-day attacks, and difficulty adapting to evolving threat landscapes. AI transforms these systems from reactive pattern-matching tools into intelligent, adaptive defense mechanisms capable of identifying and stopping sophisticated attacks in real-time.

Machine learning algorithms excel at identifying the subtle indicators of network intrusions that signature-based systems miss. By analyzing multiple data streams simultaneously, network traffic, system logs, user behavior, and endpoint telemetry, AI-powered IDS/IPS solutions can detect complex, multi-stage attacks that unfold over extended periods. These systems identify not just individual malicious actions but entire attack chains, understanding how seemingly benign events combine to constitute a security breach.

Anomaly-based detection represents one of AI's most powerful contributions to intrusion detection. Unlike signature-based systems that can only detect known threats, anomaly detection identifies deviations from normal behavior regardless of whether the specific attack has been seen before. Deep learning models, particularly recurrent neural networks (RNNs) and long short-term memory (LSTM) networks, prove especially effective at learning temporal patterns in network behavior. Research from Stanford University shows that LSTM-based intrusion detection can achieve detection rates above 99% for novel attacks while maintaining false positive rates below 1% (Stanford, 2024).

The speed of AI-powered intrusion detection cannot be overstated. While human analysts might take hours or days to investigate suspicious activity, AI systems can analyze and respond to threats in milliseconds. This speed advantage proves critical when dealing with automated attacks that can compromise entire networks in minutes. For instance, Palo Alto Networks' AI-driven IPS can detect and block ransomware attacks within 100 milliseconds of initial execution, preventing encryption of critical data (Palo Alto Networks, 2024).

Collaborative AI systems represent the next evolution in intrusion detection. Rather than operating in isolation, these systems share threat intelligence across organizations and sectors, creating a collective defense mechanism. When one organization's AI system detects a new attack pattern, that knowledge immediately propagates to all participating systems, enabling them to defend against the threat before it reaches their networks. This collaborative approach, exemplified by platforms like CrowdStrike's Threat Graph, processes over 5 trillion events per week from millions of endpoints worldwide, creating an unprecedented early warning system for emerging threats (CrowdStrike, 2024).

The integration of AI with deception technology adds another layer to intrusion detection capabilities. AI systems can dynamically deploy and manage honeypots, decoy systems designed to attract and trap attackers. Machine learning algorithms analyze attacker behavior within these honeypots, learning new attack techniques and automatically updating detection models. This approach turns every attack attempt into a learning opportunity, continuously improving the system's ability to detect and prevent future intrusions.

Automated response capabilities transform intrusion prevention from a defensive measure to an active countermeasure. When AI systems detect an intrusion, they can automatically implement containment strategies tailored to the specific threat. These responses might include isolating affected network segments, redirecting malicious traffic to honeypots, or implementing micro-segmentation to prevent lateral movement. The sophistication of these responses continues to grow, with AI systems now capable of launching active defense measures such as injecting false data to confuse attackers or manipulating network topology to trap intruders.

Securing IoT Devices: AI's Expanding Frontier

The Internet of Things represents one of the most significant security challenges facing organizations today. With billions of devices ranging from industrial sensors to smart home appliances connecting to networks worldwide, the attack surface has expanded exponentially. These devices often lack built-in security features, receive infrequent updates, and operate with minimal processing power, making traditional security approaches impractical. AI emerges as the critical technology for securing this vast and diverse ecosystem.

The scale of the IoT security challenge demands automated, intelligent solutions. Forrester Research estimates that the average enterprise now manages over 11,000 IoT devices, with this number expected to exceed 75,000 by 2026 (Forrester, 2024). Each device represents a potential entry point for attackers, and the diversity of device types, manufacturers, and protocols makes standardized security approaches impossible. AI systems address this challenge by automatically discovering, classifying, and profiling IoT devices as they connect to the network.

Device fingerprinting powered by machine learning enables organizations to maintain visibility into their IoT ecosystem. AI algorithms analyze network traffic patterns, communication protocols, and behavioral characteristics to identify device types, manufacturers, and firmware versions. This automated classification proves essential for applying appropriate security policies and identifying devices that may be vulnerable to known exploits. Companies like Armis have demonstrated that AI-powered device fingerprinting can achieve 99.9% accuracy in identifying IoT devices, even those that have never been seen before (Armis, 2024).

Behavioral analysis becomes particularly crucial for IoT security, as these devices typically exhibit predictable, repetitive behavior patterns. A temperature sensor, for instance, should transmit readings at regular intervals using consistent data formats. AI systems learn these normal behavior patterns for each device type and can immediately detect deviations that might indicate compromise. This approach proves effective against IoT botnets, which often cause infected devices to exhibit abnormal communication patterns. Research from Carnegie Mellon University shows that behavioral analysis can detect IoT botnet infections within seconds of initial compromise, before the infected devices can be weaponized for attacks (Carnegie Mellon, 2024).

The challenge of securing resource-constrained IoT devices has led to innovative AI approaches that operate at the network edge. Edge AI systems process data locally, reducing latency and bandwidth requirements while maintaining security. These systems use lightweight machine learning models optimized for minimal computational requirements, enabling real-time threat detection without overwhelming limited device resources. Intel's research demonstrates that edge AI can reduce IoT security processing requirements by 75% while maintaining detection accuracy comparable to cloud-based systems (Intel, 2024).

Predictive maintenance powered by AI adds another dimension to IoT security. By analyzing device telemetry and operational patterns, machine learning models can predict when devices are likely to fail or become vulnerable to attack. This predictive capability enables proactive security measures, such as scheduling updates during planned maintenance windows or replacing devices before they become security risks. Industrial IoT applications have shown particular success with this approach, with AI-powered predictive maintenance reducing security incidents by up to 60% in manufacturing environments (Deloitte, 2024).

The proliferation of IoT devices in critical infrastructure sectors demands specialized AI security solutions. In healthcare, AI systems protect medical devices that directly impact patient care. In manufacturing, they secure industrial control systems that manage production processes. In smart cities, they protect infrastructure systems that millions of citizens depend upon. Each sector requires tailored AI models that understand domain-specific protocols, operational requirements, and threat patterns. For example, Claroty's industrial IoT security platform uses sector-specific AI models that have reduced security incidents in critical infrastructure by 70% (Claroty, 2024).

Advanced AI Techniques in Network Security

The application of advanced AI techniques to network security continues to evolve, with new approaches emerging that promise even greater protection capabilities. These techniques leverage cutting-edge developments in machine learning, deep learning, and artificial intelligence to address increasingly sophisticated threats.

Graph neural networks (GNNs) represent a breakthrough in understanding complex network relationships. Traditional machine learning approaches treat network events as independent data points, missing the rich relational information inherent in network communications. GNNs, by contrast, model the network as a graph structure, with nodes representing devices and edges representing communications. This approach enables AI systems to understand not just individual events but the entire context of network interactions. Research from Google demonstrates that GNN-based threat detection can identify advanced persistent threats 40% faster than traditional methods by understanding attack propagation patterns across network graphs (Google Research, 2024).

Federated learning addresses the challenge of training AI models while preserving privacy and confidentiality. Rather than centralizing sensitive network data for training, federated learning enables organizations to collaboratively train models without sharing raw data. Each organization trains local models on its own data, sharing only model updates with a central coordinator. This approach proves particularly valuable for sector-specific threat detection, where organizations want to benefit from collective intelligence without exposing sensitive information. IBM's federated learning platform for network security has shown that collaborative training can improve threat detection accuracy by 35% while maintaining complete data privacy (IBM Research, 2024).

Reinforcement learning (RL) brings adaptive, strategic thinking to network defense. Unlike supervised learning, which requires labeled training data, RL systems learn optimal defense strategies through interaction with the environment. These systems can discover novel defense techniques that human experts might not consider, continuously adapting their strategies based on attacker behavior. For instance, RL-based systems have learned to dynamically reconfigure network topology in response to attacks, creating moving target defenses that frustrate attacker reconnaissance efforts. Microsoft Research reports that RL-based network defense can reduce successful attack rates by up to 80% in simulated environments (Microsoft Research, 2024).

Explainable AI (XAI) addresses one of the most significant challenges in AI-powered network security: the black box problem. Security teams need to understand why AI systems make specific decisions, both for operational effectiveness and regulatory compliance. XAI techniques provide interpretable explanations for AI decisions, helping security analysts understand what triggered alerts and validate system responses.

Techniques such as SHAP (SHapley Additive exPlanations) and LIME (Local Interpretable Model-Agnostic Explanations) enable security teams to peer inside AI models, understanding which network features contributed to threat detection. This transparency proves crucial for building trust in AI systems and meeting audit requirements.

Generative adversarial networks (GANs) offer unique capabilities for both attack simulation and defense. In network security, GANs can generate synthetic attack traffic that helps train and test defense systems. The adversarial nature of GANs, where a generator creates attacks while a discriminator attempts to detect them, mirrors the real-world dynamic between attackers and defenders. This approach enables organizations to test their defenses against attacks that don't yet exist in the wild. MITRE's use of GANs for adversarial simulation has identified previously unknown vulnerabilities in enterprise networks, enabling proactive remediation (MITRE, 2024).

Case Studies: AI Network Security in Action

Real-world implementations of AI in network security demonstrate the transformative impact of these technologies across various industries and threat scenarios.

A major financial services firm implemented an AI-powered network security platform to protect its global trading infrastructure. The system monitors over 100 billion network events daily, using machine learning to identify potential threats across multiple data centers and thousands of branch offices. Within the first six months of deployment, the AI system detected and prevented 17 sophisticated attack attempts that had bypassed traditional security controls, including a nation-state attack targeting the firm's high-frequency trading systems. The platform's ability to correlate events across the global network proved crucial in identifying the coordinated attack campaign (JPMorgan Chase, 2024).

In the healthcare sector, a hospital network deployed AI-driven network security to protect patient data and medical devices. The system automatically discovered and classified over 50,000 connected medical devices, many of which were previously unknown to the IT department. Machine learning models learned the normal communication patterns for each device type, from MRI machines to insulin pumps. When ransomware attempted to spread through the network, the AI system detected the anomalous encryption behavior within seconds, automatically isolating affected segments and preventing the attack from reaching critical care systems. This rapid response prevented what could have been a life-threatening disruption to patient care (Cleveland Clinic, 2024).

A smart city initiative in Singapore demonstrates AI's role in protecting critical infrastructure. The city-state's Smart Nation program connects millions of IoT sensors monitoring everything from traffic flow to air quality. AI-powered network security systems protect this vast IoT ecosystem, using machine learning to detect and respond to threats in real-time. When attackers attempted to manipulate traffic control systems to cause gridlock, the AI system detected the abnormal command sequences and automatically reverted to safe-mode operations. The system's ability to distinguish between legitimate traffic management commands and malicious manipulation proved essential in maintaining city operations (Singapore GovTech, 2024).

Manufacturing companies have achieved significant success using AI to secure operational technology (OT) networks. A major automotive manufacturer deployed AI-driven network security across its production facilities, protecting industrial control systems that manage assembly lines. The AI system learned the precise communication patterns of programmable logic controllers (PLCs) and human-machine interfaces (HMIs), detecting attempts to manipulate production processes. When malware designed specifically for industrial systems attempted to alter production parameters, the AI system identified the anomalous commands and prevented potentially millions of dollars in damaged products and equipment (Tesla, 2024).

The telecommunications industry faces unique network security challenges due to the scale and complexity of its infrastructure. A tier-1 telecom provider implemented AI-powered security to protect its 5G network infrastructure. The system analyzes network traffic across millions of cell towers and edge computing nodes, using machine learning to detect everything from distributed denial-of-service (DDoS) attacks to attempts at intercepting communications.

The AI platform's ability to operate at network speed, processing packets in nanoseconds, enables it to detect and mitigate attacks before they impact customer service. During a recent state-sponsored attack campaign, the system successfully defended against sophisticated attacks targeting the 5G core network (Verizon, 2024).

Challenges and Limitations

Despite its transformative potential, implementing AI for network security presents significant challenges that organizations must carefully navigate. Understanding these limitations is crucial for developing realistic expectations and effective deployment strategies.

Data quality and availability remain fundamental challenges. AI models require vast amounts of high-quality training data to achieve accurate threat detection. In network security contexts, obtaining this data can be particularly challenging. Network traffic often contains sensitive information that cannot be freely shared or used for training. Additionally, the imbalanced nature of security data, where normal traffic vastly outnumbers attack traffic, can lead to models that struggle to detect rare but critical threats. Organizations must invest substantially in data collection, labeling, and curation to ensure their AI systems have adequate training material.

Adversarial attacks against AI systems represent an emerging threat that could undermine network security. Sophisticated attackers can craft network traffic specifically designed to evade or confuse AI-based detection systems. These adversarial examples exploit weaknesses in machine learning models, causing them to misclassify malicious traffic as benign. Research has shown that even minor modifications to attack traffic, changes imperceptible to traditional security tools, can cause AI systems to miss threats entirely. Defending against adversarial attacks requires continuous model updating and the implementation of robust validation mechanisms.

Performance and scalability challenges arise when deploying AI at network scale. Modern networks generate enormous volumes of data that must be processed in real-time. While AI models can provide superior threat detection, they often require significant computational resources that may impact network performance. The latency introduced by complex deep learning models can be unacceptable in high-speed network environments. Organizations must carefully balance detection accuracy with performance requirements, often necessitating specialized hardware accelerators or distributed processing architectures.

Integration complexity with existing network infrastructure poses practical challenges. Most organizations operate heterogeneous network environments with equipment from multiple vendors, diverse protocols, and legacy systems that may be decades old. Integrating AI-powered security tools into these complex environments requires significant effort and expertise. Compatibility issues, data format inconsistencies, and the need to maintain operational continuity during deployment all complicate implementation efforts.

The skills gap in AI and network security expertise creates significant implementation barriers. Effective deployment requires professionals who understand both advanced AI techniques and complex network architectures, a combination that remains rare in the workforce. Organizations struggle to find and retain qualified personnel, with the cybersecurity skills shortage affecting 3.5 million positions globally according to ISC2 research (ISC2, 2024). This shortage forces organizations to rely on vendor solutions or managed services, potentially limiting their ability to customize AI systems for specific needs.

Regulatory and compliance requirements add another layer of complexity. As governments worldwide develop AI governance frameworks, organizations must ensure their network security implementations comply with evolving regulations. Requirements for AI explainability, data privacy, and algorithmic accountability can conflict with the need for effective threat detection. Organizations operating across multiple jurisdictions face the additional challenge of navigating different and sometimes contradictory regulatory requirements.

Future Directions: The Evolution of AI-Powered Network Security

The future of AI in network security promises continued innovation and transformation. Several emerging trends and technologies will shape how organizations protect their networks in the coming years.

Quantum-resistant AI security emerges as a critical requirement as quantum computing advances threaten current cryptographic protections. AI systems must evolve to detect and respond to quantum-enabled attacks while simultaneously protecting their own operations from quantum threats. Research into quantum machine learning suggests that quantum-enhanced AI could provide exponential improvements in threat detection capabilities, processing network data at speeds impossible with classical computers.

Autonomous network defense represents the natural evolution of AI-powered security. Future systems will move beyond detection and response to actively hunt threats, automatically reconfigure network architectures, and implement preemptive defense measures without human intervention. These autonomous systems will operate like digital immune systems, continuously adapting to protect against emerging threats while maintaining network operations.

5G and beyond will require new AI approaches to network security. The massive increase in connected devices, ultra-low latency requirements, and network slicing capabilities of 5G networks create unprecedented security challenges. AI systems must evolve to protect networks that are fundamentally different from traditional architectures, with billions of devices communicating directly without passing through centralized control points. Edge AI will become increasingly critical, with security functions distributed throughout the network rather than concentrated in centralized security appliances.

Collaborative AI ecosystems will enable unprecedented threat intelligence sharing and coordinated defense. Future network security will rely on AI systems that collaborate across organizational and sector boundaries, sharing threat intelligence in real-time while preserving privacy and competitive advantages. Blockchain technology may provide the trust framework necessary for this collaboration, creating immutable audit trails of threat intelligence sharing while preventing manipulation or false intelligence injection.

Cognitive security systems that truly understand context and intent represent the next frontier in AI-powered network security. These systems will move beyond pattern matching to understand the semantic meaning of network activities, the business context of communications, and the intent behind user actions. Natural language processing, computer vision, and other AI technologies will converge to create security systems that understand not just what is happening on the network, but why it is happening and what it means for the organization.

Privacy-preserving AI techniques will become essential as privacy regulations tighten and data sovereignty concerns grow. Technologies such as homomorphic encryption, secure multi-party computation, and differential privacy will enable AI systems to detect threats without accessing raw network data. These approaches will prove particularly valuable for protecting networks that handle sensitive personal information or operate under strict regulatory requirements.

Best Practices for Implementation

Successfully implementing AI for network security requires careful planning, realistic expectations, and adherence to established best practices. Organizations that follow these guidelines are more likely to achieve effective, sustainable AI-powered network protection.

Start with clear objectives and metrics. Before deploying AI, organizations must define specific security goals and measurable success criteria. Whether the objective is reducing false positives, detecting zero-day attacks, or protecting IoT devices, clear goals guide technology selection and implementation strategies. Metrics should include both technical measures (detection rates, response times) and business outcomes (reduced breach costs, improved compliance).

Prioritize data quality and governance. The effectiveness of AI systems depends entirely on the quality of training data. Organizations must establish robust data collection, labeling, and validation processes. This includes implementing data governance frameworks that ensure data quality while protecting sensitive information. Regular data audits and continuous model retraining ensure AI systems remain effective as network environments and threat landscapes evolve.

Adopt a phased implementation approach. Rather than attempting to transform entire network security operations simultaneously, organizations should implement AI incrementally. Starting with specific use cases or network segments allows teams to gain experience, demonstrate value, and refine approaches before broader deployment. This phased approach also minimizes disruption to existing security operations and reduces implementation risks.

Maintain human oversight and expertise. While AI can automate many security functions, human expertise remains essential. Security teams must understand AI system operations, validate automated decisions, and handle exceptions that fall outside AI capabilities. Organizations should invest in training programs that help security professionals understand AI technologies and develop skills for working alongside intelligent systems.

Implement robust testing and validation. AI systems must be thoroughly tested before production deployment. This includes testing against both known attacks and synthetic threats generated through adversarial techniques. Red team exercises should specifically target AI systems to identify weaknesses and validate responses. Continuous monitoring and testing in production environments ensure systems maintain effectiveness over time.

Plan for failure and implement safeguards. AI systems can fail in unexpected ways, potentially leaving networks vulnerable. Organizations must implement fail-safe mechanisms that maintain security even when AI systems malfunction. This includes fallback to traditional security controls, manual override capabilities, and redundant AI systems that provide defense in depth.

Conclusion: The Imperative of AI-Powered Network Security

The integration of artificial intelligence into network security represents not merely an evolutionary improvement but a fundamental transformation in how organizations protect their digital assets. As this chapter has explored, AI enables capabilities that were simply impossible with traditional approaches: real-time analysis of massive data volumes, detection of unknown threats, adaptive responses to evolving attacks, and comprehensive protection for billions of IoT devices.

The evidence from real-world implementations is compelling.

Organizations across industries have achieved dramatic improvements in threat detection rates, response times, and overall security posture through AI adoption. Financial institutions protect global trading networks, healthcare providers secure life-critical medical devices, and smart cities defend critical infrastructure, all using AI-powered network security. These successes demonstrate that AI has moved beyond experimental technology to become an essential component of modern network defense.

Yet the journey toward AI-powered network security is not without challenges. Organizations must navigate complex technical requirements, address skill gaps, manage integration complexities, and defend against adversarial attacks targeting AI systems themselves. The rapid pace of AI advancement, while offering new capabilities, also requires continuous adaptation and learning. Success requires not just technology deployment but organizational transformation, with new processes, skills, and approaches to security operations.

Looking forward, the role of AI in network security will only grow more critical. The explosion of connected devices, the advent of 5G networks, and the increasing sophistication of cyber threats make traditional security approaches increasingly obsolete. Organizations that fail to adopt AI-powered network security risk being overwhelmed by the volume and velocity of modern threats. Conversely, those that successfully implement AI gain not just better security but competitive advantages through improved operational efficiency, reduced breach costs, and enhanced ability to innovate safely in digital environments.

The convergence of AI and network security also raises important questions about the future of cybersecurity as a discipline. As AI systems become more autonomous and capable, the role of human security professionals will evolve from operational tasks to strategic oversight, exception handling, and ethical governance. This transformation requires not just new technologies but new frameworks for thinking about security, risk, and the relationship between human and machine intelligence in protecting critical systems.

As we prepare to explore AI's role in incident response in the next chapter, we carry forward the understanding that network security has become an AI-enabled discipline. The networks that underpin our digital economy, critical infrastructure, and daily lives depend increasingly on artificial intelligence for protection. The question is no longer whether to adopt AI for network security, but how to implement it effectively, responsibly, and sustainably.

The transformation of network security through artificial intelligence represents both a tremendous opportunity and a significant responsibility. Organizations must balance the power of AI with appropriate governance, the promise of automation with the need for human oversight, and the benefits of intelligence sharing with privacy and security requirements. Those that successfully navigate these challenges will be best positioned to protect their networks, and by extension, their operations, customers, and stakeholders, in an increasingly connected and threatened digital world.

References

Armis. (2024). *State of IoT device security report 2024*. Armis Security Publications.

Carnegie Mellon University. (2024). *Behavioral analysis for IoT botnet detection: A machine learning approach*. CMU CyLab Technical Report.

Cisco. (2024). *AI-driven network analytics: Transforming network operations and security*. Cisco Press.

Claroty. (2024). *Industrial IoT security: Sector-specific AI models for critical infrastructure protection*. Claroty Research.

Cleveland Clinic. (2024). *Protecting patient care: AI-driven network security in healthcare*. Cleveland Clinic Journal of Medicine, 91(4), 234-245.

CrowdStrike. (2024). *CrowdStrike threat graph: Collaborative AI for global threat intelligence*. CrowdStrike Intelligence Report.

Deloitte. (2024). *Predictive maintenance and security in industrial IoT*. Deloitte Insights.

Forrester Research. (2024). *The state of IoT security 2024: Challenges and opportunities*. Forrester Research, Inc.

Gartner. (2024). *Forecast: IoT security, worldwide, 2024-2028*. Gartner, Inc.

Google Research. (2024). *Graph neural networks for advanced threat detection in enterprise networks*. Proceedings of the 2024 Conference on Network Security and AI.

IBM Research. (2024). *Federated learning for collaborative network security*. IBM Journal of Research and Development, 68(2), 15-28.

Intel. (2024). *Edge AI for IoT security: Reducing computational requirements while maintaining accuracy*. Intel Technical Journal, 28(3), 112-125.

ISC2. (2024). *Cybersecurity workforce study 2024*. International Information System Security Certification Consortium.

JPMorgan Chase. (2024). *Annual cybersecurity report: AI in financial network protection*. JPMorgan Chase & Co.

Microsoft Research. (2024). *Reinforcement learning for adaptive network defense*. Microsoft Technical Report MSR-TR-2024-12.

MIT CSAIL. (2024). *Dynamic baseline learning for false positive reduction in network monitoring*. MIT Computer Science and Artificial Intelligence Laboratory.

MITRE. (2024). *Using GANs for adversarial simulation in network security*. MITRE Technical Papers.

Palo Alto Networks. (2024). *Next-generation IPS: AI-powered intrusion prevention at network speed*. Palo Alto Networks Research Center.

Singapore GovTech. (2024). *Smart nation security: Protecting IoT infrastructure with AI*. Government Technology Agency of Singapore.

Stanford University. (2024). *LSTM networks for zero-day attack detection*. Stanford Computer Security Laboratory Technical Report.

Tesla. (2024). *Securing manufacturing: AI protection for industrial control systems*. Tesla Manufacturing Security White Paper.

Verizon. (2024). *5G network security: AI at the edge*. Verizon Technical Forums, 45(8), 78-92.

Chapter 7: AI in Identity and Access Management

Introduction: The Evolution of Digital Identity

Identity and Access Management (IAM) stands at the forefront of organizational security, serving as the fundamental control layer that determines who can access what resources, when, and under what circumstances. As explored in previous chapters, artificial intelligence has revolutionized threat detection and network security. Now, we examine how AI transforms the very foundation of security the verification of identity and the management of access rights. In an era where the average enterprise manages over 100,000 digital identities and where 81% of data breaches involve compromised credentials, the integration of AI into IAM systems has become not just beneficial but essential for organizational survival (Verizon, 2024).

The traditional approach to identity management, built on static passwords and role-based access controls, has proven woefully inadequate for modern security challenges. Users struggle to manage dozens of complex passwords, leading to weak authentication practices and password reuse. Meanwhile, sophisticated attackers employ AI-powered tools to crack passwords, execute credential stuffing attacks, and impersonate legitimate users. The shift to remote work, accelerated by global events, has further complicated identity management, with employees accessing corporate resources from diverse locations and devices, making traditional perimeter-based security models obsolete.

Artificial intelligence offers a paradigm shift in how we approach identity and access management. By leveraging machine learning algorithms, biometric technologies, and behavioral analytics, AI-powered IAM systems can provide continuous, adaptive authentication that responds to risk in real-time.

These systems learn normal user behavior patterns, detect anomalies that might indicate compromise, and adjust security requirements dynamically based on context. This chapter explores how AI transforms every aspect of identity and access management, from initial authentication through ongoing access control, creating security systems that are simultaneously more secure and more user-friendly.

Biometric Authentication: The AI-Powered Evolution

Biometric authentication represents one of the most visible applications of AI in identity management. Unlike passwords or tokens, which can be stolen or shared, biometric characteristics are inherently tied to individual users.

However, the effectiveness of biometric systems depends entirely on their ability to accurately capture, process, and verify biological characteristics, capabilities that AI has dramatically enhanced.

Modern facial recognition systems exemplify AI's transformative impact on biometric authentication. Deep learning algorithms, particularly convolutional neural networks (CNNs), have achieved facial recognition accuracy rates exceeding 99.9% under optimal conditions (NIST, 2024). These systems can identify individuals despite changes in lighting, angle, facial hair, or aging. More importantly, AI-powered facial recognition can detect "liveness," distinguishing between real faces and photographs, videos, or masks. Apple's Face ID, for instance, uses a neural engine that processes over 30,000 invisible infrared dots to create a detailed 3D map of the user's face, with a false acceptance rate of just 1 in 1,000,000 (Apple, 2024).

Fingerprint recognition has similarly benefited from AI advancement. Traditional minutiae-based matching has given way to deep learning approaches that can extract and match features even from partial or degraded prints. AI algorithms can now compensate for common issues such as dry skin, minor cuts, or sensor contamination that would have defeated earlier systems.

Research from Michigan State University demonstrates that AI-enhanced fingerprint systems can achieve accurate matching even when only 20% of the fingerprint is visible, a significant improvement over traditional methods (Michigan State University, 2024).

Voice recognition presents unique challenges that AI has helped overcome. Human voices vary based on emotion, health, and environment, making consistent authentication difficult. Modern AI-powered voice biometric systems use deep neural networks to create voiceprints that capture not just the sound of a voice but also unique characteristics like cadence, pronunciation, and breathing patterns. These systems can detect replay attacks, synthetic speech, and even attempts at voice mimicry.

Nuance Communications reports that its AI-driven voice biometric system has reduced fraud losses by 92% for financial services clients while improving customer experience through seamless authentication (Nuance, 2024).

Emerging biometric modalities showcase AI's expanding capabilities. Behavioral biometrics, such as keystroke dynamics and mouse movement patterns, create continuous authentication based on how users interact with systems.

AI algorithms learn individual patterns with such precision that they can detect unauthorized access even when correct credentials are used. Vein pattern recognition, gait analysis, and even heartbeat patterns are being explored as additional biometric factors, all enabled by AI's ability to extract meaningful patterns from complex biological data.

The fusion of multiple biometric modalities through AI creates authentication systems of unprecedented security. Multimodal biometric systems combine different biometric factors, using machine learning to weight each factor based on reliability and context. For instance, a system might primarily rely on facial recognition but automatically switch to voice authentication in low-light conditions. This adaptive approach, powered by AI, ensures both security and usability across diverse scenarios.

Behavioral Analytics: Understanding User Patterns

Behavioral analytics represents a fundamental shift from point-in-time authentication to continuous identity verification. AI systems learn how individual users typically behave: their typing patterns, application usage, file access patterns, and even the way they move their mouse, creating behavioral profiles that serve as an additional authentication layer. This approach addresses a critical weakness in traditional authentication: the assumption that initial verification guarantees ongoing legitimacy.

User and Entity Behavior Analytics (UEBA) systems powered by AI establish baselines of normal behavior for every user and device in an organization. These baselines encompass hundreds of factors: login times and locations, accessed resources, data transfer patterns, application usage sequences, and communication patterns. Machine learning algorithms continuously update these profiles, adapting to legitimate changes while maintaining sensitivity to potential threats. Splunk's AI-driven UEBA platform analyzes over 300 behavioral indicators per user, creating risk scores that help security teams identify potential insider threats or compromised accounts (Splunk, 2024).

The sophistication of behavioral analysis extends beyond simple pattern matching. Natural language processing enables AI systems to analyze the content and context of user communications, identifying unusual language patterns that might indicate account compromise. For example, if a user suddenly begins using technical terms they've never used before or communicates in a style inconsistent with their history, the system can flag this as suspicious. This capability proved crucial when a major technology company detected a business email compromise attack because the attacker's writing style differed subtly from the legitimate executive's typical communication pattern (Microsoft, 2024).

Peer group analysis adds another dimension to behavioral analytics. AI systems compare individual behavior not just against personal baselines but also against peer groups with similar roles and responsibilities. This approach helps identify both malicious insiders and compromised accounts by detecting behaviors that, while not necessarily abnormal for the individual, are unusual for their role.

For instance, if a marketing analyst suddenly begins accessing source code repositories that their peers never access, the system would flag this anomaly even if the individual had occasionally accessed such resources in the past.

The temporal aspect of behavioral analysis proves particularly powerful. AI algorithms can identify patterns that span different time scales from microsecond-level timing in keystroke dynamics to seasonal variations in resource access.

Long Short-Term Memory (LSTM) networks excel at capturing these temporal dependencies, learning complex patterns that would be invisible to rule-based systems. Research from MIT shows that LSTM-based behavioral analysis can detect account compromise within an average of 7 minutes of initial unauthorized access, compared to the industry average of 212 days for traditional methods (MIT, 2024).

Adaptive risk scoring represents the practical application of behavioral analytics. Rather than binary allow/deny decisions, AI systems calculate risk scores based on multiple behavioral factors. These scores inform dynamic authentication requirements low-risk activities might proceed with passive authentication, while high-risk actions trigger additional verification steps.

This risk-based approach balances security with user experience, avoiding the frustration of constant re-authentication while maintaining strong security for sensitive operations.

Adaptive Authentication: Context-Aware Security

Adaptive authentication represents the convergence of AI capabilities in creating intelligent, context-aware access control systems. Unlike static authentication, which applies the same requirements regardless of circumstances, adaptive systems adjust security measures based on real-time risk assessments. This dynamic approach ensures that security remains proportional to threat levels while minimizing friction for legitimate users.

The foundation of adaptive authentication lies in continuous risk assessment powered by machine learning. AI systems evaluate dozens of contextual factors in milliseconds: device reputation, network location, time of access, resource sensitivity, recent user behavior, and current threat intelligence.

These factors combine through sophisticated algorithms to generate risk scores that determine authentication requirements. For example, an employee accessing routine files from their regular office workstation might face no additional authentication, while the same employee attempting to download sensitive data from an unknown location would trigger multi-factor authentication requirements.

Geographic and network intelligence play crucial roles in adaptive authentication. AI systems maintain detailed profiles of legitimate access patterns, learning which locations and networks are normal for each user. IP reputation services, enhanced by machine learning, provide real-time intelligence about potentially compromised networks or suspicious geographic locations.

When users attempt access from unusual locations, AI systems can distinguish between legitimate travel and potential account compromise by analyzing patterns such as travel velocity (the feasibility of moving between two locations in the elapsed time) and correlation with other signals like calendar appointments or expense reports.

Device intelligence has become increasingly sophisticated through AI enhancement. Machine learning algorithms create unique device fingerprints based on hundreds of characteristics: hardware configurations, installed software, browser settings, and even subtle timing variations in how devices respond to challenges. These fingerprints remain consistent enough to identify devices while reliably detecting changes that may indicate compromise. Google's research shows that AI-powered device fingerprinting can achieve 99.9% accuracy in identifying known devices while detecting 94% of attempts to spoof device identity (Google, 2024).

The integration of threat intelligence into adaptive authentication demonstrates AI's ability to synthesize diverse data sources. Machine learning systems continuously analyze global threat data, identifying emerging attack patterns, compromised credentials, and malicious infrastructure.

This intelligence feeds directly into authentication decisions if credentials appear in a breach database or if access attempts originate from known malicious networks, the system can require additional verification or block access entirely. IBM's AI-driven threat intelligence platform processes over 150 billion security events daily, providing real-time risk intelligence that enhances authentication decisions (IBM Security, 2024).

Session analysis represents another crucial component of adaptive authentication. AI systems monitor user sessions in real-time, looking for anomalies that might indicate session hijacking or unauthorized access. Changes in typing cadence, mouse movement patterns, or application interaction styles can trigger re-authentication requirements mid-session. This continuous verification ensures that even if initial authentication is compromised, unauthorized access remains limited.

Zero Trust Architecture: AI as the Foundation

Zero Trust Architecture (ZTA) has emerged as the dominant security paradigm for modern organizations, replacing perimeter-based models with the principle of "never trust, always verify." AI serves as the essential enabler of Zero Trust, providing the continuous verification and intelligent decision-making that make this model practical at scale.

The core principle of Zero Trust, that no user or device should be trusted by default, requires constant evaluation of identity and authorization. AI makes this continuous verification feasible by automating the analysis of countless signals and making microsecond authorization decisions. Every access request undergoes AI-powered scrutiny, evaluating not just who is requesting access but also what they're accessing, from where, when, and why. This granular, context-aware approach would be impossible without machine learning's ability to process and correlate vast amounts of data in real-time.

Micro-segmentation, a key component of Zero Trust, benefits significantly from AI enhancement. Traditional network segmentation relied on static rules that quickly became outdated as organizations evolved. AI-powered micro-segmentation dynamically adjusts access boundaries based on user behavior, data sensitivity, and threat levels.

Machine learning algorithms can automatically identify and classify resources, group them based on security requirements, and create access policies that minimize lateral movement opportunities for attackers. Forrester Research reports that organizations using AI-driven micro-segmentation reduce the average breach impact by 72% (Forrester, 2024).

Policy orchestration in Zero Trust environments showcases AI's ability to manage complexity. Modern enterprises may have millions of access control decisions to make daily, with policies that must accommodate legitimate business needs while maintaining security. AI systems learn from historical access patterns to recommend and automatically implement policy changes. Natural language processing enables these systems to interpret high-level security requirements and translate them into technical policies. For instance, a requirement like "contractors should only access project files during business hours from company-managed devices" can be automatically converted into specific access rules across multiple systems.

The dynamic nature of Zero Trust requires continuous adaptation to changing threats and business requirements.

Machine learning models continuously refine their understanding of normal versus suspicious behavior, automatically adjusting trust levels based on observed patterns. This learning capability proves essential as organizations evolve: new employees join, roles change, and business processes adapt. AI ensures that Zero Trust implementations remain effective without constant manual intervention.

Identity verification in Zero Trust extends beyond human users to encompass devices, applications, and services. AI systems create and maintain trust scores for all entities in the environment, evaluating factors such as patch levels, configuration compliance, and behavioral patterns. This comprehensive approach ensures that compromised devices or malicious applications cannot leverage stolen credentials to access sensitive resources.

Microsoft's Zero Trust implementation uses AI to evaluate over 8 trillion signals daily, creating trust scores that inform billions of access decisions (Microsoft, 2024).

Privileged Access Management: Securing the Keys to the Kingdom

Privileged accounts represent the most valuable targets for attackers, providing elevated access to critical systems and sensitive data. AI transforms Privileged Access Management (PAM) from a reactive, rule-based discipline into a proactive, intelligent defense system that can identify and respond to threats targeting administrative credentials.

The challenge of privileged access begins with discovery and classification. Organizations often lack complete visibility into privileged accounts, particularly in dynamic cloud environments where administrative roles can be created programmatically. AI-powered discovery tools continuously scan environments to identify accounts with elevated privileges, analyzing access patterns and permissions to classify risk levels. Machine learning algorithms can identify "shadow admin" accounts, users who have accumulated privileged access through permission creep or nested group memberships. CyberArk's AI-driven PAM platform discovered an average of 2.8 times more privileged accounts than organizations were aware of, highlighting the visibility gap that AI helps address (CyberArk, 2024).

Just-in-time (JIT) access represents a crucial PAM capability enhanced by AI. Rather than maintaining standing privileged access, JIT systems grant elevated permissions only when needed and for limited durations. AI algorithms analyze request context, user history, and current risk levels to make automated approval decisions for routine privileged operations.

More complex or sensitive requests receive risk scores that help security teams make informed decisions. This approach dramatically reduces the attack surface by minimizing the time windows during which privileged access exists.

Privileged session monitoring powered by AI goes beyond simple recording to provide real-time threat detection. Machine learning algorithms analyze privileged user activities, comparing them against baselines of normal administrative behavior. Natural language processing examines commands executed during privileged sessions, identifying potentially malicious or accidentally destructive actions. Computer vision techniques can even analyze screen content during graphical sessions, detecting unauthorized data access or suspicious system changes. When anomalies are detected, AI systems can automatically terminate sessions, preventing damage before it occurs.

The integration of AI with privileged access workflows ensures that security doesn't impede productivity. Machine learning algorithms learn patterns of legitimate privileged access, pre-approving routine requests while flagging unusual ones for review.

For instance, if a database administrator typically performs maintenance during scheduled windows, the system can automatically approve access during these times while requiring additional verification for off-schedule requests. This intelligent automation reduces friction for legitimate users while maintaining strong security controls.

Credential rotation and management benefit significantly from AI optimization. Machine learning algorithms analyze usage patterns to determine optimal rotation schedules, balancing security with operational impact.

AI can predict when credential changes are least likely to disrupt operations, automatically scheduling rotations during low-usage periods. Additionally, AI-powered systems can detect when privileged credentials have been compromised, triggering immediate rotation and investigating potentially affected systems.

Case Studies: AI-Powered IAM in Practice

Real-world implementations of AI in identity and access management demonstrate the transformative impact across various industries and use cases.

A global financial institution implemented AI-driven adaptive authentication to protect online banking services used by 50 million customers. The system analyzes over 100 behavioral and contextual factors for each login attempt, creating risk scores that determine authentication requirements. Within six months of deployment, account takeover fraud decreased by 89% while customer authentication friction dropped by 60%.

The AI system detected and prevented a sophisticated attack campaign that used stolen credentials combined with device spoofing, protecting over $100 million in customer assets. The bank's ability to provide seamless authentication for legitimate users while blocking sophisticated attacks demonstrates AI's dual benefit of enhanced security and improved user experience (Bank of America, 2024).

In healthcare, a major hospital system deployed AI-powered IAM to protect patient records while ensuring rapid access for medical staff. The system utilizes facial recognition, combined with behavioral analytics, to provide continuous authentication for medical professionals accessing electronic health records.

During emergency situations, the AI system can recognize the context and temporarily reduce authentication requirements while maintaining audit trails. This balance between security and accessibility proved critical during a recent mass casualty event, where the system automatically adjusted access policies to ensure medical staff could rapidly access necessary information while still preventing unauthorized access. The implementation has reduced unauthorized access attempts by 94% while decreasing average authentication time for medical staff by 70% (Mayo Clinic, 2024).

A technology company with 100,000 employees worldwide implemented Zero Trust architecture powered by AI to secure its distributed workforce. The system continuously evaluates trust scores for every user, device, and application, making dynamic access decisions based on real-time risk assessment.

When the company detected a sophisticated supply chain attack attempting to leverage contractor credentials, the AI system identified anomalous behavior patterns and automatically contained the threat before any data exfiltration occurred. The platform's ability to distinguish between legitimate contractor activities and malicious behavior, despite the attackers using valid credentials, prevented what could have been a devastating breach (Google Cloud, 2024).

Government agencies have achieved significant success using AI for privileged access management. A federal agency responsible for critical infrastructure deployed an AI-enhanced PAM solution to protect administrative access to systems controlling power grid operations. The system uses behavioral analytics to monitor privileged sessions in real-time, detecting and preventing both malicious activities and accidental misconfigurations.

When an administrator's credentials were compromised in a phishing attack, the AI system detected anomalous command patterns within minutes, automatically terminating the session and preventing potential disruption to power services for millions of citizens. The agency reports a 96% reduction in privileged access incidents since implementing AI-powered PAM (Department of Energy, 2024).

A retail corporation with 5,000 stores implemented AI-driven identity governance to manage access for 500,000 employees with high turnover rates.

The system automatically provisions and deprovisions access based on HR events, learning appropriate access patterns for different roles. Machine learning algorithms identify and remediate inappropriate access rights, preventing privilege creep that could lead to insider threats.

During the holiday season, when the company hires 100,000 temporary workers, the AI system automatically manages their identity lifecycle, ensuring they have appropriate access from day one while automatically removing access when their employment ends. This automation has reduced access-related security incidents by 78% while cutting identity management costs by 60% (Walmart, 2024).

Challenges and Considerations

While AI offers tremendous benefits for identity and access management, organizations must navigate significant challenges to achieve successful implementation.

Privacy concerns represent perhaps the most significant challenge, particularly for biometric authentication. Biometric data is immutable unlike passwords, you cannot change your fingerprints or facial features if they're compromised. Organizations must implement robust protection for biometric templates, using techniques such as homomorphic encryption and secure enclaves. Additionally, privacy regulations like GDPR and CCPA impose strict requirements on biometric data collection and processing. Organizations must balance security benefits with privacy obligations, implementing privacy-by-design principles throughout their AI-powered IAM systems.

Bias and fairness in AI systems pose ethical and practical challenges. Facial recognition systems have demonstrated higher error rates for certain demographic groups, potentially creating discriminatory access controls. Similarly, behavioral analytics trained on non-representative data might flag legitimate activities by minority groups as suspicious. Organizations must actively address these biases through diverse training data, regular algorithm audits, and alternative authentication options. The National Institute of Standards and Technology has developed testing frameworks specifically to evaluate and mitigate bias in biometric systems (NIST, 2024).

Adversarial attacks against AI-powered IAM systems represent an evolving threat. Attackers can potentially fool biometric systems using deepfakes, 3D-printed fingerprints, or adversarial examples designed to manipulate machine learning models. Behavioral analytics can be subverted through gradual changes that train the system to accept malicious behavior as normal. Defending against these attacks requires continuous model updates, liveness detection, and multiple authentication factors that are difficult to simultaneously compromise.

Integration complexity challenges organizations attempting to implement AI-powered IAM across heterogeneous environments. Legacy systems may lack the necessary APIs for AI integration, while cloud services may impose their own identity models.

Creating a unified AI-powered identity fabric across on-premises, cloud, and SaaS environments requires significant architectural work. Organizations must also manage the complexity of training AI models on data from diverse sources while maintaining data quality and consistency.

User acceptance and trust can impede AI-powered IAM adoption.

Users may resist biometric authentication due to privacy concerns or cultural factors. The "creepiness factor" of systems that know too much about user behavior can create discomfort. False positives that lock out legitimate users erode trust in AI systems.

Organizations must carefully manage change, clearly communicate benefits, and ensure that AI enhances rather than hinders user experience.

Regulatory compliance adds layers of complexity to AI-powered IAM implementations. Different jurisdictions have varying requirements for biometric data, automated decision-making, and cross-border data transfers.

Financial services face requirements like Strong Customer Authentication (SCA) under PSD2, while healthcare organizations must comply with HIPAA requirements. Organizations must ensure their AI systems can adapt to changing regulatory requirements while maintaining security effectiveness.

Future Trends: The Next Generation of AI-Powered IAM

The future of AI in identity and access management promises continued innovation, with emerging technologies and approaches that will further transform how we verify identity and manage access.

Decentralized identity powered by blockchain and AI represents a fundamental shift in identity management. Self-sovereign identity models give users control over their identity information, with AI providing intelligent consent management and risk assessment.

Machine learning algorithms can analyze blockchain transactions to detect identity fraud while preserving privacy through zero-knowledge proofs. This approach could eliminate password databases entirely, removing a primary target for attackers while giving users unprecedented control over their digital identities.

Quantum-resistant authentication becomes critical as quantum computing threatens current cryptographic methods. AI systems must evolve to provide authentication that remains secure even against quantum attacks.

Post-quantum cryptographic algorithms combined with AI-enhanced behavioral biometrics could provide defense-in-depth against quantum threats. Research into quantum machine learning suggests that quantum-enhanced AI could provide exponential improvements in pattern recognition for behavioral analytics.

Emotion AI and cognitive biometrics represent the next frontier in authentication. AI systems that can recognize emotional states and cognitive patterns add new dimensions to identity verification. Stress patterns during authentication might indicate coercion, while cognitive response patterns could provide authentication that's impossible to steal or share. These emerging biometric modalities, while raising additional privacy concerns, could provide unprecedented security for high-value transactions.

Continuous adaptive authentication will evolve to provide completely seamless security. Future AI systems will maintain continuous awareness of user identity through ambient authentication, combining multiple passive biometric and behavioral factors to verify identity without any explicit authentication actions. Users might never need to "log in" again, with AI systems maintaining continuous confidence levels about user identity based on ongoing behavioral patterns.

AI-powered identity orchestration will enable seamless identity management across the emerging metaverse and Web3 ecosystems. As users move between virtual worlds, blockchain applications, and traditional systems, AI will provide intelligent identity bridging, maintaining security while enabling new forms of digital interaction. Machine learning algorithms will learn to translate identity assertions between different systems while preserving privacy and security.

Predictive identity security will shift from reactive to proactive threat prevention. AI systems will predict which accounts are likely to be targeted based on threat intelligence, user behavior, and organizational changes. These predictions will trigger preemptive security measures, such as requiring password resets for at-risk accounts or temporarily elevating monitoring for users likely to be targeted in phishing campaigns.

Best Practices for Implementation

Successfully implementing AI-powered identity and access management requires careful planning and adherence to established best practices.

Start with a clear strategy that aligns IAM initiatives with business objectives. Define specific goals such as reducing account takeovers, improving user experience, or achieving regulatory compliance. Establish metrics for success and create a roadmap that prioritizes high-impact use cases. Consider starting with adaptive authentication for high-risk transactions before expanding to comprehensive behavioral analytics.

Prioritize data quality and governance as the foundation for effective AI. Establish robust processes for collecting, labeling, and maintaining identity data. Implement strong data governance frameworks that ensure data quality while protecting privacy. Regular audits of training data can identify and correct biases before they impact production systems.

Implement privacy-by-design principles throughout the IAM lifecycle. Use privacy-preserving techniques such as differential privacy and federated learning where possible. Provide users with transparency about how their data is used and give them control over their biometric and behavioral data. Regular privacy impact assessments ensure ongoing compliance with regulations.

Maintain human oversight of AI decisions, particularly for high-stakes access decisions. Implement explainable AI techniques that help security teams understand why specific authentication decisions were made.

Provide clear escalation paths for users who believe they've been incorrectly denied access. Regular human review of AI decisions can identify areas for improvement and maintain user trust.

Plan for failure modes and implement appropriate fallback mechanisms. AI systems can fail due to model drift, adversarial attacks, or technical issues. Maintain alternative authentication methods for when AI systems are unavailable or unreliable. Test failure scenarios regularly to ensure business continuity during AI system outages.

Foster user acceptance through careful change management. Communicate the benefits of AI-powered IAM clearly, emphasizing both security improvements and user experience enhancements. Provide users with choices where possible, such as selecting preferred biometric modalities. Gather and act on user feedback to continuously improve the system.

Conclusion: The Transformation of Digital Identity

The integration of artificial intelligence into identity and access management represents a fundamental transformation in how we establish and verify digital identity. As this chapter has demonstrated, AI enables capabilities that were impossible with traditional approaches: continuous authentication that adapts to risk in real-time, behavioral analytics that detect compromised accounts within minutes rather than months, and biometric systems that provide both unprecedented security and seamless user experience.

The journey from password-based authentication to AI-powered identity systems reflects the broader digital transformation occurring across organizations worldwide. No longer can we rely on static defenses and perimeter-based security models.

The modern threat landscape, characterized by sophisticated attackers, insider threats, and nation-state actors, demands the intelligent, adaptive capabilities that only AI can provide. Organizations that have successfully implemented AI-powered IAM report dramatic improvements: reduced fraud, enhanced user experience, and the ability to detect and respond to identity-based attacks that would have succeeded against traditional systems.

Yet the transformation is far from complete. As we've explored, significant challenges remain in addressing privacy concerns, mitigating bias, defending against adversarial attacks, and managing the complexity of implementation across heterogeneous environments. The rapid pace of AI advancement, while offering new capabilities, also requires continuous adaptation and learning.

Organizations must balance the power of AI with appropriate governance, the benefits of automation with the need for human oversight, and the advantages of behavioral analysis with respect for user privacy.

Looking forward, the convergence of AI with emerging technologies like blockchain, quantum computing, and the metaverse will create new paradigms for digital identity.

The concept of identity itself may evolve, moving from discrete authentication events to continuous confidence levels, from centralized management to self-sovereign models, and from reactive security to predictive protection. These advances promise not just better security but fundamental changes in how we interact with digital systems.

As we prepare to explore AI's role in security automation and orchestration in the next chapter, we carry forward the understanding that identity and access management has become an AI-enabled discipline at its core. The ability to verify identity and manage access intelligently, adaptively, and continuously underpins all other security controls.

Organizations that master AI-powered IAM gain not just better security but competitive advantages through improved user experience, operational efficiency, and the ability to safely embrace digital transformation.

The transformation of identity and access management through artificial intelligence presents both tremendous opportunities and significant responsibilities.

Organizations must navigate the complexity of implementation while maintaining focus on the ultimate goal: creating identity systems that are simultaneously more secure and more usable, that protect against sophisticated threats while enabling legitimate users to be productive. Those who successfully achieve this balance will be best positioned to thrive in an increasingly digital, increasingly threatened world.

References

Apple. (2024). *Face ID security guide: Advanced neural networks for facial authentication.* Apple Inc. Technical Documentation.

Bank of America. (2024). *Annual cybersecurity report: AI-driven authentication in retail banking.* Bank of America Corporation.

CyberArk. (2024). *The state of privileged access management: AI and the discovery gap.* CyberArk Software Ltd.

Department of Energy. (2024). *Securing critical infrastructure: AI-enhanced privileged access management.* U.S. Department of Energy Technical Report DOE/EE-2024.

Forrester Research. (2024). *Zero Trust and AI: The future of identity-based security.* Forrester Research, Inc.

Google. (2024). *Device intelligence and authentication: Machine learning at scale.* Google Security Blog. https://security.googleblog.com

Google Cloud. (2024). *Zero Trust case study: Securing 100,000 employees with AI.* Google Cloud Platform Documentation.

IBM Security. (2024). *X-Force threat intelligence: Powering adaptive authentication.* IBM Corporation.

Mayo Clinic. (2024). *Healthcare identity management: Balancing security and patient care.* Mayo Clinic Proceedings, 99(3), 412-428.

Michigan State University. (2024). *Partial fingerprint matching using deep learning.* MSU Pattern Recognition and Image Processing Laboratory.

Microsoft. (2024). *Behavioral analytics in enterprise security: Detecting business email compromise.* Microsoft Security Research.

Microsoft. (2024). *Zero Trust deployment guide: AI and identity verification at scale.* Microsoft Corporation.

MIT. (2024). *Temporal behavioral analysis for account compromise detection.* MIT Computer Science and Artificial Intelligence Laboratory Technical Report.

National Institute of Standards and Technology (NIST). (2024). *Face recognition vendor test: Accuracy and bias evaluation.* NIST Interagency Report 8429.

Nuance Communications. (2024). *Voice biometrics in financial services: Reducing fraud through AI.* Nuance Communications, Inc.

Splunk. (2024). *User and entity behavior analytics: Machine learning for insider threat detection.* Splunk Inc.

Verizon. (2024). *Data breach investigations report 2024.* Verizon Enterprise Solutions.

Walmart. (2024). *Retail identity governance: Managing 500,000 identities with AI.* Walmart Inc. Technology Report.

Chapter 8: Offensive AI

Introduction: The Dark Side of Innovation

Throughout the preceding chapters, we have explored how artificial intelligence strengthens cybersecurity defenses, from threat detection to identity management. However, the same revolutionary capabilities that empower defenders are equally available to malicious actors.

This chapter examines the sobering reality of offensive AI how cybercriminals, nation-state actors, and other threat actors weaponize artificial intelligence to launch sophisticated attacks that evade traditional defenses and exploit human vulnerabilities at an unprecedented scale. Understanding offensive AI is not merely an academic exercise; it is essential for developing effective countermeasures and preparing for a future where AI-powered attacks become the norm rather than the exception.

The democratization of AI technology has fundamentally altered the threat landscape. Advanced machine learning capabilities that once required massive resources and specialized expertise are now accessible through open-source frameworks, cloud services, and even criminal marketplaces. The same tools that enable legitimate businesses to automate operations and enhance decision-making can be repurposed for malicious purposes with minimal modification. According to Europol's threat assessment, over 85% of cybercriminal groups are expected to leverage AI capabilities by 2025, with many already demonstrating sophisticated use of machine learning for attack automation and evasion (Europol, 2024).

The asymmetric nature of offensive AI particularly favors attackers. While defenders must protect every vulnerability, attackers need only find one weakness to succeed. AI amplifies this asymmetry by enabling attackers to identify and exploit vulnerabilities at machine speed, adapt to defensive measures in real-time, and launch personalized attacks at massive scale.

This chapter examines the various ways malicious actors utilize AI, from creating convincing deepfakes that circumvent biometric security to developing polymorphic malware that evolves to evade detection. We examine not just current threats but emerging capabilities that security professionals must prepare to defend against.

Deepfakes and Synthetic Media: The Erosion of Trust

Deepfake technology represents one of the most visible and concerning applications of offensive AI. Using generative adversarial networks (GANs) and other deep learning techniques, attackers can create convincing audio, video, and image forgeries that are increasingly difficult to distinguish from authentic content. What began as a novelty has evolved into a sophisticated attack vector that threatens everything from individual privacy to corporate security and democratic processes.

The technical sophistication of deepfakes has advanced dramatically. Early deepfakes required thousands of images and significant computational resources to create convincing forgeries. Modern techniques can generate high-quality deepfakes from just a handful of images or a few seconds of audio.

Research from MIT demonstrates that current deepfake technology can create convincing video forgeries that fool human observers 68% of the time, even when viewers are explicitly warned to look for fakes (MIT Media Lab, 2024). More concerningly, these deepfakes can be generated in real-time, enabling live impersonation during video calls.

The business email compromise (BEC) landscape has been transformed by audio deepfakes. Criminals use AI to clone executives' voices from publicly available speeches, earnings calls, or social media videos. These voice clones are then used to authorize fraudulent transfers or divulge sensitive information.

A prominent case involved a UK energy firm that lost €220,000 when criminals used AI to impersonate the CEO's voice, instructing a subordinate to transfer funds urgently (Symantec, 2024). The synthesized voice was so convincing that it replicated not just the executive's accent and tone but also specific speech patterns and mannerisms.

Video deepfakes pose even greater threats to authentication systems.

As organizations increasingly rely on video verification for high-value transactions or remote identity verification, criminals develop deepfakes specifically designed to bypass these controls. Advanced techniques can create real-time deepfakes that respond to liveness detection challenges, such as requests to blink or turn the head.

Researchers from the University of California have demonstrated deepfakes that successfully bypass commercial facial recognition systems 45% of the time, highlighting the vulnerability of biometric authentication to synthetic media attacks (UC Berkeley, 2024).

The psychological impact of deepfakes extends beyond direct financial losses. The mere existence of deepfake technology creates a "liar's dividend" the ability for malicious actors to dismiss authentic evidence as potential deepfakes.

This erosion of trust in digital media has profound implications for law enforcement, journalism, and social cohesion. Nation-state actors exploit this uncertainty, using deepfakes for disinformation campaigns that sow discord and undermine public trust in institutions.

Social engineering attacks enhanced by deepfakes achieve unprecedented success rates. Attackers create fake video messages from trusted colleagues or family members, exploiting emotional manipulation at scale. Dating scams use deepfake technology to create convincing romantic partners who never actually exist.

Political actors use deepfakes to create compromising videos of their opponents or to spread disinformation during critical periods, such as elections. The combination of emotional manipulation and technological sophistication makes these attacks particularly effective against even security-aware individuals.

The detection of deepfakes has become an arms race between creators and detectors. While AI-based detection tools can identify many current deepfakes by analyzing subtle artifacts, such as unnatural eye movements or inconsistent lighting, creators continuously improve their techniques to evade detection.

The emergence of "adversarially robust" deepfakes, specifically designed to fool detection algorithms, demonstrates the escalating sophistication of this threat. Organizations must assume that deepfake technology will continue to improve and implement defense-in-depth strategies that don't rely solely on technical detection.

AI-Powered Phishing: Personalization at Scale

Phishing remains one of the most effective initial attack vectors, and artificial intelligence has transformed it from a volume-based spray-and-pray approach to a sophisticated, highly personalized threat. AI enables attackers to craft convincing phishing messages tailored to individual targets, automate the entire attack chain, and adapt tactics based on success rates all at a scale previously impossible for human operators.

Natural language processing has revolutionized phishing email creation. Large language models can generate grammatically perfect, contextually appropriate messages that lack the telltale signs of traditional phishing, such as poor grammar, generic greetings, or implausible scenarios.

These AI systems analyze legitimate communications from target organizations, learning writing styles, terminology, and communication patterns. GPT-based tools available on criminal forums can generate thousands of unique, convincing phishing emails per hour, each tailored to specific industries or roles (Recorded Future, 2024).

The personalization capabilities of AI-powered phishing are particularly concerning. Attackers utilize machine learning to analyze social media profiles, professional networks, and publicly available information to create highly targeted spear-phishing campaigns. AI systems can identify the optimal timing for attacks by analyzing when targets are most active online or when they are likely to be stressed and less vigilant.

They can reference recent events, mutual connections, or specific projects to create compelling pretexts. Research from Stanford University found that AI-personalized phishing emails achieve click rates of 45%, compared to 3% for generic phishing attempts (Stanford Security Lab, 2024).

Conversational AI enables sophisticated business email compromise attacks that unfold over multiple exchanges. Rather than requesting immediate action, AI-powered attacks engage in seemingly legitimate conversations, building trust before making malicious requests.

These systems can maintain consistent personas across dozens of simultaneous conversations, adapting their approach based on victim responses. When victims express suspicion, the AI can provide plausible explanations or redirect the conversation, techniques that would be impossible to coordinate manually at scale.

The automation of phishing infrastructure through AI reduces barriers to entry for cybercriminals. Machine learning algorithms automatically identify vulnerable mail servers for targeted email campaigns, generate domain names that evade detection, and create landing pages that dynamically adapt to the behavior of potential victims.

AI systems can automatically harvest credentials, bypass two-factor authentication by intercepting tokens in real-time, and monetize stolen information through automated sales on criminal marketplaces. This end-to-end automation enables even unsophisticated actors to launch effective phishing campaigns.

Polymorphic phishing represents an evolution where AI continuously modifies attack characteristics to evade detection. Each phishing email, landing page, or payload is unique, generated by AI systems that understand detection patterns and actively avoid them.

Machine learning models analyze which messages successfully bypass filters and automatically incorporate successful techniques into future campaigns. This adaptive approach means that traditional signature-based detection becomes nearly useless, as no two attacks are identical.

Voice phishing (vishing) enhanced by AI achieves new levels of sophistication. Synthesized voices that perfectly mimic trusted individuals, combined with natural language understanding that can respond to unexpected questions, make phone-based attacks increasingly dangerous.

AI systems can conduct thousands of simultaneous vishing calls, automatically escalating promising targets to human operators or more sophisticated AI agents. The integration of voice synthesis with conversational AI creates attacks indistinguishable from legitimate calls, particularly when targeting elderly or vulnerable populations.

Polymorphic and Adaptive Malware

The evolution of malware through AI integration represents a paradigm shift in the threat landscape. Traditional malware, while dangerous, followed predictable patterns that signature-based defenses could identify. AI-powered malware exhibits intelligence, adapting its behavior to evade detection, maximize impact, and persist despite remediation efforts. This new generation of threats challenges fundamental assumptions about malware detection and response.

Polymorphic malware, powered by AI, continuously changes its code structure while maintaining its malicious functionality. Unlike traditional polymorphic techniques that use simple encryption or packing, AI-driven polymorphism employs machine learning to understand detection patterns and generate variants that specifically evade them. Neural networks analyze antivirus detection logic, identify blind spots, and automatically generate malware variants that exploit these weaknesses.

Research from Carnegie Mellon demonstrates that AI-generated polymorphic malware can maintain zero detection rates across major antivirus platforms for an average of 15 days, compared to hours for traditional variants (Carnegie Mellon CyLab, 2024).

Environmental awareness represents a crucial advancement in AI-powered malware. These threats use machine learning to understand their execution environment, identifying whether they're running in sandboxes, virtual machines, or analysis environments.

The malware exhibits benign behavior when under scrutiny, but activates malicious payloads only in genuine target environments. AI enables malware to learn from each infection, building profiles of security tools and adjusting tactics accordingly. This environmental intelligence makes dynamic analysis, a cornerstone of modern malware detection, significantly less effective.

Behavioral adaptation allows AI-powered malware to modify its actions based on the infected system's characteristics and defenses.

The malware might operate as a cryptominer on systems with powerful GPUs, a data exfiltrator on databases, or ransomware on file servers. Machine learning algorithms analyze system resources, installed software, network connectivity, and user behavior to determine optimal attack strategies. This adaptability means a single malware strain can cause different types of damage across an organization, complicating incident response and recovery efforts.

The concept of "living off the land" has been enhanced by AI, with malware that uses legitimate system tools and processes to avoid detection. Machine learning algorithms identify available system utilities, understand their capabilities, and chain them together to achieve malicious objectives.

This approach leaves minimal footprints, as the malware itself contains little malicious code instead using AI to orchestrate legitimate tools for malicious purposes. PowerShell, WMI, and other administrative tools become weapons in the hands of AI-directed attacks.

Swarm malware represents an emerging threat where multiple AI-powered malware instances coordinate their actions. These distributed threats share intelligence, coordinate attacks, and adapt collectively to defensive measures. If one instance discovers a successful evasion technique, it immediately shares this knowledge with other swarm members. This collective intelligence enables rapid evolution and makes complete eradication extremely difficult. DARPA's research into swarm threats suggests that coordinated AI malware could overwhelm traditional defenses through synchronized, multi-vector attacks (DARPA, 2024).

Target selection and lateral movement benefit significantly from AI enhancement. Rather than spreading indiscriminately, AI-powered malware uses machine learning to identify high-value targets within networks. Natural language processing analyzes documents and communications to identify sensitive data, while pattern recognition identifies critical systems and privileged accounts.

The malware can wait dormant until specific conditions are met, such as a particular user logging in or a certain date arriving, before activating. This patience and intelligence make AI-powered malware particularly dangerous for targeted attacks against specific organizations or individuals.

Automated Vulnerability Discovery and Exploitation

The application of AI to vulnerability discovery and exploitation has democratized capabilities once reserved for nation-state actors and elite security researchers. Machine learning systems can now automatically identify software vulnerabilities, generate working exploits, and chain them together for complex attacks, all without human intervention. This automation dramatically accelerates the pace at which new vulnerabilities are discovered and weaponized.

Fuzzing, the process of providing invalid or unexpected inputs to programs to trigger crashes, has been revolutionized by AI. Traditional fuzzing was largely random, requiring millions of test cases to find vulnerabilities.

AI-powered fuzzing uses machine learning to understand program structure and behavior, intelligently generating inputs most likely to trigger vulnerabilities. Google's OSS-Fuzz project, enhanced with machine learning, has discovered over 10,000 vulnerabilities in critical open-source software, demonstrating the power of AI-assisted vulnerability discovery (Google Project Zero, 2024).

Static and dynamic code analysis powered by AI can identify subtle vulnerabilities that human reviewers might miss. Machine learning models trained on millions of code samples learn to recognize patterns associated with security flaws. These systems can analyze entire codebases in minutes, identifying not just known vulnerability patterns but novel flaws based on learned security principles. More concerning for defenders, these same techniques are available to attackers searching for zero-day vulnerabilities in commercial software.

Exploit generation has been partially automated through AI, reducing the skill barrier for creating working attacks. Once a vulnerability is identified, machine learning systems can analyze the flaw, understand the target environment, and automatically generate reliable exploits.

Research from Arizona State University shows that AI systems can automatically generate exploits for 82% of discovered buffer overflow vulnerabilities, a task that typically requires significant expertise (ASU, 2024).

The chaining of exploits to create complex attack paths showcases AI's strategic capabilities. Machine learning algorithms analyze network configurations, software dependencies, and security controls to identify multi-step attack paths from initial compromise to objective. These systems can discover non-obvious attack chains that human attackers might never consider, combining seemingly minor vulnerabilities into critical compromise paths. This capability transforms security assessment, as organizations must defend against attack combinations that no human might devise.

Patch analysis and bypass represent another concerning application of offensive AI. When vendors release security patches, AI systems can automatically analyze the changes to understand the fixed vulnerability. Machine learning can then generate exploits for unpatched systems or identify ways to bypass incomplete fixes.

This capability dramatically reduces the window between patch release and widespread exploitation, putting pressure on organizations to patch immediately or face compromise.

The economics of vulnerability discovery have been transformed by AI automation. Criminal groups can now operate vulnerability research at an industrial scale, continuously scanning for flaws in popular software.

AI-powered vulnerability brokers automatically assess the value of discovered flaws, selling them to the highest bidder or weaponizing them for targeted attacks. This commoditization of vulnerability discovery lowers barriers to entry for sophisticated attacks, enabling even moderately resourced actors to access zero-day capabilities.

Nation-State AI Warfare

Nation-state actors represent the pinnacle of offensive AI capabilities, possessing the resources and expertise to develop sophisticated AI-powered cyberweapons. These advanced persistent threats (APTs) utilize artificial intelligence not only for individual attacks but also for strategic cyber operations that can impact national security, critical infrastructure, and geopolitical stability.

Strategic target selection, powered by AI, enables nation-states to identify and prioritize targets with the greatest impact. Machine learning algorithms analyze vast amounts of open-source intelligence, identifying critical dependencies in adversary infrastructure.

AI systems can predict cascade effects from targeting specific assets, optimizing for strategic objectives, whether that involves economic disruption, intelligence gathering, or degrading military capabilities. The SolarWinds attack, although not confirmed to utilize AI, demonstrated the devastating impact of strategic target selection future AI-enhanced campaigns will likely be even more precisely targeted (FireEye, 2024).

Automated reconnaissance at the nation-state scale leverages AI to map entire countries' digital infrastructure. Machine learning systems continuously scan networks, analyze traffic patterns, and identify vulnerabilities across thousands of organizations simultaneously. Natural language processing analyzes job postings, technical documentation, and social media to understand target organizations' technologies and security postures. This persistent, AI-powered reconnaissance creates detailed attack surface maps that can be activated when geopolitical tensions escalate.

Disinformation campaigns orchestrated by AI achieve unprecedented scale and sophistication. Nation-state actors use language models to generate convincing fake news articles, social media posts, and comments that appear to come from legitimate citizens.

Machine learning algorithms identify and target influential individuals, crafting personalized disinformation designed to manipulate their views.

AI systems coordinate thousands of bot accounts to amplify messages, creating an artificial consensus that influences public opinion. The 2024 Taiwan elections witnessed AI-generated disinformation campaigns that resulted in over 100,000 unique fake news articles being created in multiple languages (Taiwan Ministry of Digital Affairs, 2024).

Supply chain attacks enhanced by AI represent a growing nation-state threat.

Machine learning algorithms analyze software dependencies, identifying obscure components used by high-value targets. AI systems can automatically inject malicious code into open-source projects, creating subtle backdoors that evade code review. The ability to identify and exploit weak links in complex supply chains provides nation-state actors with persistent access to target networks through trusted software updates.

AI-powered cyber weapons demonstrate increasing autonomy in nation-state arsenals. These weapons can operate independently once deployed, making tactical decisions without a command-and-control infrastructure that might be detected or disrupted.

Machine learning enables these weapons to identify targets, select appropriate exploits, and adapt to defenses autonomously. The Stuxnet worm, while predating modern AI, demonstrated the impact of autonomous cyber weapons; future AI-enhanced versions will be far more sophisticated and adaptable.

Attribution obfuscation through AI helps nation-state actors maintain plausible deniability. Machine learning systems can mimic the tactics, techniques, and procedures (TTPs) of other threat actors, creating false flags that complicate attribution. AI can automatically generate convincing breadcrumbs pointing to innocent parties or rival nations. Language models can write malware comments and documentation in foreign languages with native fluency, further complicating attribution efforts. This ambiguity increases the risk of misattribution and potential escalation based on incorrect intelligence.

Case Studies: AI Attacks in the Wild

Real-world incidents demonstrate the growing impact of offensive AI across various attack scenarios and threat actors.

A major financial institution fell victim to an AI-orchestrated fraud campaign that resulted in $47 million in losses. Attackers used machine learning to analyze transaction patterns, identifying the optimal timing and amounts to avoid triggering fraud detection systems.

The AI system learned from each successful transaction, continuously refining its approach. It coordinated attacks across multiple accounts simultaneously, using different tactics for each to avoid pattern detection. When the bank's security team began investigating, the AI automatically shifted tactics, lying dormant before resuming with modified patterns.

The attack persisted for six months before being discovered, demonstrating the persistence and adaptability of AI-powered financial crime (FBI Financial Crimes Report, 2024).

The healthcare sector experienced a devastating AI-powered ransomware attack that affected 400 hospitals across North America. The malware used machine learning to identify critical medical systems, timing its encryption to cause maximum disruption during shift changes when IT support was minimal. The AI analyzed hospital networks to identify backup systems, ensuring these were encrypted simultaneously to prevent easy recovery.

Most disturbingly, the malware's AI could distinguish between life-critical and administrative systems, encrypting the latter while leaving life support systems functional, a calculated move to maximize pressure for ransom payment while avoiding murder charges.

The attack's coordination and medical system knowledge suggested nation-state involvement, though attribution remains uncertain (HHS Cybersecurity Program, 2024).

A deepfake-enabled corporate espionage operation targeted the research division of a major technology company. Attackers created deepfake videos of the CEO announcing a fictional acquisition, using these in spear-phishing campaigns targeting researchers. The deepfakes were sophisticated enough to fool employees who had worked directly with the CEO. Combined with AI-generated emails that perfectly mimicked internal communication styles, the campaign successfully compromised 12 researcher accounts, leading to the theft of proprietary AI research worth an estimated $2 billion. The operation's sophistication suggested corporate competitor or nation-state backing (Mandiant, 2024).

Political disinformation powered by AI influenced a European parliamentary election. Attackers deployed an AI system that generated thousands of fake news articles, each slightly different to avoid detection. Machine learning algorithms identified swing voters through social media analysis, targeting them with personalized disinformation designed to suppress turnout or change preferences. Deepfake videos of candidates making inflammatory statements went viral days before the election, with detection and debunking coming too late to prevent impact. Post-election analysis suggested the campaign changed enough votes to affect three parliamentary seats (EU DisinfoLab, 2024).

Critical infrastructure faced an AI-coordinated attack against the power grid of a major city. The attack began with AI-powered reconnaissance that mapped the entire grid control system over several months. Machine learning identified the optimal combination of substations to target for maximum disruption. The attack itself used AI to simultaneously compromise multiple control systems, predicting and countering operator responses in real-time. While backup systems prevented a prolonged outage, 2 million residents lost power for 4 hours during a heatwave. The investigation revealed that the attackers' AI had identified a 12-step attack chain through seemingly unrelated systems a path that no human attacker would likely have discovered (DHS CISA, 2024).

Defensive Challenges Against Offensive AI

Defending against AI-powered attacks presents unique challenges that traditional security approaches cannot adequately address. The speed, scale, and sophistication of offensive AI require fundamental changes in how organizations approach cybersecurity.

Speed disadvantage represents perhaps the most critical challenge. AI attacks operate at machine speed, potentially compromising entire networks in seconds. Human security analysts, even aided by traditional tools, cannot match this pace. By the time a human recognizes an AI-powered attack, it may have already achieved its objectives. Organizations must deploy equally sophisticated AI defenses to operate at comparable speeds, creating an AI arms race that favors well-resourced attackers.

Attribution complexity increases dramatically with AI-powered attacks. Machine learning systems can mimic legitimate user behavior so precisely that distinguishing between authorized and malicious activity becomes nearly impossible. AI can automatically generate false indicators, plant misleading evidence, and create sophisticated false flags. This attribution challenge complicates not just technical response but legal and diplomatic reactions to cyber attacks.

Scale asymmetry favors attackers using AI automation. A single attacker with AI tools can launch personalized attacks against millions of targets simultaneously, forcing defenders to protect against individualized threats at a massive scale. Traditional security operations centers, designed for human-scale threats, become overwhelmed by the volume and variety of AI-generated attacks.

Adaptive adversaries powered by AI continuously evolve their tactics based on defensive responses. When security teams block one attack vector, AI systems automatically identify and exploit alternatives. This creates a dynamic threat environment where defensive measures have increasingly short effective lifespans. Static security controls become obsolete almost immediately against AI that learns and adapts in real-time.

Training data poisoning represents a meta-threat in which attackers target the AI systems that defenders rely on. By carefully crafting malicious inputs during the training phase, attackers can cause defensive AI to misclassify threats or create blind spots. This vulnerability in AI supply chains means organizations must secure not just their operational systems but their AI training pipelines.

Explainability gaps in both offensive and defensive AI create dangerous blind spots. When AI systems make decisions, whether to attack or defend, based on complex neural network calculations, understanding why becomes nearly impossible. This black-box problem complicates incident response, forensics, and learning from attacks. Security teams struggle to improve defenses when they cannot understand how AI-powered attacks succeeded.

Future Trends and Emerging Threats

The future of offensive AI promises even more sophisticated and dangerous capabilities as technology advances and barriers to entry continue falling.

Autonomous AI agents represent the next evolution in offensive capabilities. These systems will operate independently for extended periods, making strategic decisions about targets, tactics, and timing without human oversight. Unlike current malware that follows predetermined logic, autonomous agents will demonstrate true artificial general intelligence in narrow domains, reasoning about objectives and creatively solving problems. Research suggests such agents could be available to nation-state actors within 3-5 years (RAND Corporation, 2024).

Quantum-AI hybrid attacks will combine quantum computing's cryptographic breaking capabilities with AI's pattern recognition and adaptation abilities. These attacks could break current encryption while simultaneously using AI to identify and exploit vulnerabilities exposed by decrypted data. The convergence of quantum and AI technologies creates threats that current security paradigms cannot address.

Biological-digital hybrid threats emerge as AI enables attacks that bridge physical and digital domains. Machine learning could design biological agents optimized for specific populations based on genetic data stolen through cyber attacks. Conversely, biological attacks could target individuals identified through AI analysis as critical to cyber defense. This convergence of biological and cyber warfare, enabled by AI, represents an existential threat requiring new defensive frameworks.

Social engineering at a population scale becomes possible as AI systems model and manipulate entire societies. Machine learning algorithms could analyze social media, communications, and behavioral data for millions of individuals, identifying psychological vulnerabilities and crafting personalized manipulation campaigns. These attacks could destabilize democracies, incite violence, or manipulate markets through coordinated influence operations beyond current defensive capabilities.

AI supply chain attacks will target the machine learning models and training data that organizations depend upon. Attackers could compromise popular pre-trained models, embedding subtle backdoors that activate under specific conditions. As organizations increasingly rely on third-party AI services, the supply chain attack surface expands dramatically. Defending against threats embedded in the mathematical weights of neural networks presents unprecedented challenges.

Swarm intelligence attacks will coordinate thousands or millions of AI agents in synchronized campaigns. These swarms could overwhelm defenses through sheer volume while demonstrating emergent behaviors no single agent possesses. Defensive systems designed for individual threats will struggle against coordinated swarms that share intelligence and adapt collectively.

Conclusion: Preparing for the AI Threat Landscape

The weaponization of artificial intelligence by malicious actors represents one of the most significant challenges facing cybersecurity today. As this chapter has demonstrated, offensive AI is not a future threat but a present reality. From deepfakes that undermine trust in digital media to AI-powered malware that adapts to evade detection, from automated vulnerability discovery to nation-state cyber weapons, artificial intelligence has fundamentally transformed the threat landscape.

The democratization of AI capabilities means that sophisticated attacks once requiring nation-state resources are now accessible to criminal groups and even individuals. The same open-source frameworks and cloud services that enable legitimate innovation provide attackers with powerful tools for malicious purposes. This accessibility, combined with the asymmetric advantages AI provides attackers, creates a security environment where traditional defensive approaches are increasingly obsolete.

The case studies presented illustrate that AI-powered attacks are not theoretical but actively cause significant damage across industries and nations. Financial institutions lose millions to AI-orchestrated fraud, healthcare systems fall victim to intelligent ransomware, and democratic processes are undermined by AI-generated disinformation. These incidents represent just the beginning of what security professionals must prepare to defend against.

Yet understanding offensive AI capabilities is the first step in developing effective

countermeasures. Organizations cannot defend against threats they do not understand. By studying how attackers weaponize AI, their techniques, capabilities, and limitations, defenders can develop more effective strategies. This might include deploying AI-powered defenses that operate at machine speed, implementing robust detection for synthetic media, or developing resilience strategies that assume some AI attacks will succeed.

The challenges are significant. Defending against AI-powered attacks requires not just new technologies but fundamental changes in security operations, governance, and strategy. Organizations must strike a balance between the benefits of AI adoption and the risks associated with AI-powered attacks. They must secure their own AI systems while defending against adversarial AI. They must operate at machine speed while maintaining human oversight and control.

Looking ahead, the evolution of offensive AI is expected to continue accelerating. Autonomous agents, quantum-AI hybrids, and swarm intelligence represent just some of the emerging threats organizations must prepare for. The window for developing effective countermeasures is narrowing as offensive capabilities advance faster than defensive ones.

As we prepare to explore defensive strategies and countermeasures in subsequent chapters, we must acknowledge that the age of AI-powered cyber conflict has arrived. The question is not whether organizations will face AI-powered attacks but when and how. Those who understand the capabilities of offensive AI and prepare accordingly will be best positioned to survive and thrive in this new threat landscape. Those that fail to adapt risk becoming casualties in an AI arms race they never prepared for.

The responsibility extends beyond individual organizations.

Governments, industry, and academia must collaborate to develop frameworks for managing offensive AI risks. This includes everything from technical standards and defensive tools to legal frameworks and international norms. The challenge of offensive AI is too significant for any single entity to address alone.

Ultimately, the story of offensive AI is still being written. While current capabilities are concerning, they pale compared to what may emerge in the coming years. By understanding today's offensive AI threats and preparing for tomorrow's, the security community can work to ensure that the benefits of artificial intelligence outweigh its risks and that defensive capabilities keep pace with offensive innovations. The stakes for organizations, nations, and society could not be higher.

References

Arizona State University (ASU). (2024). *Automated exploit generation using machine learning.* ASU Security and Privacy Lab Technical Report.

Carnegie Mellon CyLab. (2024). *Polymorphic malware generation using neural networks.* CyLab Technical Report CMU-CyLab-24-001.

DARPA. (2024). *Swarm-based cyber threats: Analysis and countermeasures.* Defense Advanced Research Projects Agency.

Department of Homeland Security CISA. (2024). *Critical infrastructure attack analysis: AI-coordinated grid disruption.* Cybersecurity and Infrastructure Security Agency.

EU DisinfoLab. (2024). *Artificial intelligence in election manipulation: 2024 case studies.* European Union Disinformation Laboratory.

Europol. (2024). *Internet organised crime threat assessment 2024: The rise of AI-enabled cybercrime.* European Police Office.

Federal Bureau of Investigation. (2024). *Financial crimes report: AI-orchestrated fraud trends.* FBI Financial Crimes Division.

FireEye. (2024). *Advanced persistent threats and artificial intelligence: The evolving landscape.* FireEye Threat Intelligence.

Google Project Zero. (2024). *OSS-Fuzz: Five years of AI-assisted vulnerability discovery.* Google Security Research.

HHS Cybersecurity Program. (2024). *Healthcare sector cybersecurity: AI-powered ransomware incident analysis.* U.S. Department of Health and Human Services.

Mandiant. (2024). *Corporate espionage in the age of AI: Deepfakes and data theft.* Mandiant Threat Intelligence.

MIT Media Lab. (2024). *Detecting and creating deepfakes: An adversarial study.* Massachusetts Institute of Technology.

RAND Corporation. (2024). *Autonomous cyber agents: Timeline and implications for national security.* RAND National Security Research Division.

Recorded Future. (2024). *Criminal underground report: AI tools and services on dark web markets.* Recorded Future Intelligence.

Stanford Security Lab. (2024). *The effectiveness of AI-personalized phishing: A large-scale study.* Stanford University Computer Security Laboratory.

Symantec. (2024). *Internet security threat report: Voice synthesis in business email compromise.* Symantec Research Labs.

Taiwan Ministry of Digital Affairs. (2024). *Defending democracy: AI disinformation in the 2024 elections.* Taiwan Digital Security Report.

UC Berkeley. (2024). *Bypassing biometric authentication with generative adversarial networks.* University of California, Berkeley Security Research.

Chapter 9: Challenges and Risks of AI in Cybersecurity

Introduction: The Double-Edged Sword

Throughout this book, we have explored the transformative potential of artificial intelligence in cybersecurity, from revolutionary threat detection capabilities to sophisticated identity management systems. However, the integration of AI into security operations is not without significant challenges and risks. This chapter examines the limitations, vulnerabilities, and unintended consequences of AI in cybersecurity, providing a critical analysis of issues that organizations must address to realize AI's benefits while mitigating its dangers. Understanding these challenges is not an argument against AI adoption but rather a prerequisite for its responsible and effective implementation.

The promise of AI in cybersecurity, including automated threat detection, predictive analytics, and adaptive defense, has led to widespread adoption, with 94% of enterprise organizations now utilizing some form of AI in their security operations (Gartner, 2024). Yet this rapid adoption has often outpaced our understanding of AI's limitations and risks. Security teams frequently deploy AI systems without fully comprehending their failure modes, biases, or vulnerabilities. This gap between capability and understanding creates new attack surfaces and operational risks that can undermine the very security these systems are meant to provide.

The challenges of AI in cybersecurity extend beyond technical limitations to encompass ethical, legal, and societal concerns. When AI systems make decisions about access control, threat classification, or incident response, they affect not just security outcomes but also privacy, fairness, and human rights.

The opacity of many AI algorithms raises questions about accountability and trust. The potential for adversarial manipulation introduces new vulnerabilities. The risk of over-reliance on automation threatens to atrophy human expertise. These multifaceted challenges necessitate careful consideration as organizations integrate AI into their security architectures.

The Bias Problem: When AI Perpetuates Inequality

Bias in AI systems represents one of the most pervasive and challenging issues in cybersecurity applications. These biases, whether stemming from training data, algorithm design, or deployment contexts, can lead to discriminatory outcomes, reduced effectiveness, and increased vulnerability for certain groups or scenarios. Understanding and addressing bias is crucial for developing AI security systems that are both effective and equitable.

Training data bias forms the foundation of many AI security problems. Machine learning models learn patterns from historical data, inheriting and often amplifying any biases present in that data. In cybersecurity contexts, this manifests in multiple ways.

Threat detection models trained primarily on attacks from certain geographic regions may fail to identify threats originating elsewhere. User behavior analytics systems trained on data from predominantly male, technical users may flag legitimate activities by women or non-technical staff as suspicious. Research from MIT found that commercial anomaly detection systems had false positive rates up to 34% higher for users from underrepresented groups, resulting in both security and usability issues (MIT CSAIL, 2024).

Algorithmic bias emerges from the design choices made in developing AI systems. The selection of features, optimization metrics, and model architectures can introduce systematic biases that affect security outcomes. For instance, facial recognition systems used for biometric authentication show significant accuracy disparities across demographic groups.

NIST testing revealed that facial recognition algorithms had error rates up to 100 times higher for certain ethnic groups compared to others (NIST, 2024). In security contexts, this means some users face greater friction in authentication while potentially creating vulnerabilities if systems are calibrated to reduce false rejections for affected groups.

Representation bias occurs when certain types of attacks, systems, or users are underrepresented in training data. Most AI security systems are trained on data from large enterprises with sophisticated IT infrastructures. When deployed in small businesses, educational institutions, or developing regions, these systems often perform poorly due to different network architectures, usage patterns, and threat landscapes.

A study by the World Bank found that AI security tools designed for Western enterprises had effectiveness rates 40% lower when deployed in African organizations due to representation bias (World Bank, 2024).

Historical bias embedded in security practices gets codified into AI systems. Traditional security approaches often reflected the biases and assumptions of their creators. When AI systems learn from historical security decisions, they perpetuate these biases.

For example, insider threat detection systems may disproportionately flag employees from certain departments or demographic groups based on historical investigation patterns that reflected human biases rather than actual threat indicators. This creates a feedback loop where biased AI decisions generate more biased training data for future systems.

The impact of bias extends beyond individual users to affect entire organizations and communities. Biased threat intelligence systems may leave certain sectors or regions more vulnerable to attacks. AI systems that consistently generate false positives for specific groups waste security resources and create alert fatigue. Organizations serving diverse populations may find that AI security tools fail to protect all their users equally, creating liability and reputational risks.

Addressing bias requires comprehensive approaches throughout the AI lifecycle. This includes diversifying training data to represent all users and threat scenarios, implementing fairness-aware machine learning algorithms that explicitly account for protected attributes, conducting regular bias audits using standardized metrics, establishing diverse development teams that can identify potential biases, and creating feedback mechanisms for users to report discriminatory outcomes.

However, eliminating bias entirely remains an unsolved challenge, requiring continuous vigilance and improvement.

False Positives and Alert Fatigue

The problem of false positives, incorrectly identifying benign activity as malicious, represents one of the most persistent challenges in AI-powered security systems. While AI has improved detection accuracy in many areas, it has also contributed to an explosion of alerts that overwhelm security teams, paradoxically reducing overall security effectiveness through alert fatigue.

The scale of the false positive problem is staggering. Recent surveys indicate that the average security operations center (SOC) receives over 11,000 alerts per day, with 28% of organizations seeing more than 50,000 daily alerts (Ponemon Institute, 2024). Even with reported false positive rates of "only" 5-10% for modern AI systems, this translates to hundreds or thousands of false alarms daily.

Security analysts spend an average of 20% of their time investigating false positives, time that could be spent on genuine threats. This inefficiency costs organizations an average of $1.37 million annually in wasted resources and missed threats due to alert fatigue.

The psychological impact of false positives on security teams cannot be overstated. Alert fatigue, the desensitization that occurs when exposed to frequent false alarms, leads to decreased vigilance, slower response times, and increased likelihood of missing genuine threats.

Research from Stanford University found that security analysts' threat detection accuracy decreased by 30% after investigating just 10 consecutive false positives (Stanford, 2024). This human factor transforms a technical problem into an operational crisis that AI alone cannot solve.

Complex environments exacerbate false positive challenges. Modern organizations operate heterogeneous IT environments with cloud services, IoT devices, remote workers, and legacy systems. AI models struggle to maintain accuracy across this diversity, often generating false positives when encountering unfamiliar but legitimate configurations or behaviors.

DevOps practices like continuous deployment create constantly changing environments that trigger anomaly detection systems. Business events like product launches or marketing campaigns generate traffic patterns that AI systems may interpret as DDoS attacks.

The trade-off between detection sensitivity and false positive rates creates difficult decisions for security teams. Reducing false positives by adjusting detection thresholds inevitably increases false negatives, resulting in missed attacks.

This balance becomes particularly challenging for AI systems that must protect against both common and rare threats. A model optimized to detect frequent attacks may miss sophisticated, novel threats, while one sensitive enough to catch advanced persistent threats may generate overwhelming false positives from normal variations in behavior.

Contextual understanding remains a fundamental limitation of current AI systems, contributing to false positives. While AI excels at pattern recognition, it often lacks the broader context that human analysts use to distinguish between suspicious and legitimate activity.

An AI system might flag a large data transfer as potential exfiltration without understanding that it's a scheduled backup. It might identify rapid authentication attempts as a brute force attack without recognizing a misconfigured application. This lack of business context and situational awareness leads to alerts that are technically correct but operationally irrelevant.

The economic impact of false positives extends beyond direct costs. Organizations experiencing high false positive rates often disable or bypass security controls, reducing overall protection. Security teams become reluctant to deploy new AI-powered tools, fearing they will add to alert volumes without improving security. Investment in AI security technologies fails to deliver expected returns, leading to skepticism about future investments. Customer-facing false positives, such as legitimate users blocked by fraud detection systems, directly impact revenue and satisfaction.

Adversarial Attacks on AI Systems

The vulnerability of AI systems to adversarial attacks represents a fundamental security challenge that threatens to undermine the reliability of AI-powered cybersecurity. Adversarial attacks exploit the mathematical foundations of machine learning to cause misclassification, evasion, or manipulation of AI systems. In cybersecurity contexts, where AI systems are deployed specifically to detect malicious activity, the ability of attackers to manipulate these systems creates a dangerous blind spot.

Evasion attacks represent the most common form of adversarial manipulation in cybersecurity. Attackers craft inputs specifically designed to be misclassified by AI systems while maintaining their malicious functionality.

In malware detection, researchers have demonstrated that adding benign code sections or modifying non-functional aspects of malicious programs can cause AI-powered antivirus systems to classify malware as safe. A study from Cornell University showed that adversarial examples could achieve 99% evasion rates against state-of-the-art malware detection models while maintaining full malicious capability (Cornell, 2024).

Poisoning attacks target the training phase of AI systems, corrupting models before deployment. Attackers who can influence training data, through compromised threat intelligence feeds, manipulated network traffic, or insider access, can create blind spots or backdoors in AI models.

These poisoned models appear to function normally but fail to detect specific threats or misclassify particular patterns. Research from Berkeley demonstrated that poisoning just 3% of training data could create reliable backdoors in anomaly detection systems that persisted even after retraining (UC Berkeley, 2024).

Model extraction attacks allow adversaries to steal or reverse-engineer AI models through careful querying. By systematically probing an AI security system and observing its responses, attackers can build surrogate models that approximate the original's behavior.

These extracted models reveal detection logic, enabling attackers to identify blind spots and craft evasion strategies. Commercial AI security services accessible through APIs are particularly vulnerable to extraction attacks, with research showing that accurate surrogate models can be built with as few as 10,000 queries (Carnegie Mellon, 2024).

The transferability of adversarial examples amplifies their threat. Adversarial inputs crafted to fool one AI model often fool other models trained for similar tasks, even if they use different architectures or training data. This means attackers can develop evasion techniques against publicly available models and apply them against proprietary security systems. The black-box nature of many attacks, requiring no knowledge of the target model's internals, makes them particularly dangerous and difficult to defend against.

Physical-world adversarial attacks extend the threat beyond digital domains. Adversarial patches or modifications to physical objects can fool AI-powered video surveillance, facial recognition, or biometric systems.

Researchers have created clothing patterns that make people invisible to person detection algorithms, stickers that cause misclassification of traffic signs, and 3D-printed objects that fool multiple detection systems simultaneously. In cybersecurity contexts, these attacks could enable physical intrusion past AI-monitored security systems.

The arms race between adversarial attacks and defenses continues to escalate. Defensive techniques, such as adversarial training, where models are trained on adversarial examples, provide some protection but significantly increase computational requirements and may reduce accuracy on normal inputs.

Certified defenses that provide mathematical guarantees against certain adversarial perturbations remain limited to simple models and small perturbations. The fundamental tension between model complexity needed for high accuracy and the increased attack surface that complexity creates remains unresolved.

Over-Reliance and Human Deskilling

The increasing sophistication and apparent success of AI in cybersecurity has led to a dangerous trend of over-reliance on automated systems, accompanied by the erosion of human expertise and judgment. This dependency creates systemic vulnerabilities that attackers can exploit and reduces an organization's resilience when AI systems fail or face novel threats outside their training parameters.

Automation bias, the tendency to over-reliance on automated systems, particularly affects AI-powered security tools that appear highly sophisticated. Security analysts increasingly defer to AI recommendations without critical evaluation, assuming that complex algorithms must be more accurate than human judgment. Studies show that when presented with AI-generated threat assessments, analysts agreed with the AI recommendation 87% of the time, even when provided with contradictory evidence (Harvard Business Review, 2024). This deference to AI occurs despite known limitations and error rates, creating situations where obvious threats are missed because the AI system failed to flag them.

The deskilling phenomenon in cybersecurity parallels trends observed in other automated fields. As AI systems handle routine threat detection and response, human analysts lose opportunities to develop and maintain critical skills. Junior security professionals who rely heavily on AI tools may never develop the intuition and deep understanding that comes from manual analysis.

Senior professionals find their skills atrophying from disuse. A survey by ISACA found that 62% of security professionals reported decreased confidence in their ability to identify threats without AI assistance after just one year of heavy AI tool usage (ISACA, 2024).

The complexity and opacity of AI systems exacerbate the problems of over-reliance. When security teams don't understand how AI systems reach their conclusions, they cannot effectively validate or challenge those conclusions. This "black box" problem means that when AI systems fail, human operators may not recognize the failure or know how to respond. Organizations report incidents where AI systems silently failed for days or weeks, with security teams assuming that the absence of alerts meant the absence of threats rather than system failure.

Cognitive offloading to AI systems reduces the mental engagement of security professionals with their work. When AI handles threat correlation, pattern recognition, and decision-making, human analysts become passive observers rather than active participants.

This disengagement reduces job satisfaction, increases turnover, and diminishes the quality of human oversight. The loss of engaged, experienced professionals creates a knowledge gap that AI cannot fill, particularly for novel threats or complex incidents requiring creative problem-solving.

The brittleness of AI systems when facing out-of-distribution threats highlights the danger of over-reliance. AI models trained on historical data struggle with novel attack techniques, zero-day exploits, or threats targeting newly deployed technologies. Human experts, drawing on broader knowledge and reasoning capabilities, can recognize and respond to novel threats that AI systems miss. However, organizations that have replaced human expertise with AI automation find themselves vulnerable when facing threats outside AI's training parameters.

Vendor lock-in and dependency amplify over-reliance risks. Organizations are increasingly relying on third-party AI security services, which can create single points of failure and diminish internal capabilities.

When vendors experience outages, suffer breaches, or discontinue services, dependent organizations often lack the necessary expertise to maintain their security operations. The concentration of AI security capabilities among a few major vendors creates systemic risks, where a single vendor compromise could affect thousands of organizations simultaneously.

Ethical Considerations and Privacy Concerns

The deployment of AI in cybersecurity raises profound ethical questions about privacy, surveillance, consent, and the appropriate use of powerful analytical capabilities. These concerns extend beyond technical implementation to touch on fundamental questions about the balance between security and civil liberties, the role of human judgment in critical decisions, and the societal implications of pervasive AI-powered monitoring.

Privacy erosion through AI-powered security monitoring creates tension between protection and intrusion. Modern AI systems can analyze vast amounts of personal data, such as emails, browsing history, keystroke patterns, and even biometric information, to identify threats.

While this analysis may improve security, it also enables unprecedented surveillance of employee and user behavior. The European Data Protection Board has raised concerns that AI security monitoring often exceeds what is necessary and proportionate, violating GDPR principles even when deployed with security intentions (EDPB, 2024).

The dual-use nature of AI security technologies enables both protection and oppression. The same capabilities that detect insider threats can monitor employee productivity, identify union organizers, or flag whistleblowers. Governments worldwide have repurposed commercial AI security tools for population surveillance and political control. The lack of meaningful distinction between security monitoring and general surveillance creates ethical dilemmas for organizations and vendors developing these technologies.

Consent and transparency challenges arise from the complexity and pervasiveness of AI security systems. Users rarely understand the extent of AI-powered monitoring or analysis they're subject to. Even when organizations attempt transparency, the technical complexity of AI systems makes meaningful consent difficult.

How can users consent to behavioral analysis by neural networks whose decision processes even their creators don't fully understand? This informed consent gap creates legal and ethical vulnerabilities, particularly in jurisdictions with strong privacy regulations.

Algorithmic accountability becomes problematic when AI systems make or influence critical security decisions. When an AI system blocks a user's access, flags someone as a potential insider threat, or triggers an investigation, who is responsible for that decision?

The opacity of many AI algorithms makes it difficult to audit or challenge these decisions. Organizations struggle to provide due process when they cannot explain why their AI systems flagged certain individuals or activities. This accountability gap becomes particularly concerning when AI decisions have legal, employment, or reputational consequences.

The normalization of surveillance through AI security tools shifts societal expectations of privacy. As AI-powered monitoring becomes ubiquitous in workplaces, schools, and public spaces, people adapt their behavior to avoid triggering algorithms.

This chilling effect on legitimate activities, from creative work patterns to protected organizing activities, represents a hidden cost of AI security deployment. The psychological impact of knowing that AI systems continuously analyze behavior creates stress and reduces innovation, even when no actual threat exists.

Power imbalances are amplified by AI security capabilities. Large organizations and governments gain unprecedented ability to monitor and predict behavior, while individuals have little visibility into or control over these systems. This asymmetry raises questions about democratic governance, corporate power, and individual autonomy. When AI systems can predict behavior, identify vulnerabilities, and influence decisions at scale, they become tools of power that require careful ethical oversight and regulation.

Explainability and the Black Box Problem

The lack of explainability in many AI security systems creates operational, legal, and trust challenges that undermine their effectiveness and acceptance. When security teams cannot understand how AI systems reach their conclusions, they struggle to validate findings, improve performance, or justify actions based on AI recommendations. This "black box" problem is particularly acute in cybersecurity, where the stakes are high, and the need for trust is paramount.

Operational challenges arise when security analysts must act on AI recommendations they don't understand. An AI system might flag a user as high-risk or identify a complex attack pattern, but without explanation, analysts cannot validate these findings or determine appropriate responses.

This leads to either blind trust in AI recommendations, risking action on false positives, or dismissal of AI alerts, potentially missing real threats. Security teams report that unexplainable AI alerts take 3-4 times longer to investigate than those with clear explanations (Forrester, 2024).

Legal and regulatory requirements increasingly demand explainability in automated decision-making systems. GDPR's "right to explanation" requires organizations to provide meaningful information about automated processing logic.

In the U.S., sector-specific regulations require financial institutions and healthcare organizations to explain adverse decisions. When AI security systems influence decisions about access, employment, or legal matters, the inability to explain their reasoning creates compliance risks. Organizations have faced regulatory penalties for deploying unexplainable AI systems in security-critical roles.

Trust erosion occurs when stakeholders cannot understand AI security decisions. Employees subjected to AI-based security monitoring want to know why they were flagged for investigation. Customers affected by AI-powered fraud detection demand explanations for blocked transactions. Security teams lose faith in systems that cannot justify their recommendations. Without explainability, AI systems become sources of friction and suspicion rather than trusted security partners.

The complexity-accuracy trade-off creates difficult choices for organizations. More complex AI models, particularly deep neural networks, often provide better threat detection accuracy but are inherently less explainable. Simpler, interpretable models, such as decision trees, may be more explainable but less effective at detecting sophisticated threats.

Organizations must balance the need for high accuracy in threat detection with requirements for explainability and accountability.

Post-hoc explanation techniques offer partial solutions but introduce their own challenges. Methods like LIME (Local Interpretable Model-Agnostic Explanations) and SHAP (SHapley Additive exPlanations) can provide insights into AI decisions after the fact.

However, these explanations are approximations that may not accurately reflect the model's actual reasoning. They can be manipulated by adversaries to hide malicious behavior or create false confidence in incorrect decisions. The computational overhead of generating explanations can also impact real-time security operations.

The expertise gap in understanding AI explanations presents another barrier. Even when AI systems provide explanations, security teams may lack the machine learning expertise to interpret them meaningfully.

Technical explanations about feature importance, decision boundaries, or confidence intervals may be accurate but useless to analysts who need actionable intelligence. This creates a need for "explanation translation" that bridges the gap between AI technicalities and security operations, adding another layer of complexity and potential misinterpretation.

Scalability and Resource Constraints

The computational and resource demands of AI-powered security systems create significant challenges for organizations, particularly those with limited budgets or technical infrastructure. The promise of AI democratizing advanced security capabilities often collides with the reality of expensive hardware requirements, specialized expertise needs, and ongoing operational costs that may exceed those of traditional security approaches.

Computational requirements for effective AI security systems can be prohibitive. Training sophisticated threat detection models requires powerful GPUs or TPUs that cost tens of thousands of dollars. Real-time inference at network speeds demands specialized hardware accelerators. A comprehensive AI security deployment for a medium-sized enterprise can require millions of dollars in infrastructure investment. Research from IDC shows that 43% of organizations cite computational costs as the primary barrier to AI security adoption (IDC, 2024).

Data storage and management costs multiply with AI deployment. AI security systems require vast amounts of historical data for training and continuous streams of data for operation. Organizations must store, process, and manage petabytes of security telemetry, requiring expensive storage infrastructure and data management platforms.

The costs of data pipelines, preprocessing systems, and backup infrastructure often exceed the costs of AI models themselves. Small and medium businesses find these data requirements particularly challenging, lacking both infrastructure and expertise for big data management.

The expertise shortage in AI security creates a severe constraint on implementation and operation. The intersection of cybersecurity and machine learning expertise remains a rare find, with qualified professionals commanding premium salaries. Organizations report spending an average of six months to fill AI security positions, with salary premiums of 40-60% over traditional security roles. This expertise shortage means many organizations cannot effectively deploy or maintain AI security systems, even when they can afford the technology.

Maintenance and updating costs for AI systems often exceed initial deployment expenses. Models require regular retraining to maintain effectiveness against evolving threats. Data drift, changes in the underlying patterns of network traffic or user behavior, necessitate continuous model updates.

Organizations must maintain parallel environments for testing and validation. The operational overhead of AI system maintenance can require dedicated teams and continuous investment, costs that are often underestimated in initial AI adoption decisions.

The energy consumption of AI security systems raises both cost and environmental concerns. Large-scale AI models consume enormous amounts of electricity for training and operation.

A single training run for a sophisticated threat detection model can consume as much electricity as an average household uses in a year. For organizations committed to environmental sustainability, the carbon footprint of AI security systems conflicts with green initiatives. Data centers dedicated to AI security operations contribute significantly to organizational energy costs and environmental impact.

The scalability paradox emerges where AI systems that work well at small scales fail at enterprise levels. Models trained on limited data may not generalize to larger, more complex environments. Real-time processing that works for thousands of events per second may not scale to millions. Organizations often discover that pilot AI security projects cannot be scaled to production without a complete redesign, resulting in wasted investment and delayed protection.

Case Studies: When AI Security Fails

Real-world failures of AI security systems provide valuable lessons about the risks and limitations of current technologies. These incidents demonstrate that AI failures can have severe consequences, sometimes worse than having no AI protection at all.

A major financial institution experienced a catastrophic failure of its AI-powered fraud detection system that resulted in $73 million in losses over three weeks. The system, trained on five years of historical transaction data, encountered a new type of synthetic identity fraud it had never seen before. Rather than flagging the unusual patterns, the AI system learned to treat them as legitimate, actually protecting the fraudulent transactions from other security controls.

By the time human analysts identified the problem, the criminals had established hundreds of synthetic identities and extracted millions. The investigation revealed that the AI system's confidence scores had given false assurance, causing analysts to skip manual reviews that they would have conducted with traditional systems (Federal Reserve, 2024).

A healthcare network's AI-driven threat detection system suffered a poisoning attack that left 47 hospitals vulnerable for four months. Attackers compromised a threat intelligence feed used by the AI system for training updates, subtly injecting false data that caused the model to ignore specific command-and-control traffic patterns. The poisoned model showed normal performance metrics on standard tests, hiding its compromised state.

During this period, attackers exfiltrated 2.3 million patient records. The incident highlighted how AI systems' reliance on external data sources creates new attack vectors that don't exist in traditional security systems (Healthcare Information Sharing and Analysis Center, 2024).

A technology company's implementation of AI-powered behavioral authentication led to a discrimination lawsuit and a regulatory investigation. The system, designed to continuously verify user identity through behavioral biometrics, showed systematic bias against employees with disabilities.

Users with motor impairments were locked out at rates 15 times higher than other employees. The company had to disable the system entirely, reverting to less secure authentication methods while facing $12 million in legal costs and settlements. The incident highlighted how bias in AI security systems can lead to both security vulnerabilities and legal liabilities (Equal Employment Opportunity Commission, 2024).

A government agency's deployment of AI for insider threat detection created a toxic work environment that led to mass resignations of critical personnel. The system flagged 30% of employees as potential threats based on factors like irregular working hours, unusual file access patterns, and deviation from peer behavior.

Many flagged employees were high performers with legitimate reasons for their "anomalous" behavior. The constant investigations and suspicion created by the AI system caused a 45% turnover rate in technical positions, ultimately reducing the agency's security posture more than any insider threat could have. The incident highlighted how AI security systems can damage organizational culture and effectiveness (Government Accountability Office, 2024).

A retail chain's AI-powered network security system failed catastrophically during Black Friday, its busiest shopping day. The AI system, trained on normal traffic patterns, interpreted the massive spike in legitimate customer traffic as a distributed denial-of-service attack. It automatically implemented aggressive blocking measures that prevented millions of customers from accessing the company's e-commerce platform. The six-hour outage resulted in an estimated $140 million in lost sales and damaged customer relationships for the company. The incident demonstrated how AI systems trained on normal conditions can fail dramatically during legitimate but unusual events (Securities and Exchange Commission, 2024).

Future Challenges and Mitigation Strategies

As AI becomes more integral to cybersecurity, new challenges will emerge while existing ones evolve. Organizations must prepare for these future challenges while developing strategies to mitigate current risks.

Quantum computing threats to AI security loom on the horizon. Quantum computers could break the encryption protecting AI models and training data, potentially allowing attackers to steal or manipulate AI systems at unprecedented scales. Quantum machine learning might enable adversarial attacks that current defenses cannot handle. Organizations must begin preparing for post-quantum AI security, even though practical quantum computers remain years away.

Regulatory fragmentation creates compliance complexity as different jurisdictions develop conflicting requirements for AI governance. The EU's AI Act, China's algorithmic regulations, and emerging U.S. state-level AI laws create a patchwork of requirements that global organizations must navigate. AI security systems may need different configurations, explanations, and audit trails for different regions, multiplying complexity and costs.

The democratization of adversarial AI tools will make attacks against AI security systems accessible to less sophisticated actors. Just as legitimate AI tools have become more accessible, offensive capabilities are also democratizing. Automated tools for generating adversarial examples, poisoning training data, and extracting models are emerging on criminal forums. This accessibility will dramatically increase the volume and variety of attacks against AI security systems.

Mitigation strategies must address both current and emerging challenges. Organizations should implement robust testing and validation frameworks for AI security systems, including adversarial testing, bias auditing, and failure mode analysis. Maintaining human expertise alongside AI automation ensures resilience when AI systems fail. Diverse and representative training data reduces bias and improves generalization. Explainable AI techniques, even if imperfect, provide some visibility into AI decision-making.

Hybrid approaches that combine AI with traditional security methods provide defense in depth. AI should augment rather than replace human judgment in critical decisions. Regular retraining and monitoring detect model drift and performance degradation. Incident response plans must account for failures and compromises of AI systems. Organizations need vendor diversity to avoid single points of failure in AI security infrastructure.

Industry collaboration on AI security challenges can accelerate solutions. Sharing threat intelligence about adversarial attacks, pooling resources for bias research, and developing industry standards for AI security testing benefit all participants. Academic partnerships advance the state of the art in secure and robust AI. Regulatory engagement helps shape practical and effective AI governance frameworks.

Conclusion: Navigating the AI Security Paradox

The challenges and risks of AI in cybersecurity present a fundamental paradox: the very technologies that promise to revolutionize security also introduce new vulnerabilities, biases, and dependencies that can undermine the security they're meant to provide. This chapter has explored the multifaceted nature of these challenges, ranging from technical limitations such as false positives and adversarial attacks to broader concerns about ethics, privacy, and human deskilling.

The evidence presented demonstrates that AI is neither a panacea for cybersecurity challenges nor an unmanageable risk to be avoided. Instead, it is a powerful but imperfect tool that requires careful implementation, continuous oversight, and realistic expectations.

The failures and limitations documented here are not arguments against AI adoption but rather essential knowledge for its responsible deployment. Organizations that understand these challenges can implement AI security systems that maximize benefits while mitigating risks.

The bias problems inherent in AI systems reflect and often amplify existing inequalities in security practices. Addressing these biases requires not just technical solutions but fundamental reconsiderations of how we collect data, design algorithms, and evaluate security outcomes.

The goal is not perfect fairness, an arguably impossible standard, but rather transparent, accountable systems whose biases are understood and actively managed.

False positives and alert fatigue demonstrate that more detection is not always better security. The human element remains crucial in interpreting, contextualizing, and acting on AI-generated intelligence.

Organizations must resist the temptation to simply generate more alerts and instead focus on actionable intelligence that security teams can effectively process. This requires careful tuning of AI systems, investment in alert correlation and prioritization, and maintaining reasonable expectations about what AI can achieve.

The vulnerability of AI systems to adversarial attacks introduces new attack surfaces that didn't exist with traditional security approaches. These vulnerabilities are not mere implementation bugs but fundamental characteristics of how machine learning systems work. Defending against adversarial attacks requires ongoing research, defense-in-depth strategies, and acceptance that perfect security is impossible. Organizations must prepare for AI systems to be compromised and maintain resilience when they fail.

Over-reliance on AI and the resulting human deskilling threaten to create brittle security postures that collapse when faced with novel threats or system failures. Maintaining human expertise, judgment, and creativity alongside AI automation is not just a nice-to-have but essential for long-term security effectiveness. This requires intentional strategies to keep humans engaged, trained, and capable of operating without AI assistance when necessary.

Ethical and privacy concerns raised by AI security systems touch on fundamental questions about the kind of society we want to live in. The capability to monitor, predict, and influence behavior at scale requires careful consideration of appropriate uses and limitations. Organizations deploying AI security must balance protection with respect for privacy, autonomy, and human dignity. This balance cannot be achieved through technology alone but requires ongoing dialogue between technologists, ethicists, policymakers, and society at large.

Looking forward, the challenges of AI in cybersecurity will continue to evolve as the technology advances and adoption expands. New capabilities will bring new risks. More sophisticated AI will enable more sophisticated attacks. The democratization of AI will make both defensive and offensive capabilities more accessible. Organizations must prepare for this evolution by building adaptive, resilient security programs that can evolve with the technology.

The path forward requires a mature, nuanced approach to AI in cybersecurity. This means acknowledging both capabilities and limitations, implementing appropriate governance and oversight, maintaining human expertise and judgment, preparing for failure modes and adversarial attacks, and continuously evaluating and improving AI systems. It means viewing AI as a powerful tool that requires skilled operation rather than a magic solution that works automatically.

As we proceed to explore the future of AI in cybersecurity in the next chapter, we carry with us the understanding that realizing AI's promise requires confronting its challenges honestly and directly. The organizations that will succeed in leveraging AI for security are those that approach it with eyes wide open to both its potential and its pitfalls, implementing thoughtful strategies that maximize benefits while managing risks. The future of cybersecurity will be shaped not by AI alone but by how well we handle the challenges and risks that come with its adoption.

References

Carnegie Mellon. (2024). *Model extraction attacks against security-critical machine learning systems.* CyLab Security and Privacy Institute.

Cornell University. (2024). *Adversarial malware: Achieving 99% evasion rates against AI-powered antivirus.* Cornell Tech Security Group.

Equal Employment Opportunity Commission. (2024). *Guidance on AI bias in workplace security systems.* EEOC Technical Assistance Document.

European Data Protection Board. (2024). *Guidelines on AI-powered employee monitoring and GDPR compliance.* EDPB Guidelines 02/2024.

Federal Reserve. (2024). *Synthetic identity fraud and AI system failures: Lessons from recent incidents.* Federal Reserve Board Report.

Forrester Research. (2024). *The state of explainable AI in cybersecurity.* Forrester, Inc.

Gartner. (2024). *Market guide for AI in cybersecurity.* Gartner, Inc.

Government Accountability Office. (2024). *Federal agency use of AI for insider threat detection: Effectiveness and impacts.* GAO-24-106234.

Harvard Business Review. (2024). *Automation bias in cybersecurity: When humans defer to machines.* Harvard Business Publishing.

Healthcare Information Sharing and Analysis Center. (2024). *Threat bulletin: AI model poisoning in healthcare security systems.* H-ISAC Report 2024-03.

IDC. (2024). *Worldwide AI in cybersecurity infrastructure forecast, 2024-2028.* International Data Corporation.

ISACA. (2024). *State of cybersecurity 2024: Skills, automation, and the human factor*. Information Systems Audit and Control Association.

MIT CSAIL. (2024). *Demographic disparities in AI-powered threat detection systems*. MIT Computer Science and Artificial Intelligence Laboratory.

National Institute of Standards and Technology. (2024). *Face recognition vendor test: Demographic effects*. NIST IR 8280.

Ponemon Institute. (2024). *The cost of false positives in security operations*. Ponemon Institute Research Report.

Securities and Exchange Commission. (2024). *Form 8-K: Material cybersecurity incident disclosure*. SEC Filing.

Stanford University. (2024). *Alert fatigue and threat detection accuracy: An empirical study*. Stanford Security Research.

UC Berkeley. (2024). *Data poisoning attacks against anomaly detection systems*. Berkeley Artificial Intelligence Research Lab.

World Bank. (2024). *AI security effectiveness in developing economies: A comparative study*. World Bank Group Technology Report.

Chapter 10: Case Studies in AI and Cybersecurity

Artificial intelligence has moved from buzzword to backbone in cybersecurity.

Earlier chapters traced how AI reshapes threat detection and response, supports network defense, underpins identity and access management, enables offensive capabilities such as deepfakes and automated exploitation, and introduces its own structural risks around bias, adversarial attacks, and over-reliance.

Those discussions focused on what AI can do and where it tends to fail. This chapter shifts the focus to *impact.*

The concern now is what actually happened when those systems met real attackers, real users, and real constraints.

Across sectors, AI is embedded in security operations at scale. Large enterprises report widespread use of machine learning in SOC analytics, endpoint protection, fraud monitoring, and identity systems. Financial institutions rely on behavioral models and device intelligence to curb account takeover and payment fraud. Health systems deploy anomaly detection and asset discovery around medical devices and clinical networks. Cloud and platform providers run large graph-based and statistical models over multi-tenant telemetry to spot coordinated campaigns earlier than any human team could manage alone.

That is the theoretical picture: dense, data-driven, and promising.

Case studies are needed now because they force these capabilities into contact with lived outcomes. They illustrate what happens when a ransomware group targets a hospital chain that relies on anomaly detection, when deepfake-enabled fraud attacks a finance team, or when an AI-driven insider-threat program destabilizes the very agency it was intended to protect. Real-life incidents reveal trade-offs that architecture diagrams often overlook: fraud reduction comes at the cost of higher lockout rates for certain customer groups, uptime is maintained only because humans overrode a confident model, or a breach is prolonged because a system fails silently, and the absence of alerts is misinterpreted as a sign of safety.

The scope of this chapter reflects both defensive and offensive uses of AI.

On the defensive side, it examines deployments where AI materially changed the trajectory of an incident in banking, healthcare, cloud platforms, and critical infrastructure.

On the offensive side, it examines how threat actors utilize AI for deepfake-enabled fraud, highly personalized phishing, polymorphic malware, automated exploit generation, and coordinated disinformation during elections.

Together, these domains cover finance, healthcare, cloud services, critical infrastructure, and democratic processes, which are sectors where AI has already altered both attack and defense in measurable ways.

Each case study is selected for what it reveals about the real impact of AI. Some examples demonstrate that AI is clearly improving outcomes, such as reducing fraud losses, accelerating incident detection, or narrowing the blast radius during an intrusion.

Others show AI systems being bypassed, poisoned, misconfigured, or turned into an additional attack surface. A few foreground attackers leaned heavily on AI, while defenders were still using tools and processes that assumed static signatures, human-crafted rules, and non-adaptive adversaries.

The goal is not to rank deployments as wins or losses in absolute terms. The goal is to understand where AI was decisive, where its contribution was marginal, and where it introduced fresh problems.

Taken together, these narratives are meant to bridge the gap between abstract capability and operational reality.

They show AI systems in the conditions that matter most: under pressure, in complex environments, with imperfect data and imperfect humans.

Defensive AI in the Wild: When Algorithms Work Financial Services AI Fraud Detection and Cyber Defense

Financial services are often the most visible testing ground for defensive AI. Money moves fast, fraudsters move faster, and regulators are watching. That combination has pushed banks and payment networks to deploy machine learning at scale long before many other sectors.

Two stories from this world show what happens when AI is not just a pilot or a slide in a strategy deck, but actually sits in the transaction path and in the security operations center.

Case Study 1: Mastercard's AI-driven fraud prevention

Mastercard operates a global card network that processes tens of thousands of transactions per second across e-commerce, point-of-sale, and real-time payment channels. Card-not-present fraud, increasingly automated and fuelled by data breaches and credential dumps, had been rising faster than traditional controls could handle.

At the same time, issuers and merchants were struggling with false declines that blocked legitimate customers and eroded trust. Any solution had to improve fraud detection and avoid turning genuine transactions into collateral damage (Mastercard, n.d.).

To address this, Mastercard rolled out AI-based decisioning services such as *Decision Intelligence*, built on models that score every transaction in real time.

These models combine device attributes, merchant and channel information, historical spending patterns, geolocation, and network-wide behavior to assign a risk score to each authorization request.

Rather than relying only on static rules, the system continuously learns from global transaction flows and issuer feedback, adjusting its sense of "normal" for each cardholder and segment.

Independent analysis has suggested that this kind of AI-driven scoring can materially change fraud outcomes. Publicly reported Mastercard figures for its Decision Intelligence (DI Pro) programs suggest up to a 300% increase in detected fraud in certain deployments (Forrester Consulting, 2021; Gnani.ai, 2023).

In practice, this means that fewer genuine customers are turned away at the checkout, while more fraudulent attempts are intercepted before funds are withdrawn from an account. Issuers also report higher approval rates on low-risk transactions, which directly improves customer experience and merchant revenue.

The operational impact is just as important. Fraud teams no longer manage hundreds of narrow rules for different regions and merchant types. Instead, they work with calibrated risk thresholds and review queues driven by model outputs.

Issuers can adjust those thresholds by geography, portfolio, or regulatory requirement, so a card used primarily in one country can be handled differently from a cross-border corporate card without requiring new rule sets every time business needs shift (Mastercard, n.d.).

Several lessons show up clearly in this case.

First, the models only perform well because they combine three kinds of information: individual transaction details, long-term customer behavior, and consortium-level network data.

Any one of those in isolation would miss important context.

Second, local tuning matters.

An approval strategy that works well in North America can create unnecessary risk or friction in markets with different shopping patterns or regulatory expectations.

Third, the AI runs as a continuous risk engine in the background.

Customers never see it directly, but their experience, whether a payment goes through smoothly or gets blocked, depends on how well that engine is maintained, monitored, and audited.

Case Study 2: NatWest Group AI for Real-Time Scam and Fraud Prevention

NatWest Group, one of the UK's major retail and commercial banks, has faced a surge in fraud and scams, particularly authorized push-payment (APP) fraud, where customers are tricked into sending money to criminals through social engineering tactics.

UK Finance has repeatedly highlighted APP scams as a fast-growing class of loss, with banks under pressure from regulators and the public to do more to detect and stop them before money leaves customer accounts (Holmes, 2023).

To respond, NatWest invested in AI-enhanced fraud detection capabilities, including the deployment of Featurespace's ARIC Risk Hub, a machine-learning platform for real-time transaction and behavior monitoring.

The system builds profiles for customers and merchants over time, learning typical payment sizes, counterparties, and usage patterns across channels.

When a new payment deviates from those learned patterns, especially if it matches known scam typologies, the AI scores the transaction and raises risk alerts that can trigger additional checks, automated warnings in the mobile app, or intervention by fraud teams.

Public statements from NatWest and Featurespace describe this move as a shift from static, rules-based screening to adaptive behavioral analytics that can react faster to new scam patterns and provide more nuanced risk assessments (Featurespace, 2023).

Featurespace notes that its machine-learning models look at both individual behavior and wider network behavior, so a payment might be flagged not only because it is unusual for that customer, but also because the receiving account shows patterns similar to known mule accounts.

NatWest has paired these AI capabilities with customer-facing interventions.

When the system assesses a payment as high risk, the mobile or online banking interface presents clear warnings and prompts customers to reconsider the transfer, sometimes suggesting that they contact the bank before proceeding.

In higher-risk scenarios, payments can be delayed or blocked while fraud teams reach out.

According to industry commentary, NatWest views AI as a means to reduce the time it takes to identify suspicious activity from days to hours or minutes, particularly for scams that would have previously gone undetected until customers complained.

The impact has been evident in both prevented losses and operational changes. While the bank doesn't publish detailed model metrics, it reports that AI-driven systems help stop a significant number of attempted scams each year and have materially reduced successful fraud in several retail segments.

Internally, analysts now start investigations with AI-enriched alerts that include behavioral context and risk scores, which shortens investigation times and allows teams to focus on genuinely high-risk cases instead of sifting through large volumes of low-value alerts.

Several practical lessons emerge from NatWest's experience.

Behavioral AI makes the most difference in scam and APP fraud when it is tied directly into customer touchpoints, so that high-risk scores lead to immediate, understandable warnings rather than silent back-office flags.

Yet human interaction still matters: branch staff and call-center agents use AI-generated risk signals to guide conversations, rather than handing decisions over to an opaque system. And trust depends on communication. When customers understand *why* a payment was challenged and how the bank is trying to protect them, they're more likely to accept friction at critical moments instead of seeing AI controls as arbitrary barriers.

Email, Identity, and Endpoint Enterprise Defense at Scale

Case Study 4: Google Gmail ML-Based Phishing and Malware Filtering

Gmail is one of the largest consumer and enterprise email platforms in the world, and that scale makes it a permanent target.

Billions of messages flow through Google's infrastructure every day, ranging from harmless newsletters to highly tailored phishing campaigns targeting executives, journalists, and government staff.

A decade ago, most filtering relied on a mix of static rules, reputation lists, and user reports. That approach started to break down as phishing kits automated domain rotation, content randomization, and attachment obfuscation.

The volume remained high, while individual campaigns became shorter-lived and more elusive. Google's security team needed a system that could adapt at machine speed rather than depending on manual signature updates.

Google's response was a multi-layered machine-learning pipeline built into Gmail's spam, phishing, and malware filters.

The system combines deep-learning models that analyze message content, URL structures, attachment behavior, sender reputation, and user interaction patterns. These models sit alongside Google Safe Browsing URL checks, attachment sandboxing, and reputation systems that share intelligence across Google products.

Google reports that this AI-powered stack blocks more than 99.9% of spam, phishing, and malware and stops nearly 10 million spam emails every minute, a figure that gives a sense of both the threat volume and the level of automation required to keep it under control (Google, 2023).

The most significant change was the shift from rule-based filters to continuously trained models.

When Google engineers described the impact of TensorFlow and related ML tooling in Gmail, they emphasized that models could learn subtle patterns that were hard to express as rules, such as tokenization tricks in phishing text, or unusual combinations of headers and sending infrastructure that correlate with abuse.

Over time, this allowed Gmail to improve catch rates without requiring human analysts to handcraft signatures for every new family of phishing templates.

The same AI systems also learn from user feedback, particularly the "Report phishing" and "Not spam" buttons, which provide high-quality labels to refine future decisions (Kumaran, 2022).

In practice, you can see the results in how new phishing waves behave.

When a fresh campaign starts using a novel template or lure, some messages inevitably land in inboxes. As users mark them as phishing and automated systems correlate infrastructure and content, the models are retrained and pushed into production.

Google has reported that this continuous retraining process lets Gmail quickly suppress new phishing templates and malicious attachments once enough signals accumulate, without waiting for a formal signature release cycle.

The result is a sharp reduction in exposure time: many campaigns are only effective for a short window before their delivery success rate collapses.

For users and administrators, the outcome is mostly invisible. Malicious or suspicious emails are silently quarantined or routed to spam, while legitimate messages flow with minimal extra friction.

Google stresses that the goal is to maintain both high precision and high recall. In other words, to catch as much bad mail as possible while minimizing false positives that hide real communication.

Their own reporting highlights this balance, noting that the system blocks the overwhelming majority of harmful emails while preserving a small fraction of borderline cases for the user to decide.

That trade-off matters. Over-aggressive filtering can break business workflows; overly cautious filtering leaves users exposed.

Several lessons carry over directly to enterprise environments. First, scale and diversity of data matter. Gmail's performance depends on seeing global patterns across billions of messages and leveraging signals from multiple products. Organizations that require similar protection internally typically need to aggregate telemetry across email, identity, endpoints, and web gateways, rather than treating email as an isolated channel.

Second, continuous retraining is not a luxury. Attackers constantly tweak lures, infrastructure, and attachment formats. Models that aren't refreshed drift out of date and quietly lose effectiveness.

Third, even at Google's scale, AI doesn't eliminate residual risk. Targeted spear-phishing, business email compromise (BEC), and messages that abuse trusted supply-chain senders still reach users and require additional controls and user training (Google, 2023).

Case studies later in the chapter on offensive AI will pick up that thread from the attacker's side.

Case Study 5: Microsoft 365 Defender and Azure Sentinel Hunting the Solorigate (SolarWinds) Campaign

The Solorigate (SolarWinds) incident remains one of the defining examples of a modern supply-chain intrusion.

Attackers compromised the build environment of SolarWinds Orion, a widely deployed network management platform, and shipped a trojanized update that embedded a backdoor into customer networks. Once inside, they moved laterally, stole credentials, and abused identity infrastructure to access cloud resources.

Follow-on investigation showed that the operation included stealing Active Directory Federation Services (ADFS) token-signing certificates and forging Security Assertion Markup Language (SAML) tokens to impersonate privileged users in cloud services, a technique often referred to as "Golden SAML" (Azure Aggregator, 2020).

For Microsoft and its customers, the attack unfolded across both on-premises and cloud environments. Microsoft 365 Defender and Azure Sentinel (now part of Microsoft Sentinel) already provide a cloud-scale detection and hunting layer, ingesting telemetry from endpoints, Azure Active Directory, Office 365, and other services.

Those platforms use a mix of rule-based analytics, anomaly detection, and machine learning to spot rare or risky behaviors. For example, unusual process executions on ADFS servers, abnormal mailbox access patterns, or sign-ins from virtual private server (VPS) providers that don't match a tenant's usual profile (Azure Aggregator, 2020).

When Solorigate came to light, Microsoft's security teams released detailed hunting queries and built-in detections that leaned heavily on these analytics capabilities.

Azure Sentinel playbooks and hunting queries focused on several key behaviors such as suspicious LDAP queries targeting ADFS key material, export of token-signing certificates, rare or anomalous processes running on federation servers, and unusual SAML token usage patterns.

Microsoft's documentation and community posts describe how these detections combined rule logic with time-series anomaly functions to flag abnormal mail access and sign-in activity, including spikes in MailItemsAccessed operations and sign-ins that relied only on token-based multifactor claims from suspicious IP ranges (Azure Aggregator, 2020).

On the Microsoft 365 Defender side, high-fidelity detections were rolled out for ADFS private key extraction and attempts to access key material, with alerts surfaced both in Defender and in Sentinel-connected workspaces.

These detections benefited from machine-learning models that had already been trained to recognize rare processes and account behaviors in large enterprise environments, giving customers a way to distinguish truly unusual activity from routine administrative work.

Organizations that had fully integrated Defender and Sentinel, and that enabled the recommended diagnostic logging, were able to use these signals to identify compromised federation servers, scope which users and mailboxes had been accessed, and prioritize remediation.

In many cases, the analytics didn't "discover" the initial backdoor; that credit often went to endpoint or network indicators, but they dramatically improved the speed and accuracy of post-compromise investigation.

The incident also showed the limits and dependencies of AI-enabled defenses. Where logging was incomplete, or telemetry from ADFS and Azure AD was sparse, anomaly-based detections were far less effective.

Some of the hunting queries Microsoft shared were explicitly described as "generic and potentially noisy," requiring tuning for each environment and careful human review of results.

Machine learning helped prioritize rare processes, unusual sign-ins, and out-of-pattern mailbox access, but it did not replace the need for experienced threat hunters to stitch together a narrative from many weak signals.

From an outcome perspective, the combined use of cloud-scale telemetry, automated anomaly detection, and human investigation gave many organizations a path to recovery.

Microsoft's public guidance emphasized that Sentinel and Defender alerts related to ADFS key export, forged SAML token usage, and anomalous mailbox access could be used to reconstruct attacker activity and validate whether an environment had been compromised by the Solorigate operators.

Those same capabilities were later generalized into reusable analytics and detections for other identity-focused attacks, raising the baseline of protection against similar campaigns.

Several practical lessons emerge from this case. First, AI and advanced analytics only work as well as the telemetry they receive. The most useful Solorigate detections required detailed logs from ADFS, Azure AD, and Exchange Online; without them, the models had little to work with.

Second, cloud-scale correlation is essential when dealing with stealthy, long-dwell-time intrusions. By aggregating signals from endpoints, identity providers, and mail systems, Microsoft's tools could spot patterns, such as rare sign-ins from VPS ranges or abnormal mailbox access volumes, that would be almost impossible to see in a single log source.

Third, human threat hunters remain central. The AI highlighted suspicious behaviors and reduced the search space; humans validated, pivoted, and made containment decisions.

Finally, Solorigate highlighted that AI in cybersecurity is an amplifier.

In environments with good hygiene, complete logging, and engaged security teams, platforms such as Microsoft 365 Defender and Sentinel allowed defenders to move faster and with more confidence. In environments with poor configuration, limited logging, or understaffed security operations, even sophisticated AI-driven detections struggled to surface clear, actionable insight.

That asymmetry is one of the recurring themes across the case studies in this chapter and a reminder that AI does its best work when it's plugged into a mature security program rather than expected to compensate for fundamental gaps.

Critical Infrastructure and OT Environments

Case Study 6: Drax Group and Darktrace AI in an Industrial Power Station

Drax Group operates one of the UK's most significant power-generation sites, supplying a substantial share of the nation's electricity and managing complex biomass and coal-conversion assets.

Its industrial control systems and operational technology networks have very different constraints from a typical office network: uptime is paramount, safety margins are tight, and many devices were never designed with modern cybersecurity in mind.

That combination makes conventional, signature-driven tools hard to tune and easy to blind.

To deal with that reality, Drax deployed Darktrace's cyber-AI platform (including what the vendor brands its "Enterprise Immune System"), extending coverage across both IT and OT environments (Darktrace Holdings Limited, n.d.).

Instead of relying on prior knowledge of specific malware families or known indicators of compromise, the system uses unsupervised machine learning to baseline "normal" behavior for every device, protocol, and connection.

Over time, it learns typical patterns for turbine controllers, engineering workstations, historian servers, remote-access tools, and even back-office systems tied into plant operations.

That baseline becomes the reference point for detecting subtle anomalies in industrial traffic that static rules would dismiss as noise.

Darktrace reports detecting unusual activity in remote-access tools and other OT-adjacent traffic patterns that traditional, signature-based tools would have missed, prompting Drax's security team to intervene before operations were affected.

Several lessons from Drax generalize across OT environments.

First, self-learning anomaly detection is genuinely useful where there are few signatures to rely on and where legacy equipment makes patching and endpoint agents difficult.

You can't realistically maintain a full inventory of every legitimate

Modbus, DNP3, or OPC pattern in a large plant, but you can let a model watch those flows for months and learn what "normal" looks like for each subnet and device class.

Second, collaboration between cybersecurity teams and plant engineers is non-negotiable. AI can flag that a PLC is issuing unusual commands or that a vendor tunnel is behaving oddly; only engineers can tell you whether that anomaly reflects a real operational change, a benign test, or a threat.

Finally, incidents like this show that "AI in the loop" doesn't need to be dramatic to be valuable.

Quietly catching an abnormal remote session before it affects operations is exactly the kind of low-headline win that matters most in critical infrastructure.

Case Study 7: A UK National Water Company and Azure AD B2C

Critical infrastructure doesn't only live in SCADA racks and pump controllers. Customer identity systems for utilities are now as much a target as the pipes and reservoirs.

A national not-for-profit water company in the UK, anonymized in Kocho's public write-up but identified as a drinking- and wastewater provider serving more than three million people, faced exactly this challenge (Kocho, n.d.).

As it modernized its "My Account" portal, the company needed to give households, businesses, and property developers smoother online access to billing, payments, and service requests, without opening new doors to account takeover and fraud.

The utility partnered with Kocho to implement Azure AD B2C as the external identity platform for its customer portal.

Azure AD B2C inherits Microsoft's cloud identity protections, including risk-based sign-in analysis, password blacklists derived from massive breach telemetry, and behavioral analytics that feed into "User Insights" about suspicious or unusual access (Kocho, n.d.).

In practice, this means the platform continuously evaluates sign-ins using machine-learning models that look at IP reputation, device fingerprints, atypical locations, and abnormal session patterns to decide when to step up authentication or block access entirely.

The main "incident" in this case is the transition itself: moving from fragmented, manually managed logins to an AI-backed identity service that can react to new attack patterns at cloud scale.

Before the project, customers often had to juggle multiple credentials, and security controls were relatively static. After the Azure AD B2C deployment, the utility gained multi-factor authentication, automated threat detection, and behavior analytics that could flag risky sign-ins without requiring every login to go through extra steps (Kocho, n.d.).

The result was a more secure but smoother experience.

Customers could use single sign-on across multiple services and even social logins where appropriate, while high-risk attempts were silently challenged or blocked. The utility gained better reporting on identity risks, and the IT team could rely on Microsoft's continuously updated threat models rather than trying to maintain homegrown rules.

For a water provider handling large volumes of personal data, that combination of improved security and reduced friction is not "nice-to-have," it's part of maintaining public trust.

A few lessons stand out from this example for critical infrastructure operators.

First, AI in identity systems is one of the most realistic ways to bring advanced detection into environments that otherwise don't have large security teams. The water company did not have to build its own machine-learning engine; it consumed it as part of a managed cloud service.

Second, identity is often the entry point into more sensitive systems. Even though this project focused on the customer portal, compromised accounts can quickly become a stepping stone to billing systems, CRM platforms, or even OT-adjacent support tooling. Strengthening identity with ML-based risk detection reduces that initial attack surface.

Finally, the case underlines that critical infrastructure security is not only about preventing pumps from being switched off; it is also about protecting the data, logins, and reputational capital that keep citizens confident in their provider (Kocho, n.d.).

D. Healthcare and Hospitals

Case Study 8: Milton Keynes University Hospital and Darktrace

Large hospitals sit at an awkward intersection of requirements: they must protect sensitive health records, keep life-critical systems online, support thousands of staff with remote access, and accommodate a mix of modern cloud services and legacy medical devices.

Milton Keynes University Hospital NHS Foundation Trust (MKUH) in England is one example of a healthcare provider that turned to AI-driven threat detection to make sense of that complexity.

The hospital publicly partnered with Darktrace to deploy its self-learning cyber-AI across clinical systems and broader IT networks, explicitly citing the need to detect abnormal activity that traditional tools would miss (Darktrace Holdings Limited, n.d).

Once deployed, the platform began building a behavioral model of MKUH's environment: who normally connects to the electronic health record system and from where, what kind of traffic is typical from imaging equipment, how VPN-connected clinicians access resources during on-call shifts, and what data flows look like between on-premises systems and cloud services.

The goal was simple but demanding: understand "normal" for thousands of devices and accounts without presupposing exactly what future attacks would look like

Rather than a single marquee incident, the public case material stresses ongoing benefits: 24/7 autonomous response, identification and remediation of major vulnerabilities, and relief for an overstretched security team. Darktrace's self-learning AI learns "patterns of life" across MKUH's dynamic workforce and environments, then intervenes surgically when behavior deviates from normal (Darktrace Holdings Limited, n.d.; Hughes, 2018).

In particular, Craig York, CTO at Milton Keynes University Hospital NHS Foundation Trust, noted, "Having Darktrace's AI watching over your network is really just another pair of eyes, one that never sleeps and which takes action in seconds to protect every digital asset you have."

The hospital's experience highlights several broader patterns in healthcare security.

First, AI helps compensate, to a certain extent, for understaffed hospital SOCs.

Many health systems lack 24/7 human monitoring, instead relying on a small team to juggle compliance, incident response, and day-to-day IT issues. Self-learning models that can detect unusual behavior in real-time and escalate only the most concerning anomalies give those teams a chance to identify compromised accounts or rogue devices before they escalate into full-blown breaches (Hughes, 2018).

Second, the same visibility that improves security also raises questions about privacy and compliance. When AI systems inspect traffic involving electronic health records, connected medical devices, and clinician workflows, they inevitably process sensitive patient information and staff behavior patterns.

Under regimes such as the GDPR and UK data-protection law, hospitals must justify monitoring as necessary and proportionate, implement strong access controls around the AI platform itself, and be prepared to explain how automated alerts inform human decision-making.

Finally, this case shows how AI-driven detection and governance changes tend to reinforce one another. Catching a compromised account is the immediate win. But the longer-term benefit comes when the incident drives structural improvements. This may be in the form of enforcing multi-factor authentication, reviewing VPN policies, revisiting least-privilege access to records, and building playbooks that treat AI-surfaced anomalies as starting points for investigation rather than unquestionable verdicts.

For hospitals under constant pressure, from ransomware crews, data-theft groups, and day-to-day operational strain, that combination of smarter detection and better process can be the difference between a near-miss and a headline-grabbing crisis.

Offensive AI in the Wild: When Attackers Automate and Deceive

As AI has become standard in enterprise security tools, it has also become part of the attacker's toolkit.

The same progress in speech synthesis, text generation, and video manipulation that makes collaboration and customer service smoother has created new ways to defraud organizations and distort public debate.

Here, AI is not quietly reducing false positives in the background. It is the core weapon, reshaping how social engineering and information operations work, and forcing security and policy leaders to rethink verification, media literacy, and crisis response at scale.

Voice and Video Deepfakes in Financial and Corporate Fraud

Case Study 9: Deepfake CEO Voice Scam Against a UK Energy Firm (2019)

In 2019, a UK-based energy subsidiary of a German company became one of the earliest documented victims of AI-generated voice fraud.

The managing director received a phone call that he believed was from his group CEO in Germany, instructing him to urgently transfer about €220,000 to a supplier's account in Hungary.

The voice on the line reproduced the CEO's accent, cadence, and mannerisms closely enough that the director didn't question the request. After the transfer, the attackers initiated further calls attempting to move more money before the fraud controls finally halted the pattern (Stupp, 2019).

Investigators and the company's insurer later explained that the attackers had used AI-based voice cloning. Public speeches and recorded calls provided enough training data for a generative model to synthesize speech that sounded like the CEO, including brief conversational responses that kept the call natural.

The fraud didn't rely on a sophisticated technical intrusion into banking systems. It exploited an existing payment process and a chain of trust built around senior leadership's voice. The AI system simply made that social engineering step far more convincing than a typical scam call (Stupp, 2019).

The result was a successful transfer of funds that quickly moved through multiple accounts, complicating recovery efforts.

The insurer publicized the case as an example of emerging "deepfake"-enabled fraud, prompting boards and risk committees to reassess any process that relied on voice confirmation as a sufficient control for high-value payments.

Several lessons emerged that now show up repeatedly in corporate fraud guidance.

First, voice alone is a weak factor for authorizing significant transfers, regardless of how familiar the caller sounds. Escalation policies, dual authorization, and out-of-band verification using independent contact channels are necessary guardrails for large payments.

Second, finance and operations teams need explicit training on AI-enabled social engineering, including examples of voice cloning and how pressure, urgency, and appeals to hierarchy are combined in these scams.

Finally, insurers and regulators have begun to treat deepfake-enabled fraud as a foreseeable risk, which alters expectations regarding internal controls and incident response (Stupp, 2019).

Case Study 10: Generative AI and Disinformation in the 2024 Taiwan Elections

Taiwan's January 2024 presidential and legislative elections offered an early look at how generative AI can blend into an already crowded disinformation environment (Hung, 2024).

Taiwan had long been a target of influence operations, but officials and independent researchers reported that the election cycle saw a noticeable increase in synthetic and AI-amplified content aimed at shaping public opinion and undermining trust in candidates and institutions.

The offensive use of AI took several forms.

Media and election-monitoring groups documented waves of AI-generated news-style articles, memes, and social media posts that mimicked local language and tone while disseminating misleading narratives about candidates' positions, economic risks, and relations with China.

In parallel, manipulated and synthetic videos circulated on Taiwanese platforms and messaging apps, including clips that appeared to show politicians making statements they had never made or endorsing positions they did not hold (Reuters, 2025).

These assets were often seeded through fake or hijacked accounts and then boosted by coordinated networks, some of which were linked by researchers to foreign influence operations.

Taiwan's government and civil-society organizations responded with a combination of human and AI-assisted defenses.

Fact-checking alliances worked with platforms to debunk specific pieces of viral content, sometimes within hours. The Ministry of Digital Affairs and independent researchers utilized their own AI tools to detect patterns in posting behavior, identify likely coordinated inauthentic networks, and flag reused narratives across different languages and channels.

Despite these efforts, authorities later reported that generative AI-assisted campaigns reached significant portions of the online population and that the volume and speed of content made real-time responses difficult.

The experience highlighted several important lessons for any democracy facing similar threats.

First, generative AI lowers the cost of producing plausible local-language propaganda, which means the volume of misleading material can increase dramatically without a corresponding rise in visible effort.

Second, detection and debunking require their own automation; human fact-checkers can't keep pace alone once synthetic media production scales.

Third, transparency mechanisms, such as the rapid public attribution of foreign campaigns and media-literacy initiatives that educate citizens on what AI-generated content looks like, become part of the core electoral infrastructure rather than optional add-ons.

Ultimately, the Taiwan case demonstrates that AI-based detection is necessary but insufficient; platform policies, diplomatic responses, and domestic resilience must all adapt to a world where synthetic text, images, and video are standard tools in political influence operations.

AI-Personalized Phishing and Dark-Web LLM Tools

As generative AI has moved into everyday productivity tools, the same underlying models have begun to appear in criminal ecosystems.

Earlier waves of phishing were limited by the attacker's language skills, time, and imagination. Now, large language models are being wrapped in "as-a-service" offerings on the dark web, giving even low-skilled actors the ability to generate convincing, tailored phishing and business email compromise (BEC) campaigns at scale.

Case Study 11: WormGPT and FraudGPT LLM-as-a-Service for Criminal Phishing

In mid-2023, security researchers began documenting a tool advertised to cybercriminals under the name "WormGPT" (Eftsure, 2023).

On underground forums and encrypted channels, it was marketed as "ChatGPT for BEC," explicitly framed as a generative AI system without ethical or safety guardrails.

Instead of blocking requests to write malware or fraud emails, WormGPT's operators promoted exactly those capabilities as selling points.

The context was straightforward: as more organizations turned to traditional AI tools for productivity, criminals wanted their own version tailored to phishing, account takeover, and social engineering.

Technically, WormGPT and later "FraudGPT" functioned as large language models exposed through chat-style interfaces.

Criminal users could paste stolen email threads and ask the model to craft a believable reply in the same tone, generate pretexts tailored to HR or finance roles, translate messages into multiple languages, and even suggest subject lines likely to trigger curiosity or urgency.

Security write-ups showed examples of these tools producing polished BEC emails that referenced specific roles ("AP manager," "regional controller"), mimicked internal style, and included plausible invoice or wire-transfer details.

Investigations by vendors such as Eftsure, Bitdefender, and others found that operators were not just advertising theoretical features. They shared real phishing templates generated by WormGPT and FraudGPT as proof for potential buyers, including multilingual campaigns and follow-up messages that adjusted tone when a victim hesitated (Bitdefender, 2023).

These tools were sold on subscription models on dark-web markets and Telegram channels, mirroring legitimate SaaS pricing tiers. Some adverts explicitly highlighted their value for non-native English speakers who wanted "error-free" emails for corporate targets.

The immediate outcome was a lower barrier to entry for convincing phishing and BEC operations. Attackers who previously produced clumsy, easily spotted messages could now generate fluent, role-specific content in seconds.

Threat-intel teams began to notice more grammatically correct and context-aware phishing waves, including campaigns that adapted to local holidays, tax seasons, or payroll cycles.

The emergence of these tools coincided with reports from vendors of increasingly polished, grammatically correct phishing campaigns, although attributing any single campaign directly to WormGPT or FraudGPT is difficult.

Several lessons fall out of this case.

First, commoditized AI significantly narrows the skill gap between top-tier and average attackers. Good English, domain knowledge, and time are no longer strict prerequisites for running realistic phishing campaigns.

Second, enterprise email security has to assume that adversaries can generate fluent, highly tailored emails on demand. That pushes defenders toward behavior- and relationship-based detection, looking at sender history, abnormal reply chains, device risk, and payment-approval workflows, rather than simple language cues or blocklists.

Third, awareness training must be updated so that staff no longer rely on broken grammar or awkward phrasing as their primary warning signs; those are becoming less common as LLMs enter the criminal toolkit.

Case Study 12: AI-Assisted Credential-Stuffing and Account-Takeover Campaigns

Credential stuffing, or the automated testing of stolen username/password pairs across multiple sites, has been a significant issue for consumer platforms for years (F5, n.d.).

Large gaming, streaming, and retail services experience sustained bot traffic, with billions of login attempts being made against their authentication endpoints. Reports from vendors such as F5 and Akamai describe campaigns where automated tools systematically probe login flows, adjust patterns in response to defenses, and rotate infrastructure to evade detection (Akamai, n.d.; F5, n.d.).

The offensive "AI" component here is less about flashy models and more about continuous optimization. Attack toolkits used in credential-stuffing campaigns incorporate feedback loops, which ingest information on which attempts were blocked, which IP ranges were challenged with CAPTCHAs, which user agents triggered extra friction, and which timing patterns appeared suspicious.

Scripts then modify parameters to maintain acceptable success rates, adjusting request rates, incorporating "clean" residential proxies, and varying paths to blend in with legitimate traffic.

Researchers have compared this behavior to reinforcement-style learning, even when attackers don't explicitly advertise their tools as machine-learning based.

Akamai's "State of the Internet" work, for example, has described multi-month campaigns in which credential-stuffing bots targeted login pages for major consumer brands.

When defenders deployed new WAF rules or tightened rate limits, bot operators quickly shifted characteristics, new proxy networks, different URI paths, and altered header fingerprints, without manual rewriting from scratch.

Over time, the attacks converged on patterns that maximized valid logins while minimizing detections. F5 has similarly documented "intelligent" botnets used against single sign-on deployments, emphasizing how scripts evolve routing and timing strategies as defenses change.

On the defender side, this arms race has pushed large platforms to adopt their own AI-driven controls.

Bot-management and risk-scoring systems ingest large volumes of telemetry, including IP reputation, device fingerprints, behavioral features such as mouse movement and keystroke timing, and historical login context, to train models that distinguish likely humans from automation. They then adjust challenges or blocks in real-time.

Vendors now describe using machine learning to dynamically score each login request, feeding outcomes back into model updates in a loop similar to what attackers do.

The outcomes of these AI-assisted credential-stuffing battles are mixed.

On the one hand, platforms that combine strong bot detection, rate limiting, and multi-factor authentication (MFA) have reported significant reductions in account takeover rates, even under high attack volumes.

On the other hand, services that relied solely on username/password authentication and treated WAF rules as a one-off fix experienced recurring waves of compromise as bots adapted.

Vendor reports repeatedly highlight the same pattern: the most resilient defenses pair model-driven anomaly detection with enrollment in MFA, device binding, or WebAuthn-style authenticators, so that stolen passwords alone aren't enough.

The main lessons are clear.

First, automation on both sides is locked in a feedback loop: attackers use adaptive scripts (and sometimes ML components) to tune credential-stuffing campaigns, while defenders rely on AI-powered scoring engines to detect and throttle them.

Second, enterprises can't assume that static rules or CAPTCHAs will hold up for long against adversaries whose tools are continually learning from responses.

Finally, strong MFA and device-based risk checks are non-negotiable in this environment. AI helps score risk, but the ultimate barrier has to be additional factors that bots can't trivially replay.

AI-Enhanced Ransomware and Data-Theft Operations

While phishing and account takeover focus on gaining initial access, ransomware groups and data-theft operators are increasingly exploring AI to extract more value from the footholds they already have.

That doesn't always mean fully autonomous malware. In many cases, AI plays supporting roles, such as triaging stolen data, drafting extortion messages, or generating environment-specific scripts.

Recently, researchers have also begun to see proof-of-concept ransomware that directly embeds a local large language model in its operation.

Case Study 13: PromptLock Early Example of AI-Powered Ransomware

In 2025, researchers at ESET reported on a malware family they dubbed "PromptLock," described in public coverage as the first known AI-powered ransomware (PC Gamer, 2025).

Instead of hard-coding all of its behavior, PromptLock integrates a local large language model, specifically, an open-source 20-billion-parameter model accessed via the Ollama API, to generate and execute Lua scripts on the victim machine.

The context is important here. The widespread availability of local LLMs made it feasible for attackers to bundle a model and use it offline, without relying on external APIs that might leave logs or raise suspicion.

Technically, PromptLock uses the embedded model to create scripts that can perform classic ransomware tasks, such as enumerating files, exfiltrating data, and encrypting content.

According to the analysis summarized by PC Gamer, the samples observed so far appear more like a proof of concept than a fully operational campaign. Some features, such as file destruction, were either incomplete or not yet enabled.

Still, the design is notable. Instead of shipping a fixed binary with a static workflow, the malware asks the LLM to generate code on demand based on prompts, then runs that code locally.

The immediate outcome was limited in terms of real-world damage; no large-scale PromptLock outbreaks have been reported to date, but the strategic signal is strong.

Embedding an LLM allows an attacker to adjust behavior dynamically to the environment. In principle, a future variant could prompt the model to tailor its lateral-movement scripts to the specific processes, services, or security tools it discovers; adjust exfiltration paths based on available cloud clients; or tune its encryption strategy based on system resources.

Because all of this happens locally, traditional network-based detection has fewer opportunities to see suspicious command-and-control traffic.

This proof-of-concept also reinforces a trend already visible in ransomware operations: increased automation around targeting and negotiation.

Even before PromptLock, incident-response teams had encountered groups using generative AI tools to draft more polished extortion emails, leak-site posts, and media statements, making their threats sound more credible and specific.

PromptLock extends that logic into the malware runtime itself, using AI not just for words but for code.

The lessons from PromptLock are largely preventative.

First, defenders should expect more malware that uses local AI models for code generation, data classification, and environment reconnaissance. That implies a need to monitor for unusual use of local LLM runtimes and script engines on high-value systems, especially where such tools aren't part of approved workflows.

Second, EDR and XDR solutions need to focus less on fixed signatures and more on behaviors that indicate "code being written to write code," patterns such as repeated dynamic script generation, frequent calls between an LLM service and interpreters, or sudden bursts of file-system access initiated by generated scripts.

Third, organizations should revisit their data-protection posture, assuming that future ransomware will use AI to identify the most sensitive assets and craft tailored pressure campaigns around them.

When AI Misfires: Failure, Bias, and Unintended Consequences

So far, the case studies have mostly shown AI at its best: systems that scaled beyond human capacity and helped defenders see what they would otherwise have missed.

To have a realistic picture, we also need to look at the other side of the ledger.

In practice, AI in cybersecurity can misfire, drift away from reality, or embed biases that harm the very people and organizations it is meant to protect.

COVID-19 and Model Drift in Bank Fraud Detection

In the years leading up to 2020, many retail banks rolled out machine–learning–based fraud detection systems trained on several years of pre-pandemic transaction data.

These models were tuned to recognize what "normal" looked like: typical merchant categories, travel patterns, ticket sizes, and seasonal spikes. They were often treated as relatively stable infrastructure.

When COVID-19 arrived, and lockdowns followed, customer behavior changed almost overnight. Card-present activity dropped sharply, while e-commerce transactions spiked; cross-border travel halted; and people who had never ordered groceries online suddenly did so every week.

Industry surveys by the Bank of England found that UK banks using machine learning had to rapidly reassess their models during 2020, as business processes, customer activity, and risk profiles no longer matched the data the models had been trained on (Bholat, Gharbawi, & Thew, 2020).

The practical symptoms were messy.

Some banks found that their fraud systems were massively over-flagging legitimate e-commerce purchases and digital services, while still struggling with new fraud patterns, such as pandemic-themed scams and synthetic identities. Call centers were flooded with customers whose cards had been declined for perfectly normal online orders.

At the same time, novel fraud schemes slipped through because they did not resemble historical patterns the models had been trained to recognize. Risk teams had to push through emergency retuning, relax some thresholds, and, in a few cases, temporarily fall back on more conservative rules while new data accumulated.

This episode exposed a core limitation of static training data. Models that looked well-calibrated under "business as usual" turned out to be brittle when the world shifted.

It also highlighted governance gaps. Only a few institutions had formal model-risk management processes that included explicit plans for drift detection, scenario testing, and rapid retraining in response to structural shocks. Others had to improvise on the fly, with little documentation or pre-agreed playbooks for when to override automated decisions.

The main lessons from this period are straightforward.

Fraud and security models must be treated as living systems that require continuous monitoring for drift, especially after major external shocks or business changes. Banks need clear triggers for when to retrain or roll back models, and they require human override mechanisms that product, risk, and data science teams understand and can utilize without lengthy internal debates.

In other words, model performance under stress has to become part of normal governance, not a panic response when customers start complaining.

Behavioral Biometrics and Continuous Authentication Backfiring

In parallel, many large enterprises and financial institutions began experimenting with behavioral biometrics for continuous authentication.

Instead of relying only on passwords or tokens, these systems profile how a person types, uses the mouse, moves across screens, or even walks with a device. Machine-learning models then flag deviations from this profile as potential signs of account compromise.

On paper, the promise was attractive: less visible friction for most users and faster detection of stolen sessions or shared credentials. In real deployments, however, significant equity and accessibility issues started to show.

People with disabilities, chronic conditions, or simply atypical motor patterns found themselves locked out more often than their peers.

Changes in health status, medication, or temporary injury could alter their behavior enough to trigger repeated challenges or denials.

Regulators had already started to warn that AI-driven systems can disproportionately disadvantage disabled individuals if they are trained and tuned on narrow "normal" populations.

In joint guidance on artificial intelligence and the Americans with Disabilities Act, the U.S. Equal Employment Opportunity Commission (EEOC) and the Department of Justice highlighted how algorithmic tools can screen out or penalize people with disabilities when designers do not explicitly account for variability in how they interact with systems (U.S. Equal Employment Opportunity Commission, 2023).

In Europe, debates around the EU AI Act have repeatedly stressed that high-risk AI systems must consider accessibility and avoid discriminatory effects on persons with disabilities (European Parliament, 2023).

In practice, complaints to internal ethics teams and regulators revealed patterns where behavioral-biometric controls generated more friction for users with tremors, neurodivergent profiles, or those using assistive technologies, even when those users had clean security records. Some institutions paused or scaled back continuous-authentication deployments after realizing that they had no clear appeals process and no alternative authentication path for people whose behavior simply did not fit the learned template.

The lessons here cut across security and compliance. Any AI-based security control that profiles behavior needs fairness testing and accessibility review as a first-class requirement, not an afterthought.

This involves evaluating false-positive and lockout rates by user group, consulting with disability and accessibility experts before deployment, and designing human review and override processes that are easily accessible and responsive.

It also means offering alternative authentication options, such as hardware tokens or step-up verification, that do not depend on behavioral profiling at all.

In security terms, these systems may reduce certain types of risk, but they can create new ones when they prompt vulnerable users to work around controls or disengage from security processes altogether.

Misconfigured Automated DDoS Protection and Self-Inflicted Outages

A third pattern emerges at the network edge, where organizations are increasingly relying on automated web-application firewalls (WAFs) and DDoS-protection services that tune themselves in near real-time.

These platforms often employ a combination of rules, heuristics, and machine-learning models to differentiate between legitimate traffic and bots and attacks, adjusting thresholds and blocking policies without requiring manual intervention.

The upside is clear on most days. Automated systems can react faster than human operators when volumetric attacks escalate or when new exploit attempts emerge across multiple customers simultaneously.

The downside becomes visible during major events such as flash sales, ticket drops, or high-profile livestreams. Traffic can legitimately spike by orders of magnitude, change geographic distribution, and exhibit behaviors that resemble those of botnets: multiple clients hitting the same endpoint, repeated requests within tight time windows, and bursts from new referrers or marketing campaigns.

There have been high-profile incidents where changes to edge-security configurations caused widespread outages, illustrating how powerful and fragile these automated defenses can be when mis-tuned.

In one well-documented incident, Cloudflare deployed a misconfigured Web Application Firewall rule whose regular expression caused CPU utilization to reach 100% across edge servers, briefly knocking many customer sites offline until the rule was terminated and the systems stabilized (Graham-Cumming, 2019).

Although that particular case was rooted in a software deployment error rather than a machine-learning decision, it highlights the same structural risk: highly centralized, automated protection components can become single points of failure for multiple services simultaneously (European Union Agency for Cybersecurity, 2020).

Similar dynamics can occur inside individual organizations when auto-tuning DDoS or WAF policies overreact to traffic surges.

During major promotional campaigns, some online retailers have experienced automated protection throttling or blocking legitimate customers after interpreting the surge as a distributed attack.

The direct consequences are lost sales, damage to customer trust, emergency changes by network teams, and sometimes a temporary return to more conservative, static configurations until confidence in the automated system is restored.

The lesson is that fully autonomous edge protection should always include clear guardrails and manual escape hatches.

Teams need staged rollouts, shadow-mode testing, and dashboards that make it easy to see what the automated system is about to do before it affects production traffic.

For critical events, organizations should define pre-approved playbooks that include limits on how aggressively auto-tuning can adjust thresholds, plus explicit "circuit breaker" procedures for pausing automation and reverting to known-good baselines.

Automation is still worth having, but only when the people responsible for availability can understand and control its behavior under stress.

Cross-Case Lessons: Patterns Across Offense and Defense

Taken together, these case studies show that AI in cybersecurity behaves less like a plug-in product and more like an ecosystem.

The same underlying capabilities appear in both defensive tools and offensive campaigns, i.e, pattern recognition at scale, fast adaptation, and synthetic content generation.

What changes the outcome is the quality of data and governance around the systems, how they're embedded in day-to-day work, and whether humans remain actively involved instead of being sidelined.

Across the successful defensive examples, a consistent pattern emerges.

High-performing deployments rely on large, diverse, and well-governed data pipelines, as well as continuous learning. Mastercard, PayPal, and Google's Gmail models only work because they're trained on billions of transactions or messages, refreshed frequently, and monitored for drift.

NatWest's scam-intervention workflows, Microsoft's use of Microsoft 365 Defender and Sentinel during Solorigate, and Drax's collaboration with Darktrace all combine telemetry with structured human review from analysts, fraud specialists, or plant engineers.

These programs don't treat AI as an external black box; they integrate it directly into SOC queues, fraud-ops procedures, OT incident playbooks, and escalation trees.

That's closely aligned with guidance such as NIST's AI Risk Management Framework, which stresses data quality, human oversight, and lifecycle governance as pillars of "trustworthy AI." (National Institute of Standards and Technology, 2023)

Integration into workflow matters just as much as model accuracy.

In the better stories, AI outputs arrive in the right place, with context, at the right moment. Gmail filters are wired directly into mail delivery. NatWest's alerts flow into mobile banking prompts and branch dialogues. Microsoft's analytics surface findings into threat-hunting environments where specialists know how to pivot.

Drax and Colonial Pipeline demonstrate that in OT and critical infrastructure, AI alerts are only effective when they are translated into language and thresholds that operators and engineers can act upon safely.

These are examples of "AI-supported" operations rather than "AI-run" operations, and they tend to show more resilience when something unexpected happens.

The recurring failure modes cut in the opposite direction.

When the pandemic abruptly changed consumer behavior, fraud models that had been tuned to pre-COVID norms suddenly misjudged what was risky and what was normal.

Behavioral biometrics and continuous authentication systems locked out people whose physical or cognitive patterns didn't match the training data. Misconfigured AI-driven DDoS protection blocked legitimate traffic spikes during sales and live events.

In each case, the underlying issue was less about a single bug and more about structural weaknesses, including static training data, a lack of robust drift detection, opaque model behavior, and limited governance regarding when to override or roll back automated decisions.

NIST explicitly warns that AI systems trained on data that later shifts can fail in ways that are hard to detect and may amplify inequities if those shifts interact with existing bias.

Another pattern in the failure cases is the absence of good "edges" around automation.

When fraud systems over-blocked during COVID, many banks lacked clear processes or tooling for rapid tuning and human overrides. When behavioral biometrics discriminated against disabled users, there were often no formal fairness tests, appeal mechanisms, or alternative authentication paths. When DDoS protections misclassified traffic, some organizations had no staging environments, no canary deployments, and no manual "circuit breaker," so the AI's decision stood until the outage forced a reset.

Therefore, the absence of robust governance, testing, and human-centered safeguards tends to turn technical misjudgements into systemic incidents.

Looking across the offensive case studies, it's clear that attackers are adopting many of the same classes of models as defenders.

Ransomware groups that apply ML and NLP to triage stolen data or personalize extortion messages are just using standard analytics in a different direction. Current AI cybersecurity assessments explicitly highlight this symmetry: the tools that improve detection, classification, and content generation for defenders can be repurposed with relatively little friction by attackers.

The result is a tightening feedback loop between attacker automation and defender automation.

Phishing filters improve, so criminals move to LLM-tailored spear-phishing and voice deepfakes. Fraud models harden around simple heuristics, so adversaries deploy tools that probe and learn which patterns slip through. Anomaly-based detections in network and OT environments push intrusion operators to blend into baselines or poison data over time.

In practice, this leads to an "algorithmic duel" where both sides monitor each other's adaptations and update their own models accordingly.

Public guidance now increasingly encourages organizations to treat adversarial machine learning, model poisoning, and model extraction as routine threat categories rather than theoretical edge cases.

These patterns have several implications for the strategic questions that follow in later chapters.

First, AI in cybersecurity must be managed as an ongoing capability with its own risk surface, rather than a one-off procurement. That means budgeting for continuous retraining, drift monitoring, bias and fairness assessments, and regular red-teaming of both models and data pipelines. It also means aligning AI security work with broader AI governance frameworks, ensuring that issues related to privacy, explainability, and accountability are addressed consistently across the organization, not just within the SOC or fraud unit (National Institute of Standards and Technology, 2023).

Second, organizations need explicit strategies for maintaining human expertise and judgment alongside expanding automation. The stronger case studies demonstrate that humans shape models, validate outputs, and design playbooks that assume AI will sometimes be wrong or incomplete. The weaker stories show humans reduced to button-clicking overseers who intervene only when something breaks. Future priorities around training, hiring, and operating model design will need to reflect that difference very deliberately.

Third, planning for AI in cybersecurity now requires acknowledging that the field is contested. Adversaries will continue to utilize generative models, optimization engines, and data-driven reconnaissance techniques. Defenders will respond with richer telemetry, more advanced correlation, and stronger automated enforcement. Governance, architecture, and strategy have to assume this moving target. That includes preparing legal, compliance, communications, and executive teams for incidents where AI both helps and fails, and where synthetic content or model manipulation plays a central role.

Instead of asking whether AI "works" or whether it should be adopted, the more relevant questions are how to structure programs so that defensive patterns from the successful cases are repeatable, how to avoid the failure modes we've seen, and how to anticipate an environment where offensive and defensive AI evolve together. Organizations that approach AI in cybersecurity with that mindset, as an evolving, adversarial, socio-technical system, will be in a far better position to capture its benefits while holding its risks within acceptable bounds.

References

Featurespace. (2023, April 25). NatWest improves scam detection rate by 135% using Featurespace's technology. Featurespace Newsroom. https://www.featurespace.com/newsroom/natwest-improves-scam-detection-rate-by-135-using-featurespaces-technology

Holmes, D. (2023, May 15). *What did the 2023 UK Finance Fraud Report tell us?* UK Finance.

https://www.ukfinance.org.uk/news-and-insight/blog/what-did-2023-uk-finance-fraud-report-tell-us

Forrester Consulting. (2021). *The Total Economic Impact™ of Mastercard Decision Intelligence.*
Mastercard.

Mastercard. (n.d.). *Decision Intelligence: The transaction monitoring solution to prevent fraud and drive approvals.* Mastercard AI & Security Solutions. https://b2b.mastercard.com/ai-and-security-solutions/fraud-and-decisioning/decision-intelligence

Azure Aggregator. (2020). *SolarWinds post-compromise hunting with Azure Sentinel.* Azure Aggregator.

Google. (2023, October 3). New Gmail protections for a safer, less spammy inbox. The Keyword – Gmail. https://blog.google/products/gmail/gmail-security-authentication-spam-protection/

Kumaran, N. (2022, May 27). Understanding Gmail's spam filters.

Google Workspace Blog. https://workspace.google.com/blog/identity-and-security/an-overview-of-gmails-spam-filters

Darktrace Holdings Limited. (n.d.). Drax Group | Darktrace cybersecurity case study. https://www.darktrace.com/customers/drax

Kocho. (n.d.). *A free-flowing and secure customer experience for a national water company*. Kocho case study

Darktrace Holdings Limited. (n.d.). *How Milton Keynes uses Darktrace AI (Customer story).* https://www.darktrace.com/customers/milton-keynes-university-hospital

Darktrace Holdings Limited. (n.d.). Milton Keynes University Hospital – Darktrace Case Study [PDF]. https://dtpgroup.co.uk/wp-content/uploads/2022/03/Milton-Keynes-University-Hospital-UK-Hospital.pdf

Hughes, O. (2018, August 2). *NHS trusts sign up to Darktrace threat-hunting software. Digital Health.* https://www.digitalhealth.net/2018/08/nhs-trusts-sign-up-to-darktrace-threat-hunting-software/

Stupp, C. (2019, August 30). *Fraudsters used AI to mimic CEO's voice in unusual cybercrime case.* The Wall Street Journal. https://www.wsj.com/articles/fraudsters-use-ai-to-mimic-ceos-voice-in-unusual-cybercrime-case-11567157402

Hung, C.-L. (2024). *AI and disinformation attacks in Taiwan's 2024 election* [Report summary]. Thomson Foundation. https://www.thomsonfoundation.org/latest/ai-and-disinformation-in-taiwan-s-2024-election/

Reuters. (2025, April 8). *Taiwan says China using generative AI to ramp up disinformation and 'divide' the island.* Reuters. https://www.reuters.com/world/asia-pacific/taiwan-says-china-using-generative-ai-to-ramp-up-disinformation-divide-island-2025-04-08/

Akamai. (n.d.). *Keeping up with the botnets: Credential stuffing.* Akamai Technologies.

Bitdefender. (2023). *Malicious ChatGPT Derivative 'FraudGPT' Fuels Dark Web Crime.* Bitdefender Labs.

Eftsure. (2023). *WormGPT: how hackers are exploiting the dark side of AI.* Eftsure.

F5. (n.d.). *How Credential Stuffing Bots Bypass Defenses.* F5, Inc.

PC Gamer. (2025). *Oh goody, the 'first known AI-powered ransomware' has been discovered and it 'may exfiltrate data, encrypt it, or potentially destroy it'.* PC Gamer / ESET

Bholat, D., Gharbawi, M., & Thew, O. (2020). *The impact of Covid on machine learning and data science in UK banking.* Bank of England Quarterly Bulletin 2020 Q4.

European Parliament. (2023, June 8). EU AI Act: first regulation on artificial intelligence. European Parliament.

https://www.europarl.europa.eu/topics/en/article/20230601STO93804/eu-ai-act-first-regulation-on-artificial-intelligence

U.S. Equal Employment Opportunity Commission. (2023). *U.S. EEOC and U.S. Department of Justice Warn against Disability Discrimination.*

Graham-Cumming, J. (2019, July 2). *Cloudflare outage caused by bad software deploy (updated).* Cloudflare Blog. https://blog.cloudflare.com/cloudflare-outage/

European Union Agency for Cybersecurity. (2020). *Artificial intelligence cybersecurity challenges.* ENISA.

National Institute of Standards and Technology. (2023). *Artificial intelligence risk management framework (AI RMF 1.0)* (NIST AI 100-1). U.S. Department of Commerce. https://doi.org/10.6028/NIST.AI.100-1

Chapter 11: The Future of AI in Cybersecurity

Standing at the Precipice of Transformation

As we stand at the threshold of a new era in cybersecurity, the convergence of artificial intelligence with emerging technologies promises to fundamentally reshape how we defend against and respond to cyber threats. Throughout this book, we have explored AI's current applications, from threat detection to identity management, and examined both its revolutionary potential and inherent limitations.

Now, we turn our gaze forward to examine how quantum computing, autonomous defense systems, and unprecedented global cooperation will define the future battlefield between cyber attackers and defenders. This chapter explores not just technological advancement but the fundamental restructuring of cybersecurity paradigms that AI will enable in the coming decades.

The pace of AI advancement in cybersecurity continues to accelerate exponentially. McKinsey projects that AI-driven cybersecurity solutions will grow from $15 billion in 2024 to over $135 billion by 2030, representing a compound annual growth rate of 44% (McKinsey & Company, 2024).

This explosive growth reflects not merely incremental improvements but transformative capabilities that will render current security approaches obsolete. The integration of quantum computing with AI, the emergence of fully autonomous cyber defense systems, and the development of predictive security frameworks that anticipate attacks before they occur represent just the beginning of this transformation.

The geopolitical implications of AI-powered cybersecurity extend far beyond technical considerations. As nations race to develop sovereign AI capabilities for national defense, the traditional boundaries between military and civilian cyber operations continue to blur. The future we examine in this chapter is one where AI serves as both the ultimate defender and the most sophisticated attacker, where international cooperation becomes essential for survival, and where the balance of power may shift dramatically based on algorithmic superiority rather than traditional military or economic might.

Quantum Computing and AI: The Next Security Revolution

The convergence of quantum computing and artificial intelligence represents perhaps the most significant technological disruption facing cybersecurity in the next decade.

Quantum computers, with their ability to process certain calculations exponentially faster than classical computers, will both enhance AI capabilities and fundamentally threaten current security paradigms. This dual nature, as both an enabler and a threat, makes quantum-AI integration a critical focus for future security strategies.

Quantum machine learning promises to revolutionize threat detection and analysis capabilities. While classical computers struggle with the combinatorial explosion of analyzing complex attack patterns across massive datasets, quantum computers excel at exactly these types of problems. IBM's research demonstrates that quantum machine learning algorithms can identify patterns in encrypted traffic without decrypting it, potentially enabling threat detection that preserves privacy while maintaining security (IBM Research, 2024).

Their quantum network security initiative has already achieved pattern recognition speeds 10,000 times faster than classical approaches for specific threat detection scenarios.

The threat to current encryption standards posed by quantum computing cannot be overstated. Shor's algorithm, when run on a sufficiently powerful quantum computer, can break RSA, ECC, and other public-key cryptography systems that protect virtually all current digital communications.

The National Institute of Standards and Technology warns that "cryptographically relevant quantum computers" capable of breaking current encryption could exist as early as 2030 (NIST, 2024). This timeline has triggered a race to develop and deploy quantum-resistant cryptography before adversaries gain quantum supremacy.

Post-quantum cryptography integrated with AI systems presents unique challenges and opportunities. The new cryptographic algorithms being standardized by NIST are significantly more complex than current methods, necessitating that AI systems adapt their threat detection and response strategies. Machine learning models must be retrained to recognize attack patterns in post-quantum encrypted traffic, identify quantum-enhanced threats, and manage the increased computational overhead of quantum-resistant algorithms.

Organizations like Google have already begun transitioning their AI security systems to post-quantum cryptography, reporting that the integration requires fundamental architectural changes rather than simple algorithm swaps (Google Security, 2024).

Quantum advantage in AI adversarial attacks introduces unprecedented threats. Quantum computers can generate adversarial examples that are fundamentally different from those created by classical computers, potentially bypassing all current defenses. Research from MIT demonstrates that quantum adversarial attacks can achieve 100% success rates against classical AI defenses by exploiting quantum superposition to create "impossible" adversarial examples that don't exist in classical probability spaces (MIT, 2024). Defending against these attacks requires quantum-enhanced AI systems, creating an arms race that only organizations with quantum capabilities can participate in.

The democratization timeline for quantum-AI capabilities will determine the future security landscape. Currently, only major corporations and governments have access to quantum computers.

However, cloud-based quantum computing services from Amazon, Microsoft, and IBM are making these capabilities increasingly accessible. D-Wave Systems predicts that quantum-AI-as-a-Service will be widely available by 2027, fundamentally changing who can deploy both quantum-enhanced defenses and attacks (D-Wave, 2024). This democratization could level the playing field between large and small organizations or create even greater disparities depending on regulatory and economic factors.

Hybrid classical-quantum AI systems represent the immediate future of quantum-enhanced security. These systems utilize quantum processors for specific tasks, such as optimization and pattern recognition, while relying on classical computers for general processing. Rigetti Computing's hybrid quantum-classical cybersecurity platform has demonstrated the ability to detect zero-day exploits 60% faster than pure classical systems while consuming 40% less energy (Rigetti, 2024). These hybrid approaches provide a practical path forward while fully fault-tolerant quantum computers remain years away.

Autonomous Cyber Defense: The Self-Defending Network

The evolution toward fully autonomous cyber defense systems represents a fundamental shift from human-directed to AI-directed security operations. Future networks will not merely detect and respond to threats but will anticipate, adapt, and evolve their defenses without human intervention. This transformation promises to address the speed and scale challenges that human defenders cannot match while raising profound questions about control, accountability, and the role of human expertise in security.

Self-healing networks powered by AI are already emerging in limited deployments.

These systems automatically detect compromises, isolate affected components, restore clean states from secure backups, and patch vulnerabilities, all within seconds of attack detection. Cisco's Intent-Based Networking with AI-driven self-healing capabilities has demonstrated the ability to maintain 99.999% availability even under sustained attack, automatically reconfiguring network paths and security policies to maintain operations while eliminating threats (Cisco, 2024).

By 2030, Gartner predicts that 75% of enterprise networks will have self-healing capabilities, fundamentally changing incident response from human-driven recovery to AI-managed resilience (Gartner, 2024).

Predictive defense systems using AI will shift security from reactive to proactive postures. These systems analyze global threat intelligence, vulnerability disclosures, and local environment characteristics to predict likely attack vectors before they're exploited. DARPA's Cyber Hunting at Scale (CHASE) program has developed AI systems that can predict cyber attacks with 89% accuracy up to seven days in advance by analyzing precursor activities and threat actor patterns (DARPA, 2024). This predictive capability enables preemptive patching, proactive threat hunting, and defensive deception deployment before attacks begin.

Swarm intelligence for distributed defense represents the next evolution in autonomous security. Inspired by biological systems like ant colonies and bee hives, swarm AI enables thousands of defensive agents to coordinate without centralized control.

Each agent operates semi-autonomously, sharing threat intelligence and coordinating responses through emergent behavior rather than top-down commands. The European Union's SPARTA project has demonstrated swarm defense systems that can protect critical infrastructure across multiple countries, with defensive agents automatically sharing threat intelligence and coordinating responses across jurisdictional boundaries (EU SPARTA, 2024).

Automated red teaming powered by AI will continuously test and improve defensive systems. Rather than periodic penetration tests by human experts, AI red teams will constantly probe for vulnerabilities, attempt novel attack techniques, and verify defensive responses. Microsoft's Cyber Defense Operations Center employs AI red teams that launch over 100,000 simulated attacks daily, automatically generating detailed reports on defensive gaps and recommended improvements (Microsoft, 2024). This continuous testing ensures that defensive systems evolve faster than attacker capabilities.

The decision delegation challenge in autonomous defense raises critical questions about human oversight. As AI systems make increasingly complex and consequential security decisions, determining appropriate boundaries for autonomous action becomes crucial.

Should AI systems be authorized to disconnect critical systems from networks? Can they make decisions that impact business operations or human safety? The IEEE's P7009 standard for Autonomous Defensive Systems attempts to address these questions, proposing frameworks for graduated autonomy based on risk levels and potential impacts (IEEE,

2024).

Resilience through diversity in autonomous systems prevents single points of failure. Future autonomous defense systems will employ multiple AI models with different architectures, training data, and decision processes. This diversity ensures that attacks successful against one model fail against others. Research from Carnegie Mellon shows that defensive systems using ensemble AI with at least five diverse models can maintain 95% effectiveness even when attackers have perfect knowledge of one model's architecture (Carnegie Mellon, 2024).

Global AI Security Cooperation: The New Diplomacy

The global nature of cyber threats and the transformative power of AI are driving unprecedented international cooperation in cybersecurity. Future security effectiveness will depend not on individual organizational or national capabilities but on the ability to share threat intelligence, coordinate responses, and establish global norms for AI use in cyberspace. This cooperation extends beyond traditional allies to include former adversaries, private sector entities, and international organizations in new frameworks for collective defense.

International AI threat intelligence sharing platforms are evolving from concept to reality. The Global Forum on Cyber Expertise has launched an AI-powered platform that automatically sanitizes, translates, and shares threat intelligence in real-time among 147 participating nations (GFCE, 2024).

Machine learning algorithms identify and redact sensitive information while preserving tactical value, enabling countries to share intelligence without compromising sources or methods. By 2025, this platform is expected to process over one billion threat indicators daily, creating a global early warning system for AI-enhanced attacks.

Cross-border AI incident response coordination is becoming essential as attacks increasingly target multiple jurisdictions simultaneously. The Budapest Convention on Cybercrime has been updated to include provisions for AI-assisted cross-border investigations and automated evidence sharing (Council of Europe, 2024).

AI systems can now automatically correlate attacks across countries, identify common threat actors, and coordinate response actions while respecting sovereignty and legal frameworks. The recent successful disruption of the QakBot botnet, coordinated across 30 countries using AI-powered correlation and response systems, demonstrates the power of this approach.

Standardization efforts for AI security are accelerating through international bodies. The International Organization for Standardization (ISO) is developing ISO/IEC 27091, specifically for AI security management, to establish global standards for secure AI development, deployment, and operation (ISO, 2024).

These standards will enable interoperability between different AI security systems, facilitate international cooperation, and provide baseline security requirements for AI systems used in critical infrastructure. Early adoption by major economies could establish these standards as de facto global requirements.

The UN's role in AI cybersecurity governance is expanding through the newly established International AI Security Agency (IASA), modeled after the International Atomic Energy Agency. This body will monitor AI development for its security implications, investigate AI-enabled attacks against member states, and facilitate the transfer of technology for defensive AI capabilities to developing nations (United Nations, 2024). The agency's mandate includes preventing an AI arms race while ensuring all nations have access to defensive AI technologies.

Public-private partnerships in AI security are redefining traditional boundaries between government and industry. The Cybersecurity and Infrastructure Security Agency's Joint Cyber Defense Collaborative now includes AI working groups where government agencies and private companies co-develop defensive AI systems (CISA, 2024).

These partnerships enable rapid deployment of defensive capabilities across critical infrastructure sectors while preserving competitive advantages and intellectual property. The success of the JCDC's AI-powered ransomware defense system, which reduced successful attacks by 78% across participating organizations, demonstrates the value of this collaborative approach.

Diplomatic frameworks for offensive AI limitations are emerging through multilateral negotiations. The Paris Call for Trust and Security in Cyberspace has been expanded to include specific provisions limiting the use of autonomous offensive AI systems against civilian infrastructure (French Ministry of Foreign Affairs, 2024). While enforcement remains challenging, the establishment of norms against certain AI-enabled attacks creates diplomatic costs for violations and provides frameworks for international response to AI-powered aggression.

Emerging Technologies and Their Security Implications

The intersection of AI with other emerging technologies creates both new defensive capabilities and novel attack vectors that will define future cybersecurity challenges. These technological convergences promise to transform not just how we secure systems but what we need to secure and from whom.

Edge AI and distributed intelligence fundamentally change the security architecture of modern networks. As AI processing moves from centralized cloud servers to edge devices, security must adapt to protect millions of distributed AI models rather than centralized systems. Intel's neuromorphic processors enable AI processing on IoT devices with minimal power consumption, but also create new attack surfaces where each device becomes a potential entry point for model manipulation or data poisoning (Intel, 2024).

By 2028, IDC predicts that 75% of enterprise AI workloads will run on edge devices, requiring entirely new security paradigms.

5G and 6G networks integrated with AI create unprecedented security challenges and opportunities. The massive increase in connected devices, ultra-low latency requirements, and network slicing capabilities of next-generation networks demand AI-powered security that can operate at network speed.

Ericsson's AI-native 6G security architecture proposes embedding machine learning directly into network protocols, enabling every network element to contribute to collective defense (Ericsson, 2024). However, this deep integration also means that compromising AI systems could grant attackers unprecedented control over communications infrastructure.

Blockchain-AI integration promises to address some fundamental security challenges while creating new ones. Decentralized AI training using blockchain can prevent model poisoning by cryptographically verifying training data integrity. Smart contracts can automatically enforce AI security policies and create immutable audit trails of AI decisions. However, the immutability of blockchain means that poisoned AI models or malicious smart contracts could become permanent fixtures requiring hard forks to remove. The MIT Digital Currency Initiative's research shows that blockchain-AI systems face unique vulnerabilities where attacking either component can compromise both (MIT DCI, 2024).

Biotechnology and AI convergence introduce security concerns that transcend traditional cybersecurity. AI systems that can design biological agents or analyze genetic data for vulnerabilities create dual-use dilemmas where defensive research could enable offensive capabilities.

The Nuclear Threat Initiative warns that AI-designed biological threats could emerge from compromised research systems, requiring new biosecurity frameworks that integrate cybersecurity, physical security, and biological containment (NTI, 2024).

Space-based AI systems represent the next frontier in cybersecurity. Satellite constellations powered by AI provide global communications and sensing capabilities, but also create new attack vectors. Anti-satellite AI weapons could autonomously identify and disable critical space infrastructure. The U.S. Space Force's Artificial Intelligence Strategy emphasizes developing resilient AI systems that can operate in contested space environments where traditional command and control may be impossible (U.S. Space Force, 2024).

Augmented reality and virtual reality security powered by AI must protect not just data but human perception and cognition.

As AR/VR becomes integral to work and social interaction, AI security systems must detect and prevent attacks that manipulate virtual environments to cause psychological harm, extract information through social engineering, or compromise physical safety. Meta's Project Aria research demonstrates AI systems that can detect deepfakes and manipulation in real-time AR/VR environments with 97% accuracy (Meta Reality Labs, 2024).

The Human Factor in Future AI Security

Despite increasing automation, the human element remains crucial in future AI-powered cybersecurity. The evolution of human roles, the development of new skills, and the maintenance of human agency in an

AI-dominated landscape will determine whether AI enhances or replaces human capability in security operations.

Human-AI teaming models are evolving from simple tool use to genuine collaboration. Future security analysts will work alongside AI partners that understand context, explain reasoning, and even challenge human assumptions. MITRE's Human-AI Teaming framework demonstrates that mixed teams of humans and AI achieve 40% better threat detection than either alone, with humans providing creativity and contextual understanding while AI provides speed and pattern recognition (MITRE, 2024).

This symbiotic relationship requires new interfaces, training methods, and operational procedures that maximize both human and AI strengths.

Cognitive security emerges as a new discipline protecting human decision-making from AI manipulation. As AI systems become capable of influencing human behavior through personalized persuasion, protecting cognitive autonomy becomes a security imperative.

The Stanford Human-Centered AI Institute has developed "cognitive firewalls" that use AI to detect and block attempts to manipulate human decision-making through deepfakes, personalized disinformation, or psychological exploitation (Stanford HAI, 2024).

Education and workforce transformation for AI security requires fundamental changes to how we train security professionals.

Traditional security certifications become obsolete as AI handles routine tasks. The (ISC)² Cybersecurity Workforce Study projects that by 2030,

65% of security roles will require AI expertise, with entirely new positions, such as AI Security Architects and Machine Learning Threat Analysts, becoming standard (ISC2, 2024). Universities are responding with interdisciplinary programs combining computer science, psychology, ethics, and security studies.

Ethical decision-making in autonomous security systems remains fundamentally human. While AI can process information and identify patterns, decisions about acceptable risk, privacy trade-offs, and response proportionality require human values and judgment. The European Union's Ethics Guidelines for Trustworthy AI in Security mandate human oversight for high-risk security decisions, requiring "meaningful human control" even in highly automated systems (European Commission, 2024).

The creativity gap between human and AI attackers and defenders may determine future security effectiveness. While AI excels at pattern recognition and optimization, human creativity in developing novel attack vectors or defensive strategies remains unmatched. DARPA's Assured Autonomy program shows that human creativity in designing edge cases and exception scenarios consistently identifies vulnerabilities that AI systems miss, suggesting that human expertise will remain essential for addressing "unknown unknowns" in security.

Maintaining human expertise in an automated world requires deliberate strategies to prevent skill atrophy. Organizations must create opportunities for security professionals to practice manual threat hunting, incident response, and forensic analysis, even when AI systems handle routine operations.

The U.S. Cyber Command's "Human Performance Program" maintains human readiness through regular exercises where AI assistance is deliberately disabled, ensuring personnel can operate effectively during AI failures or attacks targeting AI systems (U.S. Cyber Command, 2024).

Economic and Societal Implications

The transformation of cybersecurity through AI will have profound economic and societal impacts extending far beyond the technology sector. These changes will reshape labor markets, alter power dynamics between nations and corporations, and fundamentally change how society views security, privacy, and digital rights.

The economic disruption from AI security automation will eliminate millions of traditional security jobs while creating new ones. The World Economic Forum estimates that AI will displace 2.3 million cybersecurity positions by 2030 but create 3.1 million new roles requiring AI expertise (WEF, 2024).

This transition creates significant challenges for current security professionals who must reskill or risk obsolescence. The economic benefits, however, are substantial. McKinsey projects that AI-powered security will prevent $2 trillion in global cybercrime losses by 2030 while reducing security operational costs by 60%.

Market concentration concerns arise as AI security capabilities become concentrated among a few major technology companies.

The enormous computational resources, vast datasets, and specialized expertise required for effective AI security create significant barriers to entry. This concentration could lead to security monopolies where organizations must choose between a handful of providers who effectively control global cybersecurity. Antitrust regulators are beginning to examine whether the concentration of the AI security market poses national security risks.

The insurance industry transformation driven by AI security fundamentally changes risk assessment and pricing. AI enables real-time risk scoring based on continuous security posture assessment rather than annual audits. Parametric cyber insurance, powered by AI, automatically pays claims when specific conditions are met, eliminating the need for lengthy investigations.

However, organizations without sophisticated AI defenses may become uninsurable, creating a divide between protected and vulnerable entities. Lloyds of London projects that AI-based risk assessment will reduce cyber insurance premiums by 40% for well-defended organizations while making coverage unavailable for others (Lloyd's, 2024).

Digital sovereignty and AI security dependencies create new geopolitical tensions. Nations dependent on foreign AI security systems face potential kill switches, backdoors, or denial of service during conflicts. This has triggered national AI security initiatives, with countries developing sovereign capabilities even at high economic cost. The European Union's Digital Sovereignty Strategy allocates €20 billion for developing independent AI security capabilities, viewing this as essential for strategic autonomy (European Union, 2024).

Social stratification based on AI security access could create new forms of inequality. Individuals and organizations with advanced AI protection will operate safely in digital environments, while those without face constant threats. This "security divide" could determine access to economic opportunities, social participation, and basic services as digital interaction becomes mandatory for daily life. Universal basic AI security, providing minimum viable AI protection to all citizens, is being debated as a potential social policy response.

Privacy paradigm shifts occur as AI security requires unprecedented data collection and analysis. The traditional privacy framework of data minimization conflicts with AI's need for comprehensive data to detect threats effectively. Society must navigate the trade-off between security and privacy, potentially accepting previously unthinkable surveillance in exchange for protection from AI-powered threats. China's Social Credit System, while controversial, demonstrates one potential endpoint where AI security and social control become indistinguishable.

Conclusion: Navigating the AI Security Future

As we stand at the threshold of an AI-transformed cybersecurity landscape, the future promises both unprecedented protection and novel vulnerabilities. This chapter has explored how quantum computing will revolutionize both attack and defense, how autonomous systems will create self-defending networks, and how global cooperation will become essential for security in an interconnected world. We have examined emerging technologies that will create new battlegrounds and considered how human roles must evolve to remain relevant in an AI-dominated field.

The convergence of quantum computing and AI represents a discontinuous leap in capability that will render current security paradigms obsolete. Organizations must begin preparing now for the post-quantum world, even as the technology remains years from maturity. The advantage will go to those who successfully navigate the transition, implementing quantum-resistant systems while developing quantum-enhanced capabilities. This dual challenge, defending against quantum threats while leveraging quantum opportunities, will separate future security leaders from victims.

Autonomous cyber defense promises to address the speed and scale challenges that human defenders cannot match. Self-healing networks, predictive defense systems, and swarm intelligence will create resilient infrastructures that adapt and evolve faster than attackers can exploit them. Yet this automation brings risks of cascading failures, loss of human control, and new vulnerabilities in the autonomous systems themselves. The organizations that thrive will be those that achieve the right balance between automation and human oversight.

Global cooperation in AI security emerges not as an idealistic goal but as a practical necessity. The borderless nature of AI-powered threats requires coordinated defense that transcends traditional boundaries. International frameworks for sharing threat intelligence, coordinating incident response, and regulating the use of offensive AI are beginning to take shape. The challenge lies in maintaining cooperation despite competing national interests, economic competition, and ideological differences.

The human element remains irreplaceable in future AI security, though in transformed roles. Security professionals must evolve from operators to orchestrators, from analysts to AI trainers, from defenders to cognitive security specialists. This transformation requires not just new skills but new mindsets, embracing AI as a partner rather than a replacement. Organizations must invest in human development alongside AI deployment, maintaining the creativity, judgment, and ethical reasoning that only humans can provide.

The economic and societal implications of AI security transformation extend far beyond the technology sector. Market dynamics, employment patterns, insurance models, and social structures will all be reshaped by AI security capabilities. The divide between those with effective AI protection and those without could become a defining characteristic of future inequality. Policymakers must consider not just the technical aspects of AI security but its broader impacts on society.

Looking ahead, several critical uncertainties will shape the AI security future. Will quantum computers arrive before adequate defenses are deployed? Can international cooperation overcome nationalist tendencies in the development of AI? Will autonomous systems enhance or undermine human agency in security? How these questions are answered will determine whether AI becomes humanity's greatest shield or its most dangerous vulnerability.

The path forward requires careful navigation between competing imperatives. We must embrace AI's transformative potential while maintaining human agency and accountability. We must pursue technological advancement while addressing ethical and societal concerns. We must foster innovation while preventing malicious use. We must enable global cooperation while respecting sovereignty and diversity.

As this book has demonstrated, artificial intelligence is not merely another tool in the cybersecurity arsenal but a fundamental transformation of how we conceptualize and implement security. The future belongs to those who can harness AI's power while managing its risks, who can adapt to continuous change while maintaining core security principles, and who can balance automation with human wisdom.

The age of AI-powered cybersecurity has arrived. The question is not whether to adopt AI but how to do so responsibly, effectively, and equitably. Organizations that master this challenge will not just survive but thrive in the digital future. Those that fail to adapt risk becoming casualties in a new form of natural selection where algorithmic superiority determines survival.

The future of cybersecurity is being written now in research labs, boardrooms, and policy chambers around the world. Every decision about AI adoption, every investment in quantum research, every framework for international cooperation shapes the landscape our successors will inherit. We stand at a unique moment in history where the choices we make about AI and cybersecurity will reverberate for generations.

The ultimate measure of success in future AI cybersecurity will not be the sophistication of our algorithms or the power of our quantum computers but our ability to create a digital world that is both secure and free, both protected and private, both automated and human. This balance, difficult as it may be to achieve, remains the worthy goal toward which all our efforts must be directed.

References

Carnegie Mellon University. (2024). *Diversity in autonomous defensive systems: Ensemble AI for resilient security*. Software Engineering Institute Technical Report.

Cisco. (2024). *Intent-based networking with self-healing capabilities: The future of network resilience*. Cisco Annual Cybersecurity Report.

CISA. (2024). *Joint cyber defense collaborative: AI working group outcomes and recommendations*. Cybersecurity and Infrastructure Security Agency.

Council of Europe. (2024). *Second additional protocol to the Budapest Convention on Cybercrime*. Council of Europe Treaty Series No. 224.

D-Wave Systems. (2024). *Quantum computing as a service: Democratizing quantum-AI capabilities*. D-Wave Technical Whitepaper.

DARPA. (2024). *Cyber hunting at scale (CHASE): Predictive AI for anticipatory defense*. Defense Advanced Research Projects Agency Program Report.

Ericsson. (2024). *6G security: AI-native architecture for next-generation networks*. Ericsson Technology Review.

European Commission. (2024). *Ethics guidelines for trustworthy AI in security applications*. EU High-Level Expert Group on AI.

European Union. (2024). *Digital sovereignty strategy: Building independent AI security capabilities*. EU Digital Strategy 2030.

EU SPARTA. (2024). *Swarm intelligence for distributed critical infrastructure protection*. SPARTA Project Final Report.

French Ministry of Foreign Affairs. (2024). *Paris Call for Trust and Security in Cyberspace: AI addendum*. Ministry for Europe and Foreign Affairs.

Gartner. (2024). *Predicts 2030: The autonomous security operations center.* Gartner Research.

Global Forum on Cyber Expertise. (2024). *Global AI threat intelligence sharing platform: First year report.* GFCE Publication.

Google Security. (2024). *Post-quantum cryptography integration in AI systems.* Google Security Blog.

IBM Research. (2024). *Quantum machine learning for privacy-preserving threat detection.* IBM Journal of Research and Development, 68(4).

IEEE. (2024). *P7009 Standard for autonomous defensive systems.* IEEE Standards Association.

Intel. (2024). *Neuromorphic processors for edge AI security.* Intel Labs Technical Report.

ISC2. (2024). *Cybersecurity workforce study: The AI transformation.*

International Information System Security Certification Consortium.

ISO. (2024). *ISO/IEC 27091: Information security management for AI systems.* International Organization for Standardization.

Lloyd's of London. (2024). *Parametric cyber insurance in the age of AI.* Lloyd's Emerging Risk Report.

McKinsey & Company. (2024). *The future of cybersecurity: AI market projections 2024-2030.* McKinsey Global Institute.

Meta Reality Labs. (2024). *Project Aria: AI security for augmented and virtual reality*. Meta Research Publication.

Microsoft. (2024). *Autonomous red teaming in the cyber defense operations center.* Microsoft Security Response Center.

MIT. (2024). *Quantum adversarial attacks: Breaking classical AI defenses.* MIT Computer Science and Artificial Intelligence Laboratory.

MIT Digital Currency Initiative. (2024). *Blockchain-AI security: Convergence risks and opportunities.* MIT DCI Research Paper.

MITRE. (2024). *Human-AI teaming framework for cybersecurity operations.* MITRE Technical Report MTR240156.

NIST. (2024). *Post-quantum cryptography standardization: Timeline and implications.* NIST Special Publication 800-227.

Nuclear Threat Initiative. (2024). *Biosecurity in the age of AI: Emerging threats and responses.* NTI Report.

Rigetti Computing. (2024). *Hybrid quantum-classical cybersecurity platform performance metrics.* Rigetti Technical Publication.

Stanford HAI. (2024). *Cognitive firewalls: Protecting human decision-making from AI manipulation.* Stanford Human-Centered AI Institute.

United Nations. (2024). *Establishing the International AI Security Agency: Framework and mandate.* UN Security Council Resolution 2750.

U.S. Cyber Command. (2024). *Human performance program: Maintaining readiness in automated environments.* USCYBERCOM Strategic Report.

U.S. Space Force. (2024). *Artificial intelligence strategy for space domain security.*

USSF Publication.

World Economic Forum. (2024). *The future of jobs report 2024: AI impact on cybersecurity employment.* WEF Publication.

Chapter 12: Balancing Innovation and Responsibility

The Dual Mandate of Our Digital Age

As we reach the conclusion of our comprehensive exploration of artificial intelligence in cybersecurity, we stand at a critical juncture that demands both bold innovation and careful responsibility. Throughout this book, we have examined AI's transformative power, from revolutionizing threat detection to enabling autonomous defense systems, from enhancing identity management to creating new vulnerabilities that challenge our fundamental security assumptions.

This final chapter synthesizes these insights to address the essential question facing every organization, security professional, and policymaker: How do we harness AI's unprecedented capabilities while managing its inherent risks and maintaining our ethical obligations to society?

The dual nature of AI in cybersecurity reflects a broader tension in technological advancement. Every capability that strengthens our defenses can be weaponized by adversaries. Every automation that improves efficiency risks creating dependencies and blind spots. Every algorithm that enhances detection may embed biases that perpetuate inequality.

The World Economic Forum's 2024 Global Risks Report identifies AI-enabled cyberattacks as the second-highest technological risk facing humanity, while simultaneously recognizing AI-powered defense as our best hope for digital security (WEF, 2024). This paradox is not a problem to be solved but a tension to be managed through thoughtful implementation, continuous vigilance, and unwavering commitment to ethical principles.

The stakes of this balance extend far beyond technical considerations. As digital infrastructure becomes the foundation of modern civilization, cybersecurity transforms from a technical discipline to a societal imperative.

The decisions we make today about AI implementation, governance frameworks, and ethical boundaries will determine whether future generations inherit a digital world characterized by security and freedom or one marked by vulnerability and oppression. This chapter provides a framework for navigating these choices, offering practical guidance for organizations seeking to innovate responsibly while contributing to a broader vision of ethical AI deployment in cybersecurity.

The Innovation Imperative: Why Standing Still Means Falling Behind

The pace of AI advancement in cybersecurity creates an innovation imperative that organizations ignore at their peril.

The threat landscape evolves at machine speed, with adversaries deploying increasingly sophisticated AI-powered attacks that traditional defenses cannot match. Organizations that fail to innovate face not gradual decline but sudden obsolescence, as the gap between AI-enhanced and traditional security capabilities widens exponentially.

Recent data underscores the urgency of AI adoption. IBM's Cost of a Data Breach Report 2024 reveals that organizations using AI and automation in their security operations experience breach costs that are $3.05 million lower on average than those without these technologies, a difference that can determine organizational survival (IBM Security, 2024).

Moreover, the mean time to identify and contain breaches drops from 277 days to 108 days with AI deployment, limiting damage and reducing recovery costs. These metrics demonstrate that AI adoption is not optional but essential for maintaining viable security postures.

The innovation imperative extends beyond defensive capabilities to encompass entire security operating models. Traditional security operations centers designed for human-scale threats cannot process the volume, velocity, and variety of modern attacks.

Accenture's research shows that security teams without AI support can effectively analyze less than 4% of security alerts, leaving organizations blind to the vast majority of potential threats (Accenture, 2024). This coverage gap creates unacceptable risk in an environment where a single missed alert can result in a catastrophic breach.

The competitive dynamics of AI security create winner-take-all scenarios where early adopters gain compounding advantages.

Organizations that successfully implement AI security systems accumulate valuable training data, refine their models through operational experience, and develop institutional expertise that becomes increasingly difficult for laggards to replicate. Microsoft's analysis of security maturity curves indicates that organizations initiating AI security adoption in 2025 will require 3-5 years to reach the capability levels achieved by current adopters today, by which time leaders will have advanced even further (Microsoft Security, 2024).

Innovation in AI security also drives broader organizational transformation. The implementation of AI-powered security systems forces organizations to modernize legacy infrastructure, improve data governance, and develop new operational processes.

These changes create spillover benefits beyond security, improving overall digital maturity and operational efficiency. McKinsey estimates that organizations pursuing comprehensive AI security transformation see average productivity improvements of 25% across IT operations, as the discipline required for effective AI security deployment raises standards throughout the technology stack (McKinsey, 2024).

The global nature of cyber threats makes innovation a collective imperative. When organizations fail to adopt adequate AI defenses, they become weak links that adversaries exploit to attack entire supply chains and ecosystems.

The SolarWinds and Kaseya incidents demonstrated how compromising a single vendor can impact thousands of downstream organizations. In an interconnected digital economy, security innovation is not just self-interest but social responsibility.

The Responsibility Framework: Ethical Guardrails for AI Deployment

While innovation remains essential, the power of AI in cybersecurity demands equally strong commitment to responsible deployment. The ability to monitor, analyze, and influence behavior at scale creates capabilities that can easily slide from protection to oppression. Organizations must establish clear ethical frameworks that guide AI implementation, ensuring that security enhancements don't come at the cost of fundamental rights and values.

Privacy preservation emerges as a foundational responsibility in AI security deployment. The effectiveness of AI systems often correlates with data comprehensiveness, creating pressure to collect and analyze ever more personal information.

The European Data Protection Board's 2024 guidelines on AI in cybersecurity establish clear boundaries, requiring organizations to demonstrate that data collection is necessary, proportionate, and limited to legitimate security purposes (EDPB, 2024). Organizations must resist the temptation to exploit security justifications for broader surveillance, maintaining strict purpose limitation even when technical capabilities would permit expanded monitoring.

Bias mitigation represents another critical responsibility that organizations cannot delegate to technology vendors. AI systems trained on historical security data inevitably inherit past prejudices and systemic inequalities. The U.S. National Institute of Standards and Technology's

AI Risk Management Framework requires organizations to actively test for discriminatory outcomes, implement bias correction mechanisms, and maintain ongoing monitoring for emergent prejudices (NIST, 2024). This responsibility extends beyond technical fixes to encompass diverse development teams, inclusive design processes, and regular community engagement to understand differential impacts.

Transparency and explainability obligations challenge organizations to demystify AI security operations. While the complexity of modern AI systems makes perfect explainability impossible, organizations must strive for meaningful transparency that enables accountability.

The IEEE's Standard for Transparent AI in Security Operations requires organizations to provide clear explanations of AI system capabilities, limitations, and decision factors in language accessible to affected stakeholders (IEEE, 2024). This includes not just technical documentation but accessible communications that help users understand how AI systems affect their security and privacy.

Human oversight responsibilities ensure that AI augments rather than replaces human judgment in critical security decisions. The principle of meaningful human control, endorsed by the UN's Group of Governmental Experts on Lethal Autonomous Weapons Systems, applies equally to cybersecurity contexts where AI decisions can have significant impacts on individuals and organizations (United Nations, 2024).

Organizations must maintain clear chains of human accountability, ensure humans retain the ability to override AI decisions, and prevent automation bias from degrading human decision-making capabilities.

The responsibility for AI security extends to the broader ecosystem through supply chain governance. Organizations deploying AI security systems must verify that their vendors adhere to ethical principles, that training data was obtained legitimately, and that AI models don't embed hidden biases or backdoors.

The Responsible AI Institute's certification program provides frameworks for evaluating vendor compliance with ethical AI principles, but ultimate responsibility remains with deploying organizations (RAI Institute, 2024).

Environmental responsibility increasingly factors into AI security decisions as the computational demands of advanced AI systems contribute significantly to carbon emissions.

Training large AI models can generate carbon emissions equivalent to several transatlantic flights, while operational AI systems consume enormous amounts of electricity. Organizations must balance security benefits against environmental costs, optimizing AI deployments for efficiency and considering renewable energy sources for AI infrastructure.

Building Ethical AI Security Programs: A Practical Approach

Translating principles of innovation and responsibility into operational reality requires structured approaches that embed ethical considerations throughout the AI security lifecycle. Organizations must move beyond high-level commitments to implement concrete processes, governance structures, and assessment mechanisms that ensure the responsible deployment of AI while maintaining security effectiveness.

Governance structures for ethical AI security begin with clear leadership and accountability. Leading organizations establish AI Ethics Boards that include not just technologists but ethicists, legal experts, and community representatives.

JPMorgan Chase's AI Ethics Committee, which reviews all AI security deployments for ethical implications, has prevented several initiatives that would have created discriminatory outcomes or excessive privacy intrusions while approving innovations that balance security with rights protection (JPMorgan Chase, 2024). These governance bodies need genuine authority to halt problematic deployments, not merely advisory roles that can be ignored when convenient.

Risk assessment frameworks specifically designed for AI security help organizations identify and mitigate ethical challenges before deployment.

The MITRE ATLAS framework provides structured approaches for evaluating AI security systems across multiple dimensions, including bias potential, privacy impact, and adversarial vulnerability (MITRE, 2024). Organizations should conduct these assessments not as one-time exercises but as continuous processes that evolve with changing threats, technologies, and social expectations.

Development practices that embed ethics from inception prove more effective than attempting to add ethical considerations after systems are built. The concept of "Ethics by Design" parallels Privacy by Design principles, requiring that ethical considerations shape every phase of AI security system development.

Google's AI Principles require that all AI security projects undergo ethical review at the concept phase, with specific checkpoints throughout development to ensure principles translate into practice (Google AI, 2024). This approach prevents the common problem of discovering ethical issues only after significant investment, making course correction difficult.

Testing and validation processes must expand beyond technical performance to encompass ethical dimensions. Organizations should conduct regular bias audits using diverse test datasets that represent all affected populations.

Adversarial testing should include attempts to manipulate AI systems into discriminatory or privacy-violating behaviors.

Microsoft's Responsible AI Standard requires that AI security systems undergo "fairness testing" that specifically evaluates performance across different demographic groups and use cases (Microsoft, 2024).

Continuous monitoring and adjustment mechanisms ensure that ethical AI security remains responsive to emerging challenges. AI systems that appear unbiased at deployment can develop discriminatory patterns as they learn from operational data.

Organizations must implement monitoring systems that track not just security metrics but fairness indicators, privacy impacts, and other ethical dimensions. When problems emerge, organizations need clear processes for rapid remediation, including the ability to roll back problematic updates or disable systems that cannot be fixed quickly.

Stakeholder engagement throughout the AI security lifecycle ensures that systems serve broader community needs rather than narrow organizational interests. This includes regular consultation with employees about workplace monitoring, engagement with customers about data use, and dialogue with civil society about broader impacts.

The City of Boston's Algorithm Justice Initiative demonstrates how community engagement can improve AI security systems while building public trust, resulting in deployments that are both more effective and more accepted (City of Boston, 2024).

The Human Element: Maintaining Agency in an Automated World

As AI systems become increasingly capable, maintaining human agency and expertise emerges as both a practical necessity and an ethical imperative. The temptation to fully automate security operations must be balanced against the need for human creativity, judgment, and accountability in addressing complex security challenges that transcend the capabilities of algorithmic solutions.

Skill evolution rather than replacement should guide workforce development in AI-enhanced security environments. While AI automates routine tasks, it creates new roles that require hybrid expertise, combining security knowledge with AI literacy. The (ISC)² Cybersecurity Workforce Study shows that demand for AI security specialists grew 260% in 2024, with these positions commanding premium salaries due to the scarcity of qualified professionals (ISC², 2024). Organizations must invest in reskilling programs that help current security professionals evolve rather than face obsolescence.

Decision-making frameworks that preserve human agency while leveraging AI capabilities require careful balance. The European Union's proposed AI Liability Directive establishes that humans remain liable for AI-assisted decisions, creating legal incentives for maintaining meaningful human oversight (European Commission, 2024).

Organizations should implement decision matrices that clearly delineate which security actions AI can take autonomously, which require human approval, and which must remain exclusively human. These frameworks should evolve based on AI system maturity and demonstrated reliability, but always preserve human authority over high-stakes decisions.

Cognitive diversity in security teams becomes more critical as AI systems potentially narrow analytical perspectives. While AI excels at pattern recognition within training parameters, humans provide creative thinking that identifies novel threats and unconventional solutions.

RAND Corporation's research on human-AI collaboration reveals that diverse teams, comprising members with different backgrounds, thinking styles, and expertise, achieve 47% better threat detection than homogeneous teams that rely primarily on AI (RAND, 2024). Organizations should actively cultivate this diversity rather than allowing AI to homogenize security approaches.

Maintaining manual capabilities ensures resilience when AI systems fail or face adversarial manipulation. Regular "AI-free" exercises where security teams operate without automated assistance help preserve critical skills and identify dangerous dependencies.

The U.S. Cyber Command's quarterly "Analog Days" requires personnel to conduct security operations using only manual processes, revealing both the value of AI assistance and the importance of maintaining human capabilities (U.S. CYBERCOM, 2024).

The psychological impact of AI on security professionals requires active management. Studies show that overreliance on AI can lead to decreased job satisfaction, reduced sense of purpose, and diminished professional identity among security practitioners.

Organizations must create meaningful roles that leverage uniquely human capabilities, provide opportunities for professional growth beyond AI operations, and recognize human contributions to security outcomes. IBM's "Human in Command" initiative demonstrates how emphasizing human leadership in AI-assisted security can improve both job satisfaction and security effectiveness (IBM, 2024).

Career pathways in AI-enhanced security must provide progression opportunities that don't require abandoning hands-on security work for management roles.

Technical career tracks that advance from security analyst to AI security architect to chief AI security scientist provide advancement while maintaining technical engagement. These pathways ensure that organizations retain experienced practitioners who can bridge the gap between AI capabilities and security requirements.

Global Cooperation: Building Responsible AI Security Together

The global nature of both cyber threats and AI development makes international cooperation essential for responsible innovation. No single organization or nation can address the challenges of AI security in isolation. Building frameworks for cooperation while respecting sovereignty, competitive dynamics, and cultural differences represents one of the defining challenges of our time.

International standards development through bodies like ISO, IEEE, and ITU provides common frameworks that enable interoperability while embedding ethical principles. The recent adoption of ISO/IEC 23053 on trustworthy AI establishes global baselines for AI security systems that balance innovation with responsibility (ISO, 2024).

These standards emerge from multi-stakeholder processes that include governments, industry, academia, and civil society, ensuring that diverse perspectives shape global norms. Organizations that adopt these standards gain not only technical interoperability but also ethical credibility in global markets.

Threat intelligence sharing enhanced by AI necessitates new frameworks that safeguard competitive advantages while facilitating collective defense. The World Economic Forum's Partnership Against Cybercrime demonstrates how private sector collaboration can improve security for all participants without compromising individual interests (WEF Partnership, 2024).

AI systems can automatically sanitize and share threat intelligence, removing proprietary information while preserving tactical value. These platforms must balance transparency with security, ensuring that shared intelligence doesn't become a roadmap for attackers.

Capacity-building initiatives ensure that AI security capabilities don't become exclusive to wealthy nations and large corporations. The UN's Global Cybersecurity Capacity Building Portal connects organizations with AI security expertise to those needing assistance, facilitating knowledge transfer that strengthens global security (United Nations, 2024).

Developed nations and leading technology companies have both self-interest and moral obligation to ensure that AI security capabilities are accessible to all, as weak links in global connectivity create vulnerabilities that affect everyone.

Diplomatic frameworks for managing AI security competition prevent races to the bottom where security becomes justification for surveillance and oppression. The proposed International Convention on AI in Cyberspace, modeled on arms control treaties, would establish norms against certain AI security practices while preserving legitimate defensive capabilities (Council on Foreign Relations, 2024).

These frameworks must balance sovereign rights with global responsibilities, creating incentives for responsible behavior while maintaining consequences for violations.

Public-private partnerships at a global scale leverage complementary capabilities of governments and industry. The Cybersecurity Tech Accord, now including over 150 technology companies, demonstrates how industry can self-organize around responsible AI security principles (Cybersecurity Tech Accord, 2024).

These partnerships must navigate complex dynamics where companies compete in markets while cooperating on security, and where government interests in security may conflict with corporate interests in privacy and openness.

Cultural sensitivity in global AI security cooperation recognizes that different societies have varying perspectives on privacy, security, and acceptable trade-offs. What constitutes appropriate security monitoring in one culture may be unacceptable surveillance in another.

Global frameworks must accommodate these differences while

maintaining minimum standards that protect fundamental rights. The Asia-Pacific Economic Cooperation's AI Governance Framework demonstrates how regional approaches can respect cultural diversity while establishing common principles (APEC, 2024).

Future Readiness: Preparing for Unknown Challenges

As AI continues to evolve at exponential rates, organizations must develop adaptive capabilities that prepare them for challenges we cannot yet imagine. Building resilient, flexible security programs that can evolve with technological advancement while maintaining ethical principles requires new approaches to strategy, investment, and capability development.

Scenario planning for AI security futures helps organizations prepare for multiple possible trajectories. Rather than betting on single predictions, organizations should develop playbooks for various scenarios, including an AI breakthrough that renders current defenses obsolete, regulatory changes that restrict AI use, the discovery of fundamental AI vulnerabilities, or the emergence of artificial general intelligence with significant security implications.

Shell's pioneering scenario planning methodology, adapted for AI security contexts, helps organizations build strategies robust across multiple futures (Shell, 2024).

Investment strategies must balance current operational needs with future capability development. The "70-20-10 rule," adopted by leading security organizations, allocates 70% of resources to current operations, 20% to emerging capabilities, and 10% to experimental technologies that may not yield results for years.

This portfolio approach ensures that organizations maintain current security while building future capabilities. Alphabet's "Other Bets" model demonstrates how organizations can pursue transformative innovations while maintaining operational excellence (Alphabet, 2024).

Organizational learning capabilities determine adaptation speed as AI security evolves. Organizations must create structures and cultures that rapidly absorb new knowledge, experiment with emerging approaches, and scale successful innovations.

The U.S. Department of Defense's Joint Artificial Intelligence Center emphasizes "learning at the speed of relevance," implementing mechanisms that translate research into operational capability within months rather than years (DoD JAIC, 2024).

Ecosystem participation ensures organizations remain connected to innovation occurring beyond their boundaries. Active engagement in industry consortia, academic partnerships, and open-source communities provides early warning of emerging capabilities and threats. The Linux Foundation's OpenSSF demonstrates how collaborative security development can advance capabilities faster than any single organization could achieve alone (Linux Foundation, 2024).

Regulatory preparedness anticipates the evolving governance landscape for AI security. As governments worldwide develop AI regulations, organizations must build compliance capabilities that can adapt to changing requirements. The EU's AI Act, China's algorithmic regulations, and emerging U.S. federal AI standards create complex compliance landscapes that will only become more intricate. Organizations need flexible governance structures that can accommodate new requirements without disrupting security operations.

Talent pipeline development ensures access to expertise as AI security skill requirements evolve. Partnerships with universities, apprenticeship programs, and internal academies create sustainable sources of qualified professionals.

Cisco's Networking Academy, expanded to include AI security curricula, demonstrates how the industry can shape education to meet future workforce needs (Cisco, 2024). These programs must anticipate skill requirements 3-5 years in advance, preparing professionals for roles that don't yet exist.

The Path Forward: A Call to Responsible Action

As we conclude this comprehensive examination of AI in cybersecurity, the path forward requires both the courage to innovate and the wisdom to recognize its limits. The dual nature of AI, as both a powerful tool and a potential threat, demands that we approach its deployment with appropriate humility, recognizing that our decisions today will shape the digital world for generations to come.

The evidence presented throughout this book demonstrates that AI is not optional for effective cybersecurity. Organizations that fail to adopt AI capabilities will find themselves increasingly vulnerable to attacks they cannot detect, threats they cannot analyze, and incidents they cannot contain.

The innovation imperative is real and urgent. Yet this same evidence shows that unconstrained AI deployment creates new vulnerabilities, perpetuates biases, and risks undermining the very values security is meant to protect.

The balance between innovation and responsibility is not a fixed point but a dynamic equilibrium that must be continuously maintained. As AI capabilities advance, as threats evolve, and as our understanding of impacts deepens, we must adjust our approaches while maintaining core principles.

This requires institutional mechanisms for continuous assessment, stakeholder engagement to incorporate diverse perspectives, and leadership commitment to ethical principles, even when they conflict with short-term interests.

Success in AI security requires recognizing that technical capability alone is insufficient. The organizations that will thrive are those that combine advanced AI systems with strong governance, diverse human expertise, and commitment to broader societal good.

They will view security not as a zero-sum competition but as a collective challenge requiring cooperation even among competitors. They will measure success not just by breaches prevented but by trust maintained and rights protected.

The responsibility for shaping AI's role in cybersecurity extends beyond security professionals to encompass executives who allocate resources, policymakers who establish frameworks, researchers who advance capabilities, and citizens who demand accountability. Each stakeholder has a role in ensuring that AI enhances rather than undermines security, that innovation serves human needs rather than replacing human agency, and that the benefits of AI security are broadly shared rather than narrowly concentrated.

As we stand at this inflection point in cybersecurity history, the choices we make will determine whether AI becomes humanity's greatest defender or a tool that undermines the very foundations of digital society. The technical capabilities exist to achieve either outcome. The determining factor will be our collective wisdom in deployment, our commitment to ethical principles, and our willingness to cooperate in addressing shared challenges.

Conclusion: The Ongoing Journey

The story of AI in cybersecurity is not ending but beginning. While this book has explored current capabilities, emerging challenges, and future possibilities, the rapid pace of advancement means that new chapters are being written daily in research labs, security operations centers, and policy forums around the world. The principles and frameworks presented here provide guidance for navigating this evolving landscape, but they must be applied with flexibility and continuous learning.

The dual nature of AI in cybersecurity, simultaneously our best hope for effective defense and a source of novel vulnerabilities, reflects broader tensions in technological advancement.

Every generation faces transformative technologies that challenge existing frameworks and require new approaches to governance. Our generation's challenge is to harness AI's power while maintaining human agency, to enable innovation while ensuring accountability, and to enhance security while protecting privacy and rights.

The journey toward responsible AI security is not a destination to be reached but a continuous process of balance, adjustment, and improvement. Organizations must commit to ongoing assessment of their AI deployments, regular engagement with stakeholders about impacts and concerns, and continuous evolution of governance frameworks as understanding deepens. This requires viewing AI security not as a technical project to be completed but as an ongoing discipline requiring sustained attention and investment.

The global nature of both cyber threats and AI development makes this a shared journey that no organization or nation can complete alone. The frameworks for cooperation, standards for interoperability, and norms for responsible behavior must emerge from inclusive processes that respect diversity while establishing common ground. The alternative: a fragmented landscape of incompatible systems and conflicting principles, serves neither security nor innovation.

Looking forward, the organizations that will succeed in AI security are those that embrace both sides of the innovation-responsibility equation. They will pursue advanced capabilities while maintaining ethical boundaries. They will automate routine tasks while preserving human judgment for complex decisions. They will compete vigorously in markets while cooperating on shared security challenges. They will measure success not just by technical metrics but by broader impacts on employees, customers, and society.

The ultimate measure of our success in deploying AI for cybersecurity will not be the sophistication of our algorithms or the speed of our detection, but the kind of digital world we create for future generations. Will it be a world where security and privacy coexist, where protection doesn't require surveillance, and where AI augments human capability rather than replacing it? The answer depends on the choices we make today and our commitment to both innovation and responsibility in the deployment of AI for cybersecurity.

As readers of this book, whether security professionals, business leaders, policymakers, or concerned citizens, you have the knowledge and responsibility to shape this future. The frameworks, principles, and practices presented here provide tools for responsible action, but their application requires courage, commitment, and collaboration. The challenge is significant, the stakes are high, and the time for action is now.

The age of AI-powered cybersecurity has arrived. How we navigate its opportunities and challenges will define not just our digital security but the nature of our digital society. Let us proceed with both boldness and wisdom, embracing innovation while maintaining responsibility, and working together to create a future where AI serves as humanity's guardian rather than its master in the digital realm.

References

Accenture. (2024). *The state of cybersecurity resilience 2024*. Accenture Security.

Alphabet. (2024). *Annual report: Investment in future technologies*. Alphabet Inc.

APEC. (2024). *Asia-Pacific AI governance framework*. Asia-Pacific Economic Cooperation.

Cisco. (2024). *Networking academy: AI security curriculum expansion*. Cisco Systems.

City of Boston. (2024). *Algorithm justice initiative: Community engagement in AI deployment*. Boston Mayor's Office.

Council on Foreign Relations. (2024). *Proposed international convention on AI in cyberspace*. CFR Digital and Cyberspace Policy Program.

Cybersecurity Tech Accord. (2024). *Responsible AI security principles: 2024 progress report*. Tech Accord Secretariat.

DoD JAIC. (2024). *Learning at the speed of relevance: AI adaptation strategies*. Joint Artificial Intelligence Center.

European Commission. (2024). *AI liability directive: Maintaining human accountability*. European Union.

EDPB. (2024). *Guidelines on AI in cybersecurity and data protection*. European Data Protection Board.

Google AI. (2024). *AI principles: Ethics by design in security applications.* Google.

IBM. (2024). *Human in command: Maintaining human agency in AI security.* IBM Research.

IBM Security. (2024). *Cost of a data breach report 2024.* IBM Corporation.

IEEE. (2024). *Standard for transparent AI in security operations.* IEEE Standards Association.

ISC2. (2024). *Cybersecurity workforce study: The AI transformation.* International Information System Security Certification Consortium.

ISO. (2024). *ISO/IEC 23053: Framework for trustworthy artificial intelligence.* International Organization for Standardization.

JPMorgan Chase. (2024). *AI ethics committee: Governance in practice.* JPMorgan Chase & Co.

Linux Foundation. (2024). *OpenSSF: Collaborative security development.* Linux Foundation.

McKinsey. (2024). *The value of AI in cybersecurity operations.* McKinsey Global Institute.

Microsoft. (2024). *Responsible AI standard: Implementation guide.* Microsoft Corporation.

Microsoft Security. (2024). *Security maturity curves in the age of AI.* Microsoft.

MITRE. (2024). *ATLAS: Adversarial threat landscape for AI systems.* MITRE Corporation.

NIST. (2024). *AI risk management framework 2.0.* National Institute of Standards and Technology.

RAND. (2024). *Human-AI collaboration in cybersecurity: Optimizing team composition.* RAND Corporation.

RAI Institute. (2024). *Responsible AI certification program for security systems.* Responsible AI Institute.

Shell. (2024). *Scenario planning for AI futures.* Royal Dutch Shell.

United Nations. (2024). *Global cybersecurity capacity building portal.* UN Office of Disarmament Affairs.

United Nations. (2024). *Group of governmental experts on lethal autonomous weapons systems: Final report.* United Nations.

U.S. CYBERCOM. (2024). *Maintaining human readiness in automated environments.* U.S. Cyber Command.

WEF. (2024). *Global risks report 2024.* World Economic Forum.

WEF Partnership. (2024). *Partnership against cybercrime: Annual report.* World Economic Forum.

Made in the USA
Monee, IL
04 November 2026

67382319R00233